Stick
Insects

of the
Continental United States
and Canada

SPECIES AND EARLY STUDIES

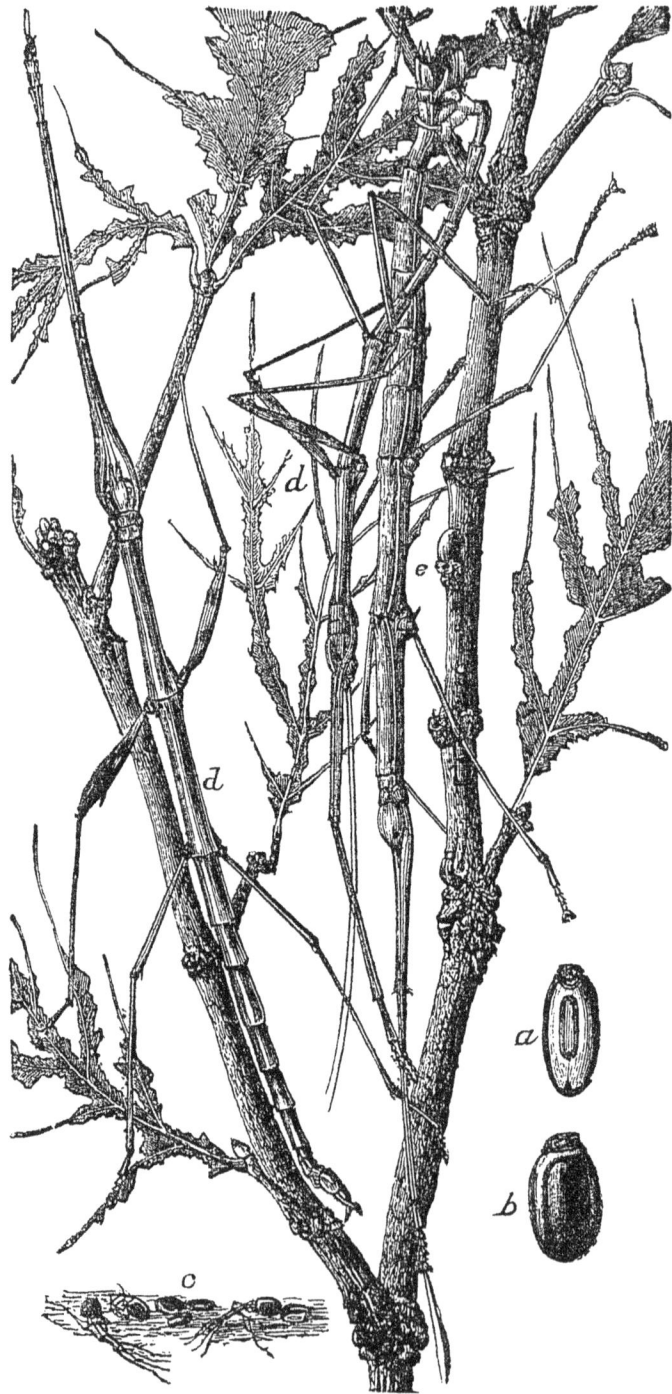

Stick Insects

of the
Continental United States
and Canada

SPECIES AND EARLY STUDIES

Edited by

Chad Arment

COACHWHIP PUBLICATIONS
LANDISVILLE, PENNSYLVANIA

Coachwhipbooks.com
Landisville, Pennsylvania

Library of Congress Cataloging-in-Publication Data

Stick insects of the continental United States and Canada : species and early studies / edited by Chad Arment.
    p. cm.
  Includes bibliographical references.
  ISBN 1-930585-23-3
  1. Stick insects—North America. I. Arment, Chad.
  QL509.6.A1S75 2006
  595.7'29—dc22
                          2005025368

Cover textures courtesy Mayang Murni Adnin.
Cover image (*Diapheromera femorata*): James Solomon, USDA Forest Service, www.forestryimages.org
Back cover image (*Timema* sp., Solano Co., California): Alex Wild, www.myrmecos.net
Back cover image (*Anisomorpha* sp., pair, Lee Co., Alabama): Lew Scharpf
Back cover image (*Megaphasma denticrus*, Newton Co., Arkansas): Sarah A. Clark
Frontispiece: *Diapheromera femorata*, attributed to a published sketch by Charles Valentine Riley

CONTENTS

Part I: Walkingsticks of the Continental U.S. and Canada

Part II: Early Studies

Species

IDENTIFYING NORTH AMERICAN STICK INSECTS

If you have collected a mature adult stick insect within the continental United States or Canada, it should not be difficult to discern its genus by examining different parts of the body. Specifically, you should look at:

The number of tarsomeres on each leg. Each leg is segmented into four parts. The coxa is directly attached to the insect's body, and is followed in turn by the femur, tibia, and tarsus. The tarsus is the segment closest to the ground. It is also segmented, each segment called a tarsomere. There will be three or five tarsomeres per tarsus. Only the western genus *Timema* has three tarsomeres (or rather five fused into three).

The insect's body. This is separated into the head, the thorax (from which the limbs emerge), and the abdomen. The thorax is also separable into the prothorax (nearest the head), the mesothorax, and the metathorax (from which the hind legs emerge). Measure the relative lengths of the prothorax and mesothorax.

Wings, if present. If the insect is an adult, and has wings, it is our only winged walkingstick, *Aplopus mayeri*. This species is found in southern Florida.

Spines on head, if present.

Length of antennae. Compare to the length of the femurs of the front legs.

Femurs of the middle and hind legs, if present. Note the presence of any spines, lobes, or swollen regions.

Proportional length and width of head.

Species determination often requires further morphological examination. You may need to examine such characters as:

The poculum. This is the cup-shaped swollen lobing of the subgenital plate, located underneath the male stick insect.

The cerci. This is a pair of short tail-like segments at the end of the body. In some species, small spine- or tooth-like extensions can be noted basally between the cerci.

There is a history of confusion among many of our native species due to variability of certain characters. Rather than a simple diagnostic key, I recommend a holistic approach to these insects. Careful examination of the morphological characters (preferably of several adult specimens from the same area), coupled with locality data and host plant identification, provides the best means to accurately identify our phasmids.

SPECIES GUIDE

The purpose of this book is to provide insect hobbyists (whether livestock breeders, entomological specimen collectors, macrophotographers, or other hobbyists) with a clearer picture of the diversity of stick insects found in the continental United States (and a few regions of southern Canada). Only one species listed, *Timema nakipa* from Baja California Norte, is not found strictly within our borders. It is included because it is the only other known species of *Timema*, and should not be overlooked in any discussion of the genus.

The species guide includes morphological characters to distinguish genera, characters that help determine species, representative distribution, and representative habitat and food plants. A few additional notes were added as appropriate.

The distribution is based on museum specimen records and published entomological records. As such, there are inherent biases (collection localities are primarily wherever the collectors traveled; most regions do not have curated entomological museum collections; many entomological collections include only a handful of stick insect specimens; not all museum specimens are identified or have proper collection details; not all museum collections solicited were able to provide requested information from their collections), but it should provide a skeleton distributional record which future research can flesh out. The data should provide rough outlines of the biogeographic ranges, but the attentive hobbyist will find many avenues for potential research. Within the representative distribution, those states or regions which may be suspect (being far outside what might be considered a normal range) are italicized.

I should also note the decision to include common names. While I understand the argument by those pointing to paleontological success with binomial nomenclature, I would point out that common names and scientific names serve different purposes. A scientific name is primarily categorical, thus subject to change with systematic revision. A common name is ethnozoological, emphasizing designation of apparent types, whether or not those types undergo systematic change. Several of our phasmids have recognized common names; for others, I merely provide an expansion from the Latin.

It would certainly be valuable for hobbyists to provide stick insect specimens to museum entomological collections. First, make certain that the museum collection has an interest in acquiring new specimens. The collections manager or curator can provide information on the best way to submit specimens. I would also recommend that specimens be given to those collections that make data freely available to researchers (even those who are not able to visit the collection in person). Due to budget and personnel constraints, many museums are not able to provide such data, but it would be a shame for useful information to have limited availability.

Collectors should provide as much information regarding a specimen as possible—identification (to genus or species); state, county, and specific geographic description of capture location; date, time, and weather conditions; how the specimen was captured;

general habitat (and host plant, if pertinent); collector's name. Collecting of specimens, of course, should be done only with proper permits, should state, park, or local requirements dictate.

For those hobbyists interested in rearing walkingsticks, our natives provide a range of interesting species. While this text is not meant as a rearing guide, some of the data may provide clues for husbandry requirements. Please note that there may be Federal or state regulations barring the interstate transport of live stick insects from other parts of the country without a permit.

HISTORICAL LITERATURE

While some hobbyists may find the historical literature repetitive, as species are added, revised, and deleted, it does provide a good foundation for understanding how our current species came to be recognized. In doing so, it also points out several directions where research is truly needed. As stick insects are of little interest to the agricultural industry, there has been only sporadic systematic research over the last several decades. (Many investigations have notably centered around speciation in the genus *Timema*.) There are still many questions about the biogeography, systematics, and life histories of our other genera that require answers.

Illustrations from the historical literature should provide a better understanding of the systematic differentiation for many currently recognized species. Techniques and field notes in the literature will offer ideas for collecting or keeping stick insects.

Genus *Anisomorpha*

DISTINGUISHING CHARACTERS:

Five tarsomeres.

Mesothorax is only three times longer (or less) than the prothorax.

Antennae longer than front leg femurs in both sexes.

SYSTEMATICS:

There are two recognized species of *Anisomorpha* in the United States. There is, however, some confusion over how well these two species are differentiated and the limits of their respective ranges. After examining a wide range of specimens, Hebard (1943) considered *A. buprestoides* to be limited to peninsular Florida and a very small section of southeastern Georgia. He believed all other specimens were *A. ferruginea*, and that this latter species might turn out just to be a variety of *buprestoides*. For this text, localities will correspond to names provided by literature and museum collections, but these may be based on inaccurate identifications. A serious review of this genus in North America is sorely needed.

Adult specimens should be used to distinguish between the species, as immature specimens have contributed to the biogeographic confusion of *Anismorpha*.

It also appears that *Anisomorpha ferruginea* ranges a bit further north than generally recognized. A Delaware specimen appeared grayer than southern specimens, but this difference in coloration is unlikely to be systematically significant.

Anisomorpha buprestoides

Southern Two-Striped Walkingstick, or "Spitting Devil"

RECOGNIZABLE CHARACTERS:

Females range up to almost 8 centimeters in length, males up to about 4.5 centimeters.

Ground color is brown or gray, with three black dorsal and subdorsal stripes separated by two distinctive yellowish or pale stripes.

Florida's "Ocala National Forest" (Marion County) morph is distinctively black and white.

Head is longer than it is wide.

Noted by Orin McMonigle (*Elytra and Antenna* website): eggs are oval, while the eggs of the next species, *ferruginea*, are log-shaped with flattened ends.

REPRESENTATIVE DISTRIBUTION:

Alabama: Baldwin Co. *(Cover image from Lee Co., either this or next species.)*

Florida: Florida Keys, Alachua Co., Brevard Co., Broward Co., Charlotte Co., Collier Co., Columbia Co., Dixie Co., Duval Co., Escambia Co., Gadsden Co., Gulf Co., Highlands Co., Hillsboro Co., Lake Co., Leon Co., Levy Co., Liberty Co., Manatee Co., Marion Co., Miami-Dade Co., Monroe Co., Nassau Co., Orange Co., Osceola Co., Palm Beach Co., Polk Co., Putnam Co., Santa Rosa Co., St. Johns Co., Union Co.

Georgia: Atlanta, Bibb Co., Coweta Co.

Louisiana: Jefferson Parish, Orleans Parish, Rapides Parish, Terrebonne Parish

Mississippi: Harrison Co., Granada Co., Jackson Co.

North Carolina: No county specified.

South Carolina: Anderson Co., Beaufort Co., Charleston Co., Hampton Co., Newberry Co., Oconee Co., Pickens Co.

Texas: Brazos Co., Galveston Co.

REPRESENTATIVE HABITAT AND FOOD PLANTS:

Open pinelands, hammock forest, saw palmetto scrub.

Sometimes found under loose bark.

Known to feed on oak, crepe myrtle, lyonia, rosemary, roses.

Will eat privet in captivity.

BEHAVIOR:

When disturbed, *Anismorpha* will expel a fine liquid mist of repugnatory chemicals which can seriously affect an eye from over a foot away.

Will aggregate in groups, often in large numbers.

The much smaller mature males are often found riding on females.

Nymphs are rarely seen, as they feed mostly in the tree-tops.

During the day, may be found resting on palmetto leaves.

While most phasmid females randomly drop their hard-capsuled eggs from where they forage among the vegetation, *A. buprestoides* females of the black-and-white morph dig small pits in the dry sandy soil, deposit their eggs in the pits, and cover them up.

Just 10-15 minutes before Hurricane Charley (August 13, 2004) arrived, a large group of *A. buprestoides* was observed in Lake County near Ocala National Forest. Tozier (2005) noted that all paired males began synchronously drumming their legs for about two minutes, possibly in response to the change in barometric pressure (though it may just have been a coincidence).

Anisomorpha ferruginea

Northern Two-Striped Walkingstick, or "Prairie Alligator"

DISTINGUISHING CHARACTERS:
Smaller than *A. buprestoides*, females averaging about 5.5 centimeters in length, males usually less than 4 centimeters.
Striping has much less contrast.
Head is barely longer than it is wide.

REPRESENTATIVE DISTRIBUTION:
Delaware: New Castle Co. (Univ. Delaware specimen confirmed, swept in 1998 survey)
Florida: Franklin Co.
Georgia: Chatham Co., Dougherty Co., Elbert Co., Thomas Co.
Illinois: Pope Co., Union Co.
Indiana: Crawford Co., Jackson Co., Posey Co.
Kentucky: Warren Co.
Lousiana: Bienville Parish, East Baton Rouge Parish, Grant Parish, Ouachita Parish
Mississippi: Callaway Co., Cape Girardeau Co., Harrison Co., Howard Co.
North Carolina: Brunswick Co., Person Co., Wake Co.
Nebraska: Extreme southeast (Hebard considered this questionable, as no specimen was preserved)
Oklahoma: Choctaw Co., Pushmataha Co.
Pennsylvania: No county specified, but more than one record noted.
South Carolina: Beaufort Co.
Texas: Harris Co., Tarrant Co.
Virginia: No county specified.

REPRESENTATIVE HABITAT AND FOOD PLANTS:
Often found in and near oak trees.
In Texas, has been found in high salt marsh grass.
Noted by Orin McMonigle (*Elytra and Antenna* website) to feed on oak, rose, and black-berry leaves in captivity.

Genus *Aplopus*

DISTINGUISHING CHARACTERS:
>   The only winged stick insect in the United States.
>   Five tarsomeres.
>   Mesothorax is four times longer (or more) than the prothorax.
>   Antennae longer than front leg femurs in both sexes.
>   If it is a juvenile, and thus wingless, *Aplopus* can be differentiated by its spines and a first abdominal segment that is much longer than it is wide.

Aplopus mayeri

Mayer's Walkingstick

RECOGNIZABLE CHARACTERS:
>   Two large spines on head, smaller spines on body.
>   Females can reach 12.5 centimeters in length.

REPRESENTATIVE DISTRIBUTION:
>   Florida: Florida Keys, Miami-Dade Co.

REPRESENTATIVE HABITAT AND FOOD PLANTS:
>   Bay cedar.

Genus *Diapheromera*

DISTINGUISHING CHARACTERS:

Five tarsomeres.

Mesothorax is four times longer (or more) than the prothorax.

Antennae longer than front leg femurs in both sexes.

Femurs of the middle and hind legs usually have a spine near the tip.

Head is about as long as wide.

In males, the femurs of the middle legs are expanded.

Diapheromera arizonensis

Arizona Walkingstick

RECOGNIZABLE CHARACTERS:

Females average 7.5 centimeters in length.

Pale yellow-brown ground coloration.

Males' thoraxes have green dorsal stripe and black ventral stripe.

REPRESENTATIVE DISTRIBUTION:

Arizona: Cochise Co., Graham Co., La Paz Co., Maricopa Co., Mohave Co., Pima Co., Yuma Co.

Texas: El Paso Co.

REPRESENTATIVE HABITAT AND FOOD PLANTS:

Mountainous regions: Baboquivari Mts., Mule Mts.

Bear grass, low trees.

Diapheromera carolina

Carolina Walkingstick

RECOGNIZABLE CHARACTERS:
Green, gray, or brownish in coloration.
Prominent black median stripe on thorax.
Head is round.

REPRESENTATIVE DISTRIBUTION:
Georgia: Gordon Co., Union Co., White Co.
North Carolina: Burke Co., Transylvania Co., Watauga Co.
South Carolina: Greenville Co., Oconee Co., Pickens Co.

REPRESENTATIVE HABITAT AND FOOD PLANTS:
Not recorded.

Diapheromera covillea

Coville's Walkingstick

RECOGNIZABLE CHARACTERS:
Horn-like spines on head.

REPRESENTATIVE DISTRIBUTION:
Arizona: Maricopa Co., Mohave Co., Pima Co., Pinal Co.
New Mexico: Dona Ana Co., Eddy Co., Otero Co.
Texas: El Paso Co., Presidio Co.

REPRESENTATIVE HABITAT AND FOOD PLANTS:
Mountainous area: Santa Catalina Mts.
Creosote bush (*Larrea tridentata*) specialist.

Diapheromera femorata

Common or Northern Walkingstick

RECOGNIZABLE CHARACTERS:
Brown or green in color. Middle femurs often banded in males.
Females are larger than males, but less than 10 centimeters in length.
Head is squarish in form.
Male's seventh abdominal segment is longer than its ninth abdominal segment.
Male cerci unspined.

REPRESENTATIVE DISTRIBUTION:
Alabama: Baldwin Co., Butler Co., Choctaw Co., Cleburne Co., Franklin Co., Houston Co., Lauderdale Co., Lee Co., Madison Co., Marion Co., Marshall Co., Mobile Co., Perry Co., Winston Co.
Arizona: Cochise Co., Cocino Co., Maricopa Co., Pima Co., Pinal Co.
Arkansas: Baxter Co., Johnson Co., Lawrence Co., Logan Co., Madison Co., Newton Co., Ouachita Co., Polk Co., Pope Co., Pulaski Co., Sharp Co., Washington Co., Yell Co.
Connecticut: Fairfield Co., New Haven Co., New London Co., Windham Co.
Delaware: Kent Co., New Castle Co.
District of Columbia
Florida: Alachua Co., Gadsden Co.; Hamilton Co., Jefferson Co., Liberty Co.
Georgia: Baker Co., Bibb Co., Decatur Co., DeKalb Co., Dougherty Co., Houston Co., Meriwether Co., Morgan Co., Pickens Co., Rabun Co., Stephens Co., Whitfield Co.
Illinois: Adams Co., Champaign Co., Coles Co., Cook Co., Du Page Co., Edgar Co., Gallatin Co., Hardin Co., Jackson Co., Lake Co., Lawrence Co., Lee Co., Massac Co., McHenry Co., Pope Co., Rock Island Co., Union Co., Vermilion Co., Washington Co., White Co.
Indiana: Carroll Co., Cass Co., Clark Co., Greene Co., Knox Co., Kosciusko Co., Marion Co., Morgan Co., Putnam Co., Ripley Co., St. Joseph Co., Starke Co., Tippecanoe Co., Vigo Co.
Iowa: Appanoose Co., Clay Co., Crawford Co., Dallas Co., Muscatine Co., Story Co., Winnebago Co., Woodbury Co.
Kansas: Clark Co., Doniphan Co.
Kentucky: Adair Co., Campbell Co., Casey Co., Fayette Co., Harrison Co., Jefferson Co., Jessamine Co., Johnson Co., Kenton Co., Mason Co., Meade Co., Menifee Co., Powell Co., Russell Co., Scott Co.
Louisiana: Caddo Parish, Natchitoches Parish
Maine: Cumberland Co., Kennebec Co.

Maryland: Allegany Co., Cecil Co., Frederick Co., Georges Co., Harford Co., Howard Co., Montgomery Co., Prince George's Co.

Massachusetts: Essex Co., Hampden Co., Hampshire Co., Middlesex Co., Worcester Co.

Michigan: Allegan Co., Berrien Co., Cheboygan Co., Clinton Co., Crawford Co., Dickinson Co., Genesee Co., Gratiot Co., Hillsdale Co., Huron Co., Ingham Co., Iosco Co., Kalamazoo Co., Kent Co., Lapeer Co., Livingston Co., Menominee Co., Midland Co., Newaygo Co., Oakland Co., Oceana Co., Ogemaw Co., Oscoda Co., Ottawa Co., Saginaw Co., Shiawassee Co., St. Joseph Co., Washtenaw Co.

Minnesota: Aitkin Co., Anoka Co., Becker Co., Beltrami Co., Cass Co., Clearwater Co., Crow Wing Co., Dakota Co., Hennepin Co., Hubbard Co., Nicollet Co., Olmsted Co., Pine Co., Polk Co., Sherburne Co., Todd Co., Wadena Co.

Mississippi: Lauderdale Co., Pontotoc Co.

Missouri: Boone Co., Cole Co., Crawford Co., Grundy Co., Jasper Co., Jefferson Co., Lewis Co., Marion Co., Miller Co., Newton Co., Oregon Co., Osage Co., Pettis Co., Phelps Co., Pike Co., Pulaski Co., Randolph Co., St. Charles Co., St. Louis Co., Scott Co., Shannon Co., Stoddard Co., Vernon Co.

Nebraska: Cass Co.

New Hampshire: Belknap Co., Cheshire Co., Hillsborough Co., Mirrimack Co., Rockingham Co., Strafford Co.

New Jersey: Burlington Co., Gloucester Co., Sussex Co.

New Mexico: Dona Ana Co., Otero Co., Sandoval Co., Santa Fe Co., Valencia Co.

New York: Albany Co., Cattaraugas Co., Dutchess Co., Essex Co., Greene Co., Nassau Co., Niagara Co., Orange Co., Rockland Co., Suffolk Co., Tompkins Co., Ulster Co., Warren Co., Westchester Co., Wyoming Co., Yates Co.

North Carolina: Cherokee Co., Graham Co., Halifax Co., Person Co., Wake Co.

North Dakota: Cass Co., Grand Forks Co., Pembina Co.

Ohio: Cuyahoga Co., Franklin Co., Geuaga Co., Greene Co., Greer Co., Henry Co., Lucas Co., Mercer Co., Monroe Co., Muskingum Co., Scioto Co., Wayne Co.

Oklahoma: Custer Co., Delaware Co., Jackson Co., LeFlore Co., Logan Co., Mayes Co., McCurtain Co., Muskogee Co., Ottawa Co., Payne Co., Sequoyah Co., Wagoner Co.

Pennsylvania: Armstrong Co., Blair Co., Butler Co., Carbon Co., Centre Co., Cumberland Co., Dauphin Co., Huntingdon Co., Lebanon Co., Luzerne Co., Lycoming Co., Mifflin Co., Montour Co., Pike Co., Somerset Co., Union Co., Westmoreland Co., York Co.

Rhode Island: Providence Co., Washington Co.

South Carolina: Charleston Co., Greenville Co., Pickens Co., Richland Co.

South Dakota: Brookings Co., Lincoln Co., Marshall Co., Washabaugh Co.

Tennessee: Cumberland Co., Fentress Co., Lawrence Co., Roane Co., White Co.

Texas: Brewster Co., Cameron Co., Dallas Co., Jeff Davis Co., Starr Co.

Utah: Kane Co., Salt Lake Co.

Vermont: Addison Co., Chittenden Co., Rutland Co., Windsor Co.

Virginia: Amherst Co., Bath Co., Clark Co., Fairfax Co., Frederick Co., Madison Co., Montgomery Co., Orange Co., Pittsylvania Co., Prince George Co., Roanoke Co., Shenandoah Co., Warren Co.

West Virginia: Hardy Co., Pendleton Co.

Wisconsin: Adams Co., Bayfield Co., Columbia Co., Dodge Co., Door Co., Douglas Co., Dunn Co., Eau Claire Co., Fond du Lac Co., Green Co., Jackson Co., Kewaunee Co., Marathon Co., Marinette Co., Marquette Co., Menominee Co., Osconto Co., Pierce Co., Richland Co., Rock Co., St. Croix Co., Sauk Co., Sawyer Co., Shawano Co., Termpealeua Co., Vernon Co., Washburn Co., Waupaca Co., Waushara Co., Wood Co.

Manitoba: Norden, Selkirk

Ontario: Turkey Point

Quebec

REPRESENTATIVE HABITAT AND FOOD PLANTS:
Oak, black locust, wild cherry.

BEHAVIOR:
Adults of northern walkingsticks exhibit negative geotaxis, seeking high ground from which to feed. This apparently is the primary basis for dietary preference of tree leaves. They will feed on berry (*Rubus*) leaves if they fall from the tree.

Diapheromera persimilis

Similar Walkingstick

RECOGNIZABLE CHARACTERS:
Slender body, no spine on hind femur.
Males usually brown (rarely with green limbs), females often green or light brown.

REPRESENTATIVE DISTRIBUTION:
Arkansas: Polk Co.

Kansas: Cherokee Co., Crawford Co., Douglas Co., Reno Co., Riley Co., Sedgwick Co.

Louisiana: Bienville Parish, Caddo Parish, Calcasieu Parish, Rapides Parish

Nebraska: Lancaster Co., Saunders Co.

Oklahoma: Alfalfa Co., Creek Co., Ellis Co., Grady Co., Kingfisher Co., Major Co., Pawnee Co., Payne Co., Pittsburg Co., Tulsa Co.

Texas: Anderson Co., Aransas Co., Bandera Co., Bee Co., Blanco Co., Burnet Co., Calhoun Co., Cameron Co., Chambers Co., Cherokee Co., Colorado Co., Dallas Co., Eastland Co., Ellis Co., Fort Bend Co., Galveston Co., Grayson Co., Gregg Co., Grimes Co., Harris Co., Johnson Co., Kerr Co., Nueces Co., Parker Co., San Patricio Co., Shackelford Co., Tyler Co., Uvalde Co., Van Zandt Co., Victoria Co.

REPRESENTATIVE HABITAT AND FOOD PLANTS:
Undergrowth or grass at edges of mixed forests, tall weeds, high grass, prairie.

Diapheromera tamaulipensis

Tamaulipas Walkingstick

RECOGNIZABLE CHARACTERS:
Females have horn-like spines on head.
Ninth abdominal segment in males is longer than its width.

REPRESENTATIVE DISTRIBUTION:
Texas: Bexar Co., Childress Co., Comal Co., Eastland Co., Frio Co., Hidalgo Co., Kerr Co., LaSalle Co., Medina Co., Moore Co., Nolan Co., Starr Co., Terrell Co., Uvalde Co., Val Verde Co., Victoria Co., Ward Co.

REPRESENTATIVE HABITAT AND FOOD PLANTS:
Weeds, prairie grass, oak scrub, mimosas.

Diapheromera torquata

Twisted Walkingstick

RECOGNIZABLE CHARACTERS:
Small, slender body.
Adult male's poculum is twisted asymmetrically into an almost vertical position.
Male cerci are simple and unspined.

The middle femur in males is relatively thickened, but is not enlarged to the extent of many other *Diapheromera*.

Immature specimens are a light green, turning light brown with maturity.

SYSTEMATICS:
According to Hebard (1943), nearest relative is the Mexican species *D. erythropleura*.

REPRESENTATIVE DISTRIBUTION:
Texas: Brewster Co.

REPRESENTATIVE HABITAT AND FOOD PLANTS:
Chisos Mountains of the Big Bend Region.
High grass, brush oak, acacia.

Diapheromera velii

Prairie Walkingstick

RECOGNIZABLE CHARACTERS:
Middle femurs not banded in males, and male cerci have small spines.
Hind femurs in both sexes have prominent spine.
Male's seventh abdominal segment same length as ninth abdominal segment.
Female femurs often have black tips.
Male poculum is bilobed.

SYSTEMATICS:
In certain specimens from southern Texas and New Mexico, the male's poculum has a very broad lip. This and a few additional characters provided grounds for the description of a subspecies, *D. v. eucnemis*.
The variety *mesillana* is no longer considered valid.
A specimen from Illinois used in describing this species was actually *Manomera blatchleyi*.

REPRESENTATIVE DISTRIBUTION:
Colorado: Bent Co., Prowers Co., Sedgwick Co., Washington Co., Weld Co.
Indiana: Kosciusko Co.
Iowa: Humboldt Co., Johnson Co., Linn Co., Worth Co.

Kansas: Barber Co., Bourbon Co., Comanche Co., Douglas Co., Ford Co., Graham Co., Grant Co., Hamilton Co., Harper Co., Kearny Co., Kiowa Co., Lane Co., Logan Co., Meade Co., Montgomery Co., Norton Co., Osborne Co., Pratt Co., Reno Co., Rooks Co., Russell Co., Sedgwick Co., Seward Co., Sheridan Co., Stevens Co., Sumner Co., Thomas Co., Trego Co., Wallace Co., Washington Co., Wichita Co.

Louisiana: Caddo Parish

Minnesota: Hennepin Co., Pine Co., Pipestone Co., Polk Co., Todd Co., Wabasha Co.

Missouri: Grundy Co., Jasper Co., Randolph Co., Scotland Co.

Nebraska: Arthur Co., Box Butte Co., Cass Co., Cherry Co., Cuming Co., Custer Co., Dixon Co., Frontier Co., Hitchcock Co., Knox Co., Lancaster Co., Red Willow Co., Sioux Co., Thomas Co.

New Mexico: Bernalillo Co., Chaves Co., Dona Ana Co., Eddy Co., Guadalupe Co., Lea Co., Luna Co., Otero Co., Sandoval Co., San Juan Co., Santa Fe Co., Sierra Co., Socorro Co.

Oklahoma: Beaver Co., Beckham Co., Blaine Co., Carter Co., Cimarron Co., Cleveland Co., Comanche Co., Custer Co., Ellis Co., Harmon Co., Jackson Co., Kingfisher Co., Kiowa Co., Logan Co., Major Co., Mayes Co., Payne Co., Sequoyah Co., Texas Co., Woods Co., Woodward Co.

South Dakota: Brookings Co., Haakon Co.

Texas: Bee Co., Bexar Co., Brewster Co., Brooks Co., Cameron Co., Comal Co., Culberson Co., Dallam Co., Dallas Co., Dimmit Co., Donley Co., Duval Co., Eastland Co., Ector Co., El Paso Co., Gregg Co., Hemphill Co., Hidalgo Co., Howard Co., Hudspeth Co., Jeff Davis Co., Jim Wells Co., LaSalle Co., Lubbock Co., Midland Co., Nueces Co., Presidio Co., Randall Co., Reeves Co., Refugio Co., Runnels Co., Starr Co., Uvalde Co., Val Verde Co., Victoria Co., Ward Co., Webb Co., Wilbarger Co., Willis Co., Wilson Co.

REPRESENTATIVE HABITAT AND FOOD PLANTS:

Prefers tall grass and short brush.

In arid regions, may be found in stabilized sand dunes.

Sometimes found in low-hanging mesquite trees.

Found on bluestem grass (*Andropogon*), bush clover (*Lespedeza*), broom pea (*Dalea scoparia*), broom snakeweed (*Xanthocephalum sarothrae*), *Astragalus*, and prairie willow (*Salix humilis*).

In some areas, may be a vegetation specialist. For example, in Colorado's sandhill grazing ranges, it feeds on wild alfalfa (*Psoralea tenuiflora*).

BEHAVIOR:

Sometimes found in large aggregations, as males fight and compete for females.

Defensive strategies sometimes include regurgitation and reflex bleeding.

Genus *Manomera*

DISTINGUISHING CHARACTERS:

Five tarsomeres.

Mesothorax is four times longer (or more) than the prothorax.

Antennae longer than front leg femurs in both sexes.

Head distinctly longer than wide.

No lobes or swellings on femurs.

Manomera blatchleyi

Blatchley's Walkingstick

RECOGNIZABLE CHARACTERS:

Last abdominal segment twice as long as wide, blunt teeth at base of male's cercus, no teeth on middle femur. Coloration may be greenish, brownish, grayish, or purplish.

REPRESENTATIVE DISTRIBUTION*:

Connecticut: Fairfield Co., New Haven Co.

Delaware: New Castle Co.

Illinois: Champaign Co., Coles Co., Cook Co., Lake Co., Mason Co., McLean Co., Washington Co.

Indiana: Starke Co.

Iowa: Davis Co., Fremont Co.

Kansas: Douglas Co., Riley Co.

Maryland: Montgomery Co.

Missouri: Atchison Co.

New Jersey: Cape May Co., Monmouth Co., Passaic Co., Union Co.

New York: Nassau Co.

North Carolina: Wake Co.

Ohio: Ottawa Co.

Oklahoma: Payne Co.

* There is speculation that specimens from IA, KS, MO, and OK are *D. persimilis*. Kansas specimens at UGA were confirmed as *Manomera*, so I consider this range valid at present.

Virginia: Fairfax Co., Greene Co.
Wisconsin: Dane Co., Walworth Co.

REPRESENTATIVE HABITAT AND FOOD PLANTS:
Goldenrod, asters.

Manomera brachypyga

Short-Rumped Walkingstick

RECOGNIZABLE CHARACTERS:
Last abdominal segment about as long as wide, blunt teeth at base of male's cercus.

REPRESENTATIVE DISTRIBUTION:
Florida: Collier Co., Dixie Co., Hendry Co., Miami-Dade Co.

REPRESENTATIVE HABITAT AND FOOD PLANTS:
Undergrowth in pine woods.

Manomera tenuescens

Slender-Bodied Walkingstick

RECOGNIZABLE CHARACTERS:
Last abdominal segment twice as long as wide, sharp teeth at base of male's cercus, small tooth on middle femur.

REPRESENTATIVE DISTRIBUTION:
Alabama: Houston Co.
Florida: Charlotte Co., Dixie Co., Duval Co., Miami-Dade Co., Orange Co., Suwannee Co.
North Carolina: Carteret Co., Cumberland Co., Johnston Co., Moore Co., Orange Co., Wake Co.
South Carolina: Barnwell Co., Colleton Co., Jasper Co.

REPRESENTATIVE HABITAT AND FOOD PLANTS:
Underbrush of open pine woods. Huckleberry, wire grass, saw palmetto.

Genus *Megaphasma*

DISTINGUISHING CHARACTERS:

Five tarsomeres. Antennae longer than front leg femurs in both sexes.
Mesothorax is four times longer (or more) than the prothorax.
Femurs of the middle and hind legs have numerous spines underneath.

Megaphasma denticrus

Giant Walkingstick

RECOGNIZABLE CHARACTERS:

Largest phasmid in North America. Specimens known to reach 15 centimeters.
Greenish to reddish-brown in coloration.

REPRESENTATIVE DISTRIBUTION:

Alabama: Yell Co.
Arkansas: Carroll Co., Johnson Co., Logan Co., Montgomery Co., Newton Co. (*cover*)
Illinois: LaSalle Co., Randolph Co.
Indiana: Clark Co.
Iowa: Boone Co., Fremont Co., Page Co., Webster Co.
Kansas: Anderson Co.
Kentucky: Jefferson Co.
Louisiana: East Baton Rouge Parish, St. Landry Parish
Mississippi: Hinds Co.
Missouri: Crawford Co., Dallas Co., Greene Co., Iron Co., Jasper Co., Miller Co., Morgan Co., Stone Co., Taney Co.
New Mexico: Dona Ana Co.
Oklahoma: Adair Co., Cherokee Co., Latimer Co., LeFlore Co.
Texas: Anderson Co., Bandera Co., Bastrop Co., Bexar Co., Brewster Co., Burleson Co., Burnet Co., Comal Co., De Witt Co., Grimes Co., Kerr Co., Lee Co., Milam Co., Real Co., Travis Co., Victoria Co., Wharton Co., Williamson Co.
Wisconsin: Sauk Co.

REPRESENTATIVE HABITAT AND FOOD PLANTS:

Grass, grape vines, oak, elm, and mesquite.

Genus *Parabacillus*

DISTINGUISHING CHARACTERS:
Five tarsomeres.
Mesothorax is four times longer (or more) than the prothorax.
Antennae shorter than front leg femurs in both sexes.

Parabacillus coloradus

Colorado Short-Horned Walkingstick

RECOGNIZABLE CHARACTERS:
Slender, up to about 7 centimeters in length.
Found in various shades of brown, sometimes with paler stripes on the head.
In males, the length of the last abdominal segment is about two times its width.
Hebard (1934) suggested that northern populations may be parthenogenic.
There has been confusion in the overlapping ranges between *coloradus* and *hesperus*.
   Further study will be needed to establish the true boundaries or intergrade zone.

REPRESENTATIVE DISTRIBUTION:
Arizona: Cochise Co., Coconino Co., Mohave Co., Pima Co., Pinal Co., Sta. Cruz Co.,
   Yavapai Co.
Colorado: Alamosa Co., Boulder Co., Fremont Co., Garfield Co., Huerfano Co., Larimer Co.,
   Las Animas Co., Mesa Co., Moffat Co., Montezuma Co., Otero Co.
Kansas: Hamilton Co.
Nebraska: Cheyenne Co., Kimball Co., Lincoln Co.
New Mexico: Bernalillo Co., Chaves Co., Colfax Co., Curry Co., Eddy Co., McKinley Co.,
   Mora Co., Quay Co., Roosevelt Co., Socorro Co.
Oklahoma: Ellis Co., Harper Co., Texas Co.
South Dakota: Brule Co., Jones Co., Walworth Co.
Texas: Brewster Co., Dallam Co., Hemphill Co., Jeff Davis Co., Lubbock Co., Presidio Co.,
   Terrell Co.
Utah: Cache Co., Carbon Co., Grand Co., Tooele Co., Salt Lake Co., Washington Co.
Wyoming: Laramie Co.

REPRESENTATIVE HABITAT AND FOOD PLANTS:
Mountainous regions and grasslands.
Grasses.

BEHAVIOR:
Egg capsules are similar in shape and coloration to grass-seeds. They are affixed by the female to substrates with an adhesive.

Parabacillus hesperus

Western Short-Horned Walkingstick

RECOGNIZABLE CHARACTERS:
In males, the last abdominal segment is about as wide as long.
P. hesperus from Santa Cruz Island are distinctly smaller than the mainland population.
Males are medium sized, and very slender. Females are longer and more robust.
Usually straw-colored, but some are light brown or light red-brown.
Hebard (1934) suggested that northern populations may be parthenogenic.

REPRESENTATIVE DISTRIBUTION:
Arizona: Cochise Co., Coconino Co., La Paz Co., Navajo Co., Pima Co., Pinal Co., Santa Cruz Co., Yuma Co.
California: Contra Costa Co., Los Angeles Co., Riverside Co., San Bernardino Co., San Diego Co., Santa Barbara Co.
Nevada: Clark Co., Lincoln Co.
New Mexico: Grant Co.
Oregon: Harney Co., Morrow Co.
Texas: Randall Co.
Utah: Beaver Co., Washington Co.

REPRESENTATIVE HABITAT AND FOOD PLANTS:
Often associated with mountains. Chaparral.
Range grasses, burroweed, globemallow (*Sphaeralcea*), buckwheat (*Eriogonum*).

Genus *Pseudosermyle*

DISTINGUISHING CHARACTERS:
Five tarsomeres.
Mesothorax is four times longer (or more) than the prothorax.
Antennae longer than front leg femurs in both sexes.
Femurs of the middle legs show no spine or lobing.

Pseudosermyle catalinae

Santa Catalina Walkingstick

RECOGNIZABLE CHARACTERS:
Gray body with darker metathorax and first few abdominal segments.
Female cerci relatively short, only one and a half times longer than broad.
Much smaller than mainland population of *P. straminea*.

REPRESENTATIVE DISTRIBUTION:
California: Santa Barbara Co. (Santa Catalina Island only.)

REPRESENTATIVE HABITAT AND FOOD PLANTS:
Chaparral and grass patches.

Pseudosermyle straminea

Gray Walkingstick

RECOGNIZABLE CHARACTERS:
Female cerci two and a half to three times longer than broad.

ETYMOLOGY:
Straminea means straw-colored.

REPRESENTATIVE DISTRIBUTION:

Arizona: Cochise Co., Coconino Co., Pima Co., Santa Cruz Co.

Arkansas: No county recorded.

California: Inyo Co., Los Angeles Co., Riverside Co., San Bernardino Co., San Diego Co.

Colorado: Mesa Co., Montezuma Co., Otero Co.

Illinois: Henry Co.

Nevada: Lincoln Co., Nye Co.

New Mexico: Eddy Co., Grant Co., Santa Fe Co.

Oklahoma: Cimarron Co., Harmon Co.

Texas: Brewster Co., Culberson Co., Duval Co., Eastland Co., Hidalgo Co., Hudspeth Co., Jeff Davis Co., Kenedy Co., Lubbock Co., Parker Co., Randall Co., Shackelford Co., Terrell Co., Val Verde Co., Yoakum Co.

Utah: Beaver Co., Garfield Co., Iron Co., Juab Co., San Juan Co., Tooele Co., Washington Co.

REPRESENTATIVE HABITAT AND FOOD PLANTS:

Sagebrush, grass, burroweed, aster (*Haplopappus*), rabbit-weed.

Pseudosermyle strigata

Striped Walkingstick

RECOGNIZABLE CHARACTERS:

Deeper notch in male cercus than in *P. straminea.*

REPRESENTATIVE DISTRIBUTION:

Alabama: Baldwin Co., Mobile Co.

Arizona: Cochise Co., Graham Co., La Paz Co., Pima Co., Pinal Co., Yavapai Co., Yuma Co.

Arkansas: Logan Co., Polk Co.

Louisiana: Bienville Parish, Calcasieu Parish, Natchitoches Parish, Rapides Parish

Mississippi: Adams Co., Forrest Co., Lincoln Co.

Texas: Anderson Co., Bee Co., Brazos Co., Dallas Co., Fayette Co., Galveston Co., Grimes Co., Harris Co., Hidalgo Co., Jefferson Co., Robertson Co., Tyler Co., Victoria Co.

REPRESENTATIVE HABITAT AND FOOD PLANTS:

Mountainous regions and grasslands.

Undergrowth of pine forest, tall grasses, prairie-grass.

Genus *Sermyle*

DISTINGUISHING CHARACTERS:
Five tarsomeres.
Mesothorax is four times longer (or more) than the prothorax.
Antennae longer than front leg femurs in both sexes.
Femurs of the middle legs are prominently lobed.
Fifth abdominal segment is prominently lobed.

Sermyle mexicana

Mexican walkingstick

RECOGNIZABLE CHARACTERS:
Noticeable lobing on middle leg femurs and fifth abdominal segment.

REPRESENTATIVE DISTRIBUTION:
Texas: Cameron Co.

REPRESENTATIVE HABITAT AND FOOD PLANTS:
Huisache (*Acacia*) vines.

Genus *Timema*

DISTINGUISHING CHARACTERS:
Three tarsomeres.
Much smaller and more robust in form than other North American walkingsticks.

RECOGNIZABLE CHARACTERS:
Many species occur in several color morphs with little intergradation. After death, *Timema* often fade to drab brown.
Species of *Timema* are either bisexual or parthenogenic. Most parthenogenic species are closely related to a bisexual species. Even in parthenogenic species, a male may rarely be found; in bisexual species, however, males guard females from competitors, so both sexes should be easily found within a known population.

NATURAL HISTORY AND BEHAVIOR:
Often found at higher elevations than other phasmids can tolerate.
Timema females ingest soil, which is defecated onto eggs as they are laid. The egg is coated with soil, then dropped to the ground or placed carefully (depending on species). This may protect the eggs against parasites and dessication.
When disturbed, some *Timema* release an "acrid" chemical odor.

SPECIATION:
While *Timema* is unlikely to be confused with any other native phasmid, the species themselves can be difficult to distinguish, especially if using dried specimens with no locality data. A diagnostic key is outside the scope of this book, as the primary characters are microscopic and prone to variability. Recent additions in taxonomy suggest that there are still unrecognized species left to discover.
In order to adequately identify specimens, make certain you have 1) multiple sexed live specimens from the same locality, 2) identification of the host plant on which the specimens were feeding, and 3) locality data for the collection site. *Timema* species are often host-plant specific or found only in certain locations. Coloration is too variable to be a principle diagnostic character, but if used in conjunction with these three data, you should be able to come up with a reasonable identification.
Hobbyists interested in the systematics of *Timema* are strongly encouraged to obtain the relevant papers (especially by Vickery and Sandoval) listed in the references. There have also been several interesting studies on *Timema* speciation throughout the West Coast, including discussion of parthenogenesis. Those papers are listed, as well.

Timema bartmani

Bartman's Timema

RECOGNIZABLE CHARACTERS:
Bisexual, so both sexes will be readily found.
Color morphs: ground color is pale greenish brown or beige. Some have greenish brown bodies with beige head and limbs. All morphs have a yellow dorsal stripe.

REPRESENTATIVE DISTRIBUTION:
California: San Bernardino Co.

REPRESENTATIVE HABITAT AND FOOD PLANTS:
White fir (*Abies concolor*) specialist; feeds on both needles and bark.
Fed on California lilac (*Ceanothus*), oak (*Quercus*), and pine (*Pinus*) in captivity.

Timema boharti

Bohart's Timema

RECOGNIZABLE CHARACTERS:
Bisexual, so both sexes will be readily found.
Coloration includes light brown, gray, and green morphs. Darker mottling.

REPRESENTATIVE DISTRIBUTION:
California: Fresno Co., Riverside Co., San Bernardino Co., San Diego Co.

REPRESENTATIVE HABITAT AND FOOD PLANTS:
Found on *Yucca,* pinyon pine (*Pinus* sp.), chamise (*Adenostoma*), California lilac (*Ceanothus*), quackgrass (*Elymus*), scrub oak (*Quercus dumosa*), and buckwheat (*Eriogonum*).

Timema californicum

California Timema

RECOGNIZABLE CHARACTERS:
Bisexual, so both sexes will be readily found.
Males up to about 1.5 centimeters in length, females reaching up to a bit longer than 2 centimeters.
Color forms include green, pink, or green with pink legs (the latter often found in males).

REPRESENTATIVE DISTRIBUTION:
California: Alameda Co., Contra Costa Co., Fresno Co., Kern Co., Los Angeles Co., Marin Co., Mariposa Co., Monterey Co., Napa Co., Riverside Co., San Bernardino Co., San Luis Obispo Co., San Mateo Co., Santa Clara Co., Santa Cruz Co., Sonoma Co.

REPRESENTATIVE HABITAT AND FOOD PLANTS:
Oaks, fir trees, chamise (*Adenostoma*), California lilac (*Ceanothus*), toyon (*Heteromeles arbutifolia*), madrona (*Arbutus*), manzanita (*Arctostaphylos*), woolly leaf (*Eriophyllum*), yerba santa (*Eriodictyon californicum*), coyote brush (*Baccharis pilularis*), silk tassel bush (*Garrya elliptica*).

Timema chumash

Chumash Timema

RECOGNIZABLE CHARACTERS:
Bisexual, so both sexes will be readily found.
Usually green, sometimes brown. Pale speckling.

REPRESENTATIVE DISTRIBUTION:
California: Los Angeles Co., Riverside Co., San Bernardino Co.

REPRESENTATIVE HABITAT AND FOOD PLANTS:
Oaks, chamise (*Adenostoma*), California lilac (*Ceanothus*), mountain mahogany (*Cercocarpus*).

Timema coffmani

Coffman's Timema

RECOGNIZABLE CHARACTERS:
Bisexual, so both sexes will be readily found.
Coloration is typically pale reddish-brown, with darker head and prothorax. Two less common color morphs are either gray or yellow ground colors. Dark markings found on all morphs.

REPRESENTATIVE DISTRIBUTION:
Arizona: Mohave Co.

REPRESENTATIVE HABITAT AND FOOD PLANTS:
Utah juniper (*Juniperus osteosperma*) specialist.

BEHAVIOR:
Will rest underneath logs on the ground under their juniper-feeding spots.

Timema cristinae

Cristina's Timema

RECOGNIZABLE CHARACTERS:
Bisexual, so both sexes will be readily found.
Highly variable in color. Males can be yellow, yellow-green, or reddish. Females can be these colors, as well as gray or creamy yellow. Pale abdominal stripes are usually found, but there are unstriped morphs.

REPRESENTATIVE DISTRIBUTION:
California: Santa Barbara Co.

REPRESENTATIVE HABITAT AND FOOD PLANTS:
Chamise (*Adenostoma*), California lilac (*Ceanothus*), mountain mahogany (*Cercocarpus*), chaparral pea (*Pickeringia*).

Timema dorotheae

Dorothy's Timema

RECOGNIZABLE CHARACTERS:
Bisexual, so both sexes will be readily found.
Pale brown in coloration, darker dorsal stripe.

REPRESENTATIVE DISTRIBUTION:
Arizona: Mohave Co.

REPRESENTATIVE HABITAT AND FOOD PLANTS:
Hualpai Mountains.

Timema douglasi

Douglas Timema

RECOGNIZABLE CHARACTERS:
Parthenogenic, so males will rarely be found.
Green background color, with three dark green dorsal stripes enclosing two broad
yellowish-green stripes.

REPRESENTATIVE DISTRIBUTION:
California: El Dorado Co.*, Humboldt Co., Mendocino Co., Plumas Co.*, Santa Cruz Co.,
Tehama Co.*
Oregon: Curry Co.

(* probable distribution based on specimens formerly considered *T. californicum*, but
too far north and only females found.)

REPRESENTATIVE HABITAT AND FOOD PLANTS:
Old-growth fir forests near prairie grass.
Douglas fir (*Pseudotsuga douglasii*) is the primary host plant, with lesser numbers
found on redwood (*Sequoia*) and California lilac (*Ceanothus*).

Timema genevievae

Genevieve's Timema

RECOGNIZABLE CHARACTERS:
Parthenogenic, so males will rarely be found.
Coloration is grayish-brown with yellow speckling. Some light striping on dorsal aspect.

REPRESENTATIVE DISTRIBUTION:
California: Alameda Co., Colusa Co.*, Santa Clara Co., Stanislaus Co., Tehama Co.*

(* probable distribution based on specimens formerly considered *T. podura*, but too far north and only females found.)

REPRESENTATIVE HABITAT AND FOOD PLANTS:
Feeds on chamise (*Adenostoma fasciculatum*).
Has been found on mountain mahogany (*Cercocarpus*), but may not feed on it.

Timema knulli

Knull's Timema

RECOGNIZABLE CHARACTERS:
Bisexual, so both sexes will be readily found.
A larger *Timema*, green with two dark green dorsal stripes.
Removed from synonymy with *T. californicum* in 2001.

REPRESENTATIVE DISTRIBUTION:
California: Monterey Co.

REPRESENTATIVE HABITAT AND FOOD PLANTS:
Santa Lucia mountains.
Redwood (*Sequoia*) specialist.

Timema landelsensis

Landels-Hill Timema

RECOGNIZABLE CHARACTERS:
Bisexual, so both sexes will be readily found.
Green coloration, with pale spots on the sides of the abdomen.

REPRESENTATIVE DISTRIBUTION:
California: Monterey Co.

REPRESENTATIVE HABITAT AND FOOD PLANTS:
Specialist on manzanita (*Arctostaphylos*).

Timema monikensis

Santa Monica Mountains Timema

RECOGNIZABLE CHARACTERS:
Parthenogenic, so males will rarely be found.
Coloration may be green, or gray with dark markings, both forms with small pale spotting.

REPRESENTATIVE DISTRIBUTION:
California: Los Angeles Co.

REPRESENTATIVE HABITAT AND FOOD PLANTS:
Chaparral along sides of the Mulholland Highway.
Mountain mahogany (*Cercocarpus*), scrub oak (*Quercus dumosa*), chamise (*Adenostoma*), and redheart (*Ceanothus spinosus*).

Timema morongensis

Morongo Valley Timema

RECOGNIZABLE CHARACTERS:
Bisexual, so both sexes will be readily found.
A larger *Timema*, females up to 3 centimeters.

REPRESENTATIVE DISTRIBUTION:
California: Riverside Co.

REPRESENTATIVE HABITAT AND FOOD PLANTS:
Buckwheat (*Eriogonum*).

Timema nakipa

Nakipa Timema

RECOGNIZABLE CHARACTERS:
Coloration is green, tan, or light brown.

REPRESENTATIVE DISTRIBUTION:
Baja California Norte.

REPRESENTATIVE HABITAT AND FOOD PLANTS:
Manzanita (*Arctostaphylos*) and California lilac (*Ceanothus*).

ETYMOLOGY:
The Nakipa tribe once inhabited this region.

Timema nevadense

Nevada Timema

RECOGNIZABLE CHARACTERS:
Bisexual, so both sexes will be readily found.
Color morphs may be green, brown, or gray and white.

REPRESENTATIVE DISTRIBUTION:
California: San Bernardino Co.
Nevada: Clark Co.

REPRESENTATIVE HABITAT AND FOOD PLANTS:
California juniper (*Juniperus californica*) specialist, but has been taken on pine.

BEHAVIOR:
Will rest underneath rocks on the ground.

Timema petita

Petite Timema

RECOGNIZABLE CHARACTERS:
Bisexual, so both sexes will be readily found.
Small species, even for *Timema*.
Dark green dorsally, with paler underbelly. Black markings on head and abdomen.

REPRESENTATIVE DISTRIBUTION:
California: Monterey Co.

REPRESENTATIVE HABITAT AND FOOD PLANTS:
California lilac (*Ceanothus*).

Timema podura

Sierra Nevada Mts. Timema

RECOGNIZABLE CHARACTERS:
Bisexual, so both sexes will be readily found.
Coloration in shades of brown, often with darker mottling.

REPRESENTATIVE DISTRIBUTION:
California: Fresno Co., Kern Co., Los Angeles Co., Monterey Co., Riverside Co., San
     Benito Co., San Bernardino Co., San Diego Co., Stanislaus Co., Tulare Co., Tuolomne Co.
Baja California

REPRESENTATIVE HABITAT AND FOOD PLANTS:
Chamise (*Adenostoma fasciculatum*), California lilac (*Ceanothus*), oaks, threefold
     (*Trixis*), mountain mahogany (*Cercocarpus*), and *Yucca*.

BEHAVIOR:
T. podura will rest inside *Yucca* leaves, though they don't necessarily feed on them.

Timema poppensis

Poppe Road Timema

RECOGNIZABLE CHARACTERS:
Bisexual, so both sexes will be readily found.
This species is more elongate and slender than most *Timema*.
Coloration is pale green with some dark markings.

REPRESENTATIVE DISTRIBUTION:
California: Napa Co.

REPRESENTATIVE HABITAT AND FOOD PLANTS:
Primarily found on Douglas fir, but sometimes found on *Sequoia*.

Timema ritensis

Santa Rita Mts. Timema

RECOGNIZABLE CHARACTERS:
Bisexual, so both sexes will be readily found.
Light to dark brown in color, with some marginal orangish speckling.

REPRESENTATIVE DISTRIBUTION:
Arizona: Graham Co., Pima Co., Santa Cruz Co.

REPRESENTATIVE HABITAT AND FOOD PLANTS:
Pinaleno Mts., Santa Catalina Mts., Santa Rita Mts.
Alligator juniper (*Juniperus deppeana*) specialist.

Timema shepardi

Shepard's Timema

RECOGNIZABLE CHARACTERS:
Parthenogenic, so males will rarely be found.
Coloration is pale green with some light spotting.

REPRESENTATIVE DISTRIBUTION:
California: Mendocino Co., Napa Co.

REPRESENTATIVE HABITAT AND FOOD PLANTS:
Specializes on manzanita (*Arctostaphylos*).

Timema tahoe

Tahoe Timema

RECOGNIZABLE CHARACTERS:
   Parthenogenic, so males will rarely be found.
   Several color morphs known. Body can be greenish with yellow dorsal stripe, yellow-green with white dorsal stripe, yellow with white dorsal and lateral stripes, or violet-pink with pale dorsal and lateral stripes.

REPRESENTATIVE DISTRIBUTION:
   Nevada: Carson City Co., Douglas Co., Whashoe Co.

REPRESENTATIVE HABITAT AND FOOD PLANTS:
   White fir (*Abies concolor*).

References

Arnett, Ross H., Jr. 1993. *American Insects*. Gainesville, FL: The Sandhill Crane Press.

Beamer, Raymond H. 1932. The giant walking-stick (*Megaphasma detricus* (Stal.) found in Kansas. *Journal of the Kansas Entomological Society* 5(1): 28.

Bedford, Geoffrey O. 1978. Biology and ecology of the Phasmatodea. *Ann. Rev. Entomol.* 23: 125-149.

Blatchley, W. S. 1920. *Orthoptera of Northeastern America*. Indianapolis, IN: Nature Publ.

Brimley, C. S. 1938. *The Insects of North Carolina*. Raleigh, NC: NC Dept. Agriculture.

Capinera, John L. 1985. Determination of host plant preferences of *Hemileuca oliviae* (Lepidoptera: Saturniidae), *Paropomala wyomingensis* (Orthoptera: Acrididae), and *Diapheromera veli* (Orthoptera: Phasmatidae) by choice test and crop analysis. *Journal of the Kansas Entomological Society* 58(3): 465-471.

Caudell, Andrew Nelson. 1904. Two orthoptera hitherto unrecorded from the United States. *Proceedings of the U. S. National Museum* 27: 949-952.

Caudell, A. N. 1905. *Aplopus mayeri*, new species. *Journal of the New York Entomological Society* 8: 83-85.

Caudell, A. N. 1918. Regarding *Diapheromera veliei* Walsh and *Manomera blatchleyi* Caudell (Orth.: Phasmidae). *Entomological News* 29: 258-260.

Crespi, B. J., and C. P. Sandoval. 2000. Phylogenetic evidence for the evolution of ecological specialization in *Timema* walking-sticks. *Journal of Evolutionary Biology* 13: 249-262.

Davis, W. T. 1923. A new walking-stick insect from eastern North America. *Journal of the New York Entomological Society*. 31: 52-55.

Essig, E. O. 1926. *Insects of Western North America*. New York: MacMillan Co.

Gregory, T. Ryan. 2002. Genome size of the northern walkingstick, *Diapheromera femorata* (Phasmida: Heteronemiidae). *Canadian Journal of Zoology* 80: 1303-1305.

Gunning, Gerald E. 1987. Behavioral observations of the walking stick, *Anisomorpha buprestoides* (Phasmatodea: Phasmatidae). *Florida Entomologist* 70(3): 406-408.

Gustafson, Joel F. 1966. Biological observations on *Timema californica* (Phasmoidea: Phasmidae). *Annals of the Entomological Society of America* 59(1): 59-61.

Hebard, Morgan. 1931. The races of *Diapheromera veliei* (Orthoptera, Phasmidae, Heteronemiinae). *Entomological News* 42(3): 65-67.

Hebard, Morgan. 1931. The Orthoptera of Kansas. Proceedings of the Academy of Natural Sciences of Philadelphia 83: 119-227.

Hebard, Morgan. 1934. Studies in orthoptera which occur in North America north of the Mexican boundary. *Transactions of the American Entomological Society* 60: 281-293.

Hebard, Morgan. 1937. Studies in orthoptera which occur in North America north of the Mexican boundary. *Transactions of the American Entomological Society* 63: 347-354.

Hebard, Morgan. 1943. The Dermaptera and orthopterous families Blattidae, Mantidae and Phasmidae of Texas. Transactions of the American Entomological Society 68: 239-310+.

Helfer, Jacques R. 1987. *How to Know the Grasshoppers, Crickets, Cockroaches and Their Allies*. Mineola, NY: Dover.

Hetrick, L. A. 1949. Field notes on a color variant of the two-striped walkingstick, *Anisomorpha buprestoides* (Stoll). *The Florida Entomologist* 32(2): 74-77.

Knauer, K.H. 1966. *Seasonal life history and behavior of the northern walkingstick*. Ms. Thesis, unpublished. Lafayette, IN: Purdue University.

Law, Jennifer H., and Bernard J. Crespi. 2002. Recent and ancient asexuality in *Timema* walking-sticks. *Evolution* 56(8): 1711-1717.

Law, Jennifer H., and Bernard J. Crespi. 2002. The evolution of geographic parthenogenesis in *Timema* walking-sticks. *Molecular Ecology* 11: 1471-1489.

Littig, Kent S. 1942. External anatomy of the Florida walkingstick *Anisomorpha buprestoides* Stoll. *The Florida Entomologist* 25(3): 33-41.

Nosil, P., and B. J. Crespi. 2004. Does gene flow constrain adaptive divergence or vice versa? A test using ecomorphology and sexual isolation in *Timema cristinae* walking-sticks. *Evolution* 58(1): 102-112.

Nosil, Patrik, Bernard J. Crespi, and Cristina P. Sandoval. 2002. Host-plant adaptation drives the parallel evolution of reproductive isolation. *Nature* 417: 440-443.

Nosil, P., B. J. Crespi, and C. P. Sandoval. 2003. Reproductive isolation driven by the combined effects of ecological adaptation and reinforcement. *Proceedings of the Royal Society, London B* 270: 1911-1918.

Peck, Stewart B., and Clifford Beninger. 1989. A survey of insects of the Florida Keys: cockroaches (Blattodea), mantids (Mantodea), and walkingsticks (Phasmatodea). *Florida Entomologist* 72(4): 612-617.

Rentz, David C. 1963. Notes on a collection of *Timema boharti* Tinkham. The Pan-Pacific Entomologist 39(2): 74.

Rentz, D. C. F. 1978. A new parthenogenic *Timema* from California. *The Pan-Pacific Entomologist* 54(3): 173-177.

Rentz, D. C. F., and David B. Weissman. 1981. *Faunal Affinities, Systematics, and Bionomics of the Orthoptera of the California Channel Islands*. Berkeley, CA: Univ. of California Press.

Sandoval, Cristina P. 1994. Differential visual predation on morphs of *Timema cristinae* (Phasmatodeae: Timemidae) and its consequences for host range. *Biological Journal of the Linnean Society* 52: 341-356.

Sandoval, Cristina P. 1994. The effects of the relative geographic scales of gene flow and selection on morph frequencies in the walking-stick *Timema cristinae*. *Evolution* 48(6): 1866-1879.

Sandoval, Cristina P., and Vernon R. Vickery. 1996. *Timema douglasi* (Phasmatoptera: Timematodea), a new parthenogenetic species from southwestern Oregon and northern California, with notes on other species. *The Canadian Entomologist* 128: 79-84.

Sandoval, Cristina P., and Vernon R. Vickery. 1999. *Timema coffmani* (Phasmatoptera: Timematodea) a new species from Arizona and description of the female of *Timema ritensis*. *Journal of Orthoptera Research* 8: 49-52.

Sandoval, C., D. A. Carmean, and B. J. Crespi. 1998. Molecular phylogenetics of sexual and parthenogenetic *Timema* walking-sticks. *Proceedings of the Royal Society, London B* 265: 589-595.

Scudder, Samuel H. 1901. The species of *Diapheromera* (Phasmidae) found in the United States and Canada. *Psyche* 9: 187-189.

Seely, James A., Adam Asquith, and Gerry P. Zegers. 1991. Size-related fecundity and assortive mating in *Diapheromera veliei* (Phasmatodea: Heteronemiidae). *Annals of the Entomological Society of America* 84(3): 283-286.

Sivinski, John. 1978. Eggs and oviposition of the stick insect *Parabacillus coloradus* (Phasmatodea: Heteronemiidae). *The Florida Entomologist* 61(2): 99.

Sivinski, John. 1978. Intrasexual aggression in the stick insects *Diapheromera veliei* and *D. covilleae* and sexual dimorphism in the Phasmatodea. *Psyche* 85: 395-405.

Sivinski, John. 1980. The effects of mating on predation in the stick insect *Diapheromera veliei* Walsh (Phasmatodea: Heteronemiidae). *Annals of the Entomological Society of America* 73(5): 553-556.

Somes, M. P. 1916. The Phasmidae of Minnesota, Iowa and Missouri (Orth.). *Entomological News* 27: 269-271.

Stark, Bill P., and David L. Lentz. 1986. Morphology of the egg capsule in *Megaphasma dentricus* (Phasmatodea: Heteronemiidae). *Journal of the Kansas Entomological Soc.* 59(2): 398-401.

Strohecker, H. F. 1951. Three new species of North American orthoptera. *Annals of the Entomological Society of America* 44(2): 169-172.

Strohecker, H. F. 1966. New *Timema* from Nevada and Arizona. *The Pan-Pacific Entomologist* 42: 25-26.

Thomas, Michael C. 2003. Featured creatures: *Anismorpha buprestoides*. Florida Dept. of Plant Industry. http://creatures.ifas.ufl.edu/misc/walkingstick.htm

Tilgner, Erich H., and Joseph V. McHugh. 1997. *Diapheromera carolina* Scudder (Phasmatodea: Heteronemiidae), first description of the female form and new range records. *Transactions of the American Entomological Society* 123(3): 191-196.

Tinkham, Ernest R. 1948. Faunistic and ecological studies on the Orthoptera of the Big Bend Region of Trans-Pecos Texas, with especial reference to the Orthopteran zones and faunae of midwestern North America. *The American Midland Naturalist* 40(3): 521-663.

Tozier, Christopher. 2005. Behavioral activity of *Anisomorpha buprestoides* possibly associated with Hurricane Charley (Phasmatodea: Phasmatidae). *Florida Entomologist* 88(1): 106.

Ueckert, Darrell N., and Richard M. Hansen. 1972. Diet of walkingsticks on sandhill rangeland in Colorado. *Journal of Range Management* 25(2): 111-113.

Vickery, Vernon R. 1993. Revision of *Timema* Scudder (Phasmatoptera: Timematodea) including three new species. *The Canadian Entomologist* 125: 657-692.

Vickery, Vernon R. 1996. Additional information on *Timema* species. *The Canadian Entomologist* 126(1): 443.

Vickery, Vernon R., and Cristina P. Sandoval. 1997. *Timema bartmani* (Phasmatoptera: Timematodea: Timematidae), a new species from southern California. *The Canadian Entomologist* 129: 933-936.

Vickery, Vernon R., and Cristina P. Sandoval. 1998. *Timema monikensis*, species nov. (Phasmatoptera: Timematodea: Timematidae), a new parthenogenetic species in California. *Lymon Entomological Museum and Research Laboratory* (McGill University, Quebec, Canada) *Note No.* 22.

Vickery, Vernon R., and Cristina P. Sandoval. 1999. Two new species of *Timema* (Phasmatoptera: Timematodea: Timematidae), one parthenogenetic, in California. *Journal of Orthoptera Research* 8: 45-47.

Vickery, Vernon R., and Cristina P. Sandoval. 2001. Descriptions of three new species of *Timema* (Phasmatoptera: Timematodea: Timematidae) and notes on three other species. *Journal of Orthoptera Research* 10(1): 53-61.

Wilkins, Orin P., and Osmond P. Breland. 1951. Notes on the giant walking stick, *Megaphasma denticrus* (Stal). *The Texas Journal of Science* 3(2): 305-310.

Collections Queried with Successful Replies:

University of Arizona, Tucson, AZ
University of California-Berkeley, Berkeley, CA
Los Angeles Natural History Museum, Los Angeles, CA
California Academy of Sciences, San Francisco, CA
University of Colorado, Boulder, CO
University of Delaware, Newark, DE
University of Central Florida, Orlando, FL
University of Georgia, Athens, GA
Illinois Natural History Survey, Champaign, IL
Kansas State University, Manhattan, KS
University of Kentucky, Lexington, KY
Michigan State University, East Lansing, MI
University of Missouri-Columbia, Columbia, MO
University of Nebraska-Lincoln, Lincoln, NE

North Carolina State University, Raleigh, NC
Cleveland Museum of Natural History, Cleveland, OH
Oklahoma State University, Stillwater, OK
Clemson University, Clemson, SC
Texas A&M University, College Station, TX
Washington State University, Pullman, WA
University of Wisconsin-Madison, Madison, WI

Checklists and Guides:

USGS - Northern Prairie Wildlife Research Center. Colorado National Monument, CO, Arthropod Species. www.npwrc.usgs.gov.
USGS - Northern Prairie Wildlife Research Center. Great Sand Dunes National Monument, CO, Arthropod Species. www.npwrc.usgs.gov.
USGS - Northern Prairie Wildlife Research Center. Mesa Verde National Park, CO, Arthropod Species. www.npwrc.usgs.gov.
USGS - Northern Prairie Wildlife Research Center. Dinosaur National Monument, CO/UT, Arthropod Species. www.npwrc.usgs.gov.
USGS - Northern Prairie Wildlife Research Center. Canyonlands National Park, UT, Arthropod Species. www.npwrc.usgs.gov.
University of Minnesota - Insects of Cedar Creek Natural History Area. cedarcreek.umn.edu

Websites:

Phasmatodea.org
Elytra and Antenna — www.angelfire.com/oh3/elytraandantenna/USInsects/
Herper.com — to contact the editor.

Early Studies

The Phasmidæ, or Walkingsticks, of the United States

Andrew Nelson Caudell,
Of the Department of Agriculture

The Phasmidæ is one of the most interesting families of the order Orthoptera. It is poorly represented in the United States, and the species, being mimetic in nature, are not commonly met with. Our forms are all apterous and are confined in their distribution to the southern half of the country, with the exception of the species of the genus *Diapheromera*, one of which extends into Canada. The name "walking-stick" is commonly applied to these insects, and the common northern species, *Diapheromera femorata* Say, is the best known representative of the family. There is a popular belief extant in some parts of the country that these insects are very poisonous to stock when eaten by them. For this reason they have been called the "mule killer," though this name is more often applied to species of the family Mantidæ, which are said to be especially fatal to that useful animal. Among other popular names given to the walkingsticks are Devil's riding horse, Prairie alligator, Stick bug, Witch's horse, Devil's darning needle, Scorpion, and Musk mare, the latter applied only, I believe, to the species of the genus *Anisomorpha*.

Nowhere do we find more striking instances of protective resemblance than those afforded by members of this family of curious insects. In the tropics, where these insects abound, such amazing adaptations as the wonderful Walkingleaf, *Phyllium scythe*, and other large, winged forms are found. In the United States the species are all wingless and mimic different kinds of twigs, especially so the more slender species of the genera *Diapheromera*, *Bacunculus*, and *Parabacillus*.

The Phasmidæ are insects of very deliberate motion, especially the females. They do not depend upon locomotion for protection from their enemies, but to their deceptive resemblance and, in some cases, to the power of emitting an offensive spray from special glands situated on the prothorax.

The species are exclusively herbivorous, none being known to take animal food. One exception is recorded where some partially starved leaf insects nibbled at the foliaceous expansions of their fellows, but not enough to injure them in any way. The female of one of our species has been recorded as eating off the head of the male while under the influence of sexual excitement, but the insect in question was most surely not a Phasmid but a Mantid, as this habit is not at all uncommon among some members of that family.

From: *Proceedings U.S. National Museum*, Vol. XXVI, No. 1335, pp. 863-885, plus plates.

Regeneration of limbs is quite common among the Phasmidæ. Such limbs are much smaller and may always be distinguished by the absence of one tarsal joint, all regenerated limbs being tetramerous. According to Scudder, if the leg be removed nearer to the body than the trochantero-femoral articulation the limb will not be replaced.

The eggs of our species are dropped at random on the ground. Oviposition takes place in the fall of the year with our common northern species and the eggs lie over winter, and sometimes even through a second, before the nymphs issue. When the young walkingstick is in the egg, ready to emerge, the meso- and metathorax are not remarkably elongate, but before the little creature is fairly out of its narrow prison the thoracic segments assume their usual proportions. It is said to be a most curious sight by those who have observed this almost instantaneous development.

In my studies of these insects specimens of all of our species have been examined, except *Diapheromera mesillana* and *carolina*, and *Pseudosermyle stramineus*. The material of the U. S. National Museum forms the basis of this paper. Specimens were loaned for study by the Colorado and Oklahoma experiment stations. For various kindnesses I wish to express my sincere thanks to Professors Scudder and Bruner and Mr. J. A. G. Rehn.

The family Phasmidæ may be defined as follows:

> Body elongate, subcylindrical; abdomen with ten segments, the basal one usually coalesced to the posterior part of the metathorax, sometimes entirely invisible;[a] all of the legs equally ambulatory; wings wholly absent in the United States species, the location of the metathoracic pair, and sometimes the mesothoracic pair also, generally indicated by a stationary wing-like pad, bearing a gland, presumably a scent gland; tarsi five-jointed, except in *Timema*, terminated by two claws, between which is a large arolium; ovipositor concealed by the subgenital plate; cerci inarticulate.

The species occurring in the United States fall into four subfamilies, separated as follows.

---

[a] In descriptive work the first abdominal segment is spoken of as the intermediary segment and the abdomen is considered as consisting of nine segments. Thus the basal or first abdominal segment as used in the following pages is really the true second one. Likewise the seventh, eighth, and ninth segments are, respectively, the eighth, ninth, and tenth ones. The generally inconspicuous nature of the true basal segment, which is sometimes even wholly invisible, makes this nomenclature seem advisable.

a. Antennæ not more than one-half as long as the anterior femora ..... Clitumninæ
aa. Antennæ distinctly longer than the anterior femora.
　　b. Mesothorax never less than four times as long as the prothorax, generally more;
　　　　tibiæ not furnished at the apex beneath with a sunken areola ..... Bacunculinæ
　bb. Mesothorax never more than three times as long as the prothorax, generally
　　　　less; tibiæ furnished at apex beneath with a sunken areola.
　　　c. Coxæ visible from above; tarsi five jointed ..... Anisomophinæ
　　　cc. Coxæ invisible from above; tarsi three jointed ..... Timeminæ

Subfamily Clitumninæ

The insects representing this subfamily in the United States are very slender wingless walkingsticks with antennæ much shorter than the anterior femora in both sexes. The legs are slender and unarmed and the tibiæ are carinate beneath to the apex. The median segment is short and inconspicuous. Pronotum short as in *Bacunculinæ*. Cerci moderate, incurved in the male and straight in the female.

We have but one genus, which is here characterized as new.

Parabacillus, new genus.

Bacillus Scudder (not Latreille), *Psyche*, VI, 1893, p. 372.

Antennæ less than one-half as long as the anterior femora, composed of six or seven segments in the male and probably about that number in the female, but there, as also sometimes in the male, the segments are so closely connate as to be inseparable, except the first and second, which are very distinct.[a] Head subpyriform, horizontal. Eyes small, round. Thorax with the pronotum about one-fifth as long as the mesonotum. Legs, smooth, unarmed, long and slender. Cerci as in *Diapheromera*.

Dr. Scudder considered the species of this genus to belong to the subfamily Bacillinæ and placed them in the old world genus *Bacillus*. But the absence of an areola at the apex of the tibiæ below refers them to the subfamily Clitumninæ. In many particulars the genus seems closely allied to the genus *Paraclitumnus* of Brunner von Wattenwye. We have a single species of the genus.

---

[a] *Bacillus hispanicus* Bolivar, belongs to this genus, but the antennæ are composed of sixteen distinct segments. The *Bacillus palmeri* of the author, recently described from Mexico, is also a member of this genus.

Parabacillus coloradus Scudder.

Plate LVII, fig. 1; Plate LVIII, fig. 1.

Bacillus coloradus Scudder, *Psyche*, VI, 1893, p. 372; *Proc. Davenp. Acad. Sci.*, IX, 1902, p. 21, pl. I, fig. 4.
Bacillus carinatus Scudder, *Psyche*, VI, 1893, p. 372.

The following description is that of the author[a] which is quoted in full:

Bacillus coloradus Scudder (pl. 1, fig. 4), Baker's ranch, Beulah, Sapello Canyon, 8000' on Monarda stricta (Willmatte P. Cockerell); La Trementina (Alice Blake). The following description was taken from the first specimen, which is that figured:

Testaceous, more or less clouded with fuscous dorsally. Head striped feebly with fuscous, especially above and with five subequidistant delicate longitudinal carinæ; whole thorax and abdomen similarly carinate, but otherwise smooth except for very minute rather sparsely scattered ferruginous granules between the dorsal and subdorsal carinæ; second joint of antennæ small and globular, the remainder consisting of a hardly articulate, slightly depressed, lanceolate, bluntly pointed mass.

Length of body, 48 mm.; antennæ, 4.5 mm.; mesothorax, 10.5 mm.; metathorax, 8.5 mm.; abdomen, 25 mm.; hind femora, 12 mm.; width of metathorax in middle, 1.5 mm.

The above description is from a female specimen. The males are more slender, with longer antennæ and legs.

From a study of a series of specimens, both male and female, from Nebraska, Colorado, New Mexico, Arizona, and California I conclude that there is but one species. They show a certain amount of variation in color and size, but afford no specific characters. The antennæ of a mature pair from California measure 5 mm. in the female and 7 mm. in the male. One male from Arizona has antennæ measuring 12 mm. in length. The color varies from almost wholly infuscated to a light brown. One female from California has an extreme length of very nearly 70 mm. But there are all stages of gradation between these extremes of color and size and no characters present themselves to warrant the recognition of more than the one species.

[a] *Proc. Davnp. Acad. Sci.*, XIV, 1902, p. 21.

Subfamily Bacunculinæ.

The members of this subfamily are long, slender, stick-like insects with the meso-thorax at least five times as long as the prothorax; antennæ, except in *Sermyle*, more than twice as long as the anterior femora; tibiæ without a sunken areola at apex beneath.

The slender body at once distinguishes this subfamily from the others of our fauna except Clitumninæ. The long antennæ, however, readily separates it from that group. We have four genera of Bacunculinæ occurring in the United States. The following table will serve to separate them:

a. Head subquadrate or subcylindrical, usually distinctly longer than broad, attached obliquely or horizontally. (Plate LVII, fig. 4.) Male cerci subequal throughout or apically trifid.

    b. Middle femora of the male not much swollen, not thicker than the posterior ones; posterior femora unarmed in both sexes.

        c. Male cerci apically trifid; head carinate or longitudinally rugose between the eyes; antennæ rarely twice as long as the anterior femora ..... *Pseudosermyle*, new genus.

        cc. Male cerci simple; head smooth; antennæ more than twice as long as the anterior femora ..... *Bacunculus* Burmeister.

    bb. Middle femora of the male much swollen, distinctly thicker than the posterior ones; posterior femora armed beneath on the median line near the apex with a single spine, in the male very prominent, in the female often very small and sometimes wholly absent ..... *Diapheromera* Gray.

aa. Head ovate, short, scarcely longer than broad, attached vertically (Plate LVII, fig. 2a); male cerci spatulate, much broader apically than at the base (Plate LVII, fig. 2b) ..... *Megaphasma*, new genus.

Pseudosermyle, new genus.

Head subcylindrical, distinctly longer than broad, horizontally attached to the thorax and in front between and behind the eyes either carinate or longitudinally rugose; antennæ no more, or but little more, than twice as long as the anterior femora; legs unarmed; basal segment of the abdomen generally subquadrate in the female, twice or more than twice as long in the male. Cerci of the female simple, of the male apically trifid.

This genus, of which *P. banksii* may be considered the type, is most nearly allied to *Sermyle* Stål, but differs in the character of the male cerci, which are simple in the latter genus.[a] The head of the only species of *Sermyle* examined, a female from Guatemala, is very much shorter in proportion than found in the species of *Pseudosermyle*. It is also somewhat closely allied to *Bacunculus*, and the most stable character for its separation from that genus, exclusive of the male genital characters, seems to be the dorsally carinate or rugose head.

The males of *Pseudosermyle strigata* and *arbuscula* are unknown and it may be that these species will eventually prove to belong to *Sermyle*, but until the male sex is made known it is deemed safest to include them here.

Pseudosermyle is represented in the United States by five species, which may be separated by the following tables. The first table is based wholly upon the characters of the female:

a. Body multicarinate or longitudinally rugose.
  b. Cerci short, no more than three times as long as the greatest width; supraanal
       plate subtruncate or obtusangulate at the apex.
     c. Femora short and stout (Plate LVIII, fig. 4), the posterior ones about
          nine mm. in length ..... *arbuscula* Rehn.
     cc. Femora longer and more slender (Plate LVIII, fig. 3 *a*), the posterior
          ones about twenty mm. in length ..... *truncata*, new species.
  bb. Cerci long, six times as long as the greatest width; supraanal plate acutely
       angulate at the apex ..... *strigata* Scudder.
aa. Body smooth ..... *stramineus* Scudder.

Pseudosermyle banksii does not appear in the above table for the reason that the female is unknown. The species of which the males are known may be separated by the following table, which is based wholly upon the characters of that sex:

a. Seventh abdominal segment distinctly inflated on the posterior half.
  b. Long and slender, length about 60 mm. ..... *banksii*, new species.
  bb. Shorter and less slender, length about 40 mm. ..... *truncata*, new species.
aa. Seventh abdominal segment not inflated ..... *stramineus* Scudder.

---

[a] The male of *Sermyle mexicanus* Saussure, the type of *Sermyle*, is not positively known, but
a male specimen that Stål thought quite surely belonged to that genus had simple cerci, as
in *Bacunculus*. Besides this, other Mexican species referred to this genus have simple cerci.

Pseudosermyle arbuscula Rehn.

Sermyle arbuscula Rehn, *Can. Ent.*, XXXIV, 1902, p. 273.

The following description of this species is taken in full from the author's article referred to above:

Type, female, San Diego, California, May 7, 1901.

This species does not seem to be very closely related to any of the previously known species of the genus. From *azteca* Saussure, it is differentiated by having the femora carinate and striate; from *saussurii* Stål, by the nonampliate sixth abdominal segment; and from *strigata* Scudder, by the more robust limbs and the less strongly striate body. With *mexicana* and *linearis* Saussure, no affinity exists.

General form slender, the thoracic portion rather robust. Head rather elongate, bearing two central longitudinal rugæ, which become obscure caudad, the whole surface of the head rather tuberculate, the tubercles being longitudinally disposed; eyes subspherical, slightly exerted; antennæ longer than cephalic femora; the proximal segment large and broad, with the distal section contracted, this segment over twice as large in bulk as the next. Pronotum, mesonotum, and metanotum tuberculate, the tubercles resolving into longitudinal series, this being more apparent on the metanotum, the mesonotum and metanotum being centrally carinate; pronotum rather narrow, not quite equaling the head in length; mesonotum long (with pronotum equaling the cephalic femora), the lateral margins slightly tuberculate; metanotum very considerable shorter than the mesonotum, comparatively robust, expanding in the caudal portion. Abdomen rather slender, multistrigate, none of the segments exhibiting any special ampliation; ventral surface between the sixth and seventh segments exhibiting a pair of flattened longitudinal processes. Cephalic femora heavy, with the proximal diastema (found in many representatives of this family) rather well marked, the remaining section of the segment being indated and with three prominent angles; tibiæ as long as the femora, quadrate slightly tapering; first tarsal joint about as long as the succeeding ones. Intermediate femora short, triangular in section, equaling the metanotum (and median segment) in length; tibiæ depressed, about equaling the femora in length; first tarsal joint considerably less than the succeeding joints in length. Caudal femora short, reaching the middle of the third abdominal segment, roughly triangular in section; tibiæ rather longer, reaching to the apex of the first segment. General color, reddish brown, washed with ashy gray on the cephalic limbs.

Measurements.

	mm.
Length of body	54
Length of pronotum	3
Length of mesonotum	12
Length of metanotum (with median segment)	8.7
Length of abdomen	28
Length of cephalic femora	14
Length of intermediate femora	7.5
Length of caudal femora	8.7

The supraanal plate of this species is shown at Plate LVII, fig. 3, and for this drawing I am indebted to the describer. This species seems remarkable for the extreme brevity of the posterior femora.

Pseudosermyle truncata, new species.

Plate LVIII, figs. 3, 3a, 3b.

Color grayish brown. Head above with two pairs of prominent carinæ, the carinæ of each pair subparallel at base, flaring somewhat just beyond the middle and then rapidly converging slightly beyond the eyes by the incurving of the outer carina. Just anterior of the termination of these carinæ is an elevated, posteriorly bifurcated tubercle and between the two pairs of carinæ is a minute mesial carina extending halfway along the length of the head. Antennæ basally thicker than in *strigata*. Pronotum above with a slight mesial longitudinal incision and with a shallow transverse furrow just behind the middle which does not extend to the borders, which are strongly carinate; disk with two subdorsal carinæ, less distinct behind the transverse furrow, and with a couple of indistinct, less elevated carinæ between them and the border of the pronotum; mesonotum and metanotum, together with the intermediary segment and the abdomen carinated as in *strigata*, but the whole body is much less covered with tubercles, the abdomen being almost entirely destitute of them and the thorax supplied more sparingly than in that species. Legs much more robust than in *strigata* and showing traces of fuscous bands more noticeable on the middle femora. Supraanal plate broader than in *strigata* and subtruncate apically. Cerci short and comparatively broad, about three times as long as broad.

Length of body, 73 mm.; mesothorax, 16.5 mm.; metathorax, 10.5 mm.; middle femora, 15 mm.; hind femora, 20 mm.

One female, Dos Cabezos, Arizona, June, 1891.

Type.—No. 6613, U. S. N. M.

One immature female specimen, in poor condition, from Bright Angel, Arizona, is referred to this species. It has the posterior femora extending only to the middle of the fourth abdominal segment and the basal five segments of the abdomen are furnished posteriorly above with two prominently elevated tubercles, one on each side.

The U. S. National Museum also contains one female and six male specimens from Los Angeles County, California, that evidently belong here. The female is apparently immature, probably being in the last stage. It is 54 mm. long, and the posterior femora are 16 mm. in length. The males differ from the females in being entirely smooth except for the two main carinæ on the anterior part of the head between the eyes, and in being smaller and quite slender. The cerci project obliquely downward, are trifid apically, the center branch forming the terminus of the main body of the cerci, and engage each other at their tips. Plate LVIII, fig. 3, represents the cerci of the male of this species. In immature specimens the cerci are simple, being merely flattened and slightly concave.

The measurements of these male specimens are as follows: Length of body, 40 mm.; antennæ, 27 mm.; mesothorax, 9.5 mm.; metathorax, including the intermediary segment, 7.5 mm.; fore femora, 13.5 mm.; middle femora, 12 mm.; hind femora, 15 mm.; width of middle of meso-thorax, 1.5 mm.

These Californian specimens are much lighter colored than those from Arizona, and may represent a new species, but without additional material it is not deemed advisable to describe them as such.

The type specimen was received at the Department of Agriculture on June 17, 1891. The following note regarding it is quoted from the notebook of the Division of Entomology:

Rec. from F. W. Anderson, Asst. Ed. Am. Agr., N. Y., 1 specimen, female, of a *Diapheromera*, new to the collection, received from Los Cabezos, Arizona, with the statement that it is more deadly to stock than loco-weed if eaten by them. It is called in that section "Campo mucho."

This species, while in general resembling *strigata*, is really very distinct. The broader supraanal plate with its subtruncate apex, short broad cerci, larger legs and smoother body, will at once distinguish it from that species.

Pseudosermyle strigata Scudder.

Plate LVI, fig. 3; Plate LVIII, fig. 8.

Sermyle strigata Scudder, *Cat. Orth. U. S.*, 1900, pp. 14, 94-95, pl. I, fig. 3.

The author's description is as follows:

Whole body dull ashy gray. Head furnished above with four longitudinal rows of small tubercles. Whole thorax mesially carinate and also furnished above on either side with a pair of carina, all the carinæ equidistant and furnished, as well as the intermediate spaces, with small sparsely scattered tubercles. Abdomen and intermediary segment similarly marked, but with an additional pair of subdorsal carinæ and with fewer and much more obscure granulations, mostly confined to the carinæ. Hind femora reaching to the end of the fifth abdominal segment. Abdomen nowhere expanded.

Length of body, 72 mm.; antennæ, 30 mm.; mesothorax, 18.5 mm.; metathorax, 10.5 mm.; abdomen, 35.5 mm.; hind femora, 22.5 mm.; width of middle of mesothorax, 3 mm.

Three males. Texas, Boll, Lincecum.

This species appears to fall near *S. azteca* Sauss., but differs by the carinate thorax with its dull coloring.

The cerci, as shown in the table of species, are very long, being six times longer than broad.

Pseudosermyle stramineus Scudder.

Plate LVIII, fig. 2.

Bacunculus stramineus Scudder, *Proc. Davenp. Acad. Sci.*, IX, 1902, p. 20, pl. I, fig. 1.

Described by the author as follows:

Bacunculus stramineus Scudder, sp. nov. (pl. I, fig. 1). Body very slender, flavo-testaceous, the sides of the thorax, the undersurface of the metathorax, and most of the undersurface of the middle femora white or hoary, at least in the male, the tibiæ more or less tinged with green in the female; the terminal abdominal segments are more or less hoary (male) or green (female). Head a little longer than the pronotum, somewhat tumid in the female, laterally striped with white in the male, in the latter with a pair of longitudinal rugæ following behind the inner margin of the antennal scrobes; antennæ pale green (female) or testaceous, becoming apically infuscated (male), very slender and shorter than the body. Body smooth, the thorax with a feeble median carina. Seventh abdominal segment of male nearly as long as the eighth and ninth together, the ninth slightly longer than the eighth, the seventh segment not inflated, bearing beneath a bulbous body not reaching the extremity of the eighth segment with a cap which a little surpasses it; ninth segment cylindrical, equal, truncate, bearing a pair of cerci, straight, rather stout, but compressed, equal and apically very briefly and bluntly bifid plates, nearly as long as the segment.

Length of body, male, 50 mm., female, 42 mm.; antennæ, male, 22 mm., female, 26 mm.; head, male, 2.5 mm., female, 2.5 mm.; thorax, male, 23 mm., female, 18.5 mm.; mesothorax, male, 12.5 mm., female, 9 mm.; abdomen, male, 23.5 mm., female, 22 mm.; fore femora, male, 14 mm., female, 10.5 mm.; middle femora, male, 11.5 mm., female, 8 mm.; hind femora, male, 14 mm., female, 10.5 mm.; width of metathorax in middle, male, 1 mm., female, 1.5 mm. 1 male, 1 female. Between Mesilla Park and Little Mountain, July 1. (A. P. Morse.)

The female is probably not quite mature.

Pseudosermyle banksii, new species.

Body very slender, testaceous, paler below. Head pale, slightly longer than the pronotum and distinctly swollen anteriorly, the sides marked with a longitudinal black stripe and with the usual longitudinal carinæ on top between and behind the eyes. Body smooth, with scarcely a trace of a median carina; mesothorax much longer than the metathorax. Seventh segment of the abdomen slightly shorter than the eighth and ninth together and considerably swollen on the posterior half, and here furnished with the usual ventral appendage, which is slightly longer than the eighth segment; eighth and ninth segments subequal in length, the latter the larger and equal. The cerci are as long as the last abdominal segment, moderately slender, slightly compressed, curving very slightly downward and inward, and are apically trifid, the center branch curving inward quite abruptly and forming the terminus of the main body of the cerci.

Length of body, 64 mm.; antennæ, 50 mm.; mesothorax, 16.5 mm.; metathorax, including the intermediary segment, 12 mm.; fore femora, 25 mm.; middle femora, 22 mm.; hind femora, 25 mm.; width at the middle of the mesothorax, 1.25 mm.

One male from Brazos County, Texas, collected in September by Mr. Nathan Banks, in whose honor the species is named. Also a male from Buna, Jasper County, Texas, on November 15, 1902, by Dr. A. D. Hopkins. The latter specimen was taken on pine.

Type.—No. 6616, U.S.N.M.

This insect may prove to be the male of *Sermyle strigata* Scudder, but more material is needed before it can be proven. The very slender form, however, seems to militate against this.

Bacunculus Burmeister.

Bacunculus Burmeister, *Handb. Ent.*, II, 1838, p. 566.

Burmeister established *Bacunculus* as a subgenus of *Bacteria*. As represented in the United States, the genus is defined as follows:

Very closely allied to *Diapheromera*. Head smooth in both sexes, subcylindrical anteriorly swollen, elongate, more than twice as long as broad, and horizontally attached to the thorax. Antennæ much more than twice as long as the anterior femora. Prothorax about one-sixth as long as the mesothorax; mesothorax slightly longer than metathorax. Legs of male unarmed, slender, filiform; middle femora of male not at all swollen as they are in *Diapheromera*; legs of female usually unarmed, but the middle and posterior femora are sometimes armed below on the median line next the apex with a distinct, though usually minute, spine. Body of male more slender than in *Diapheromera* and the cerci of similar shape and relative proportion as in that genus.

The unswollen middle femora of the males make it easy to distinguish this genus from *Diapheromera*, but from female specimens alone it is more difficult. The more elongate and anteriorly swollen head together with the more generally unarmed legs will usually serve, however, to distinguish the females with considerable certainty.

In the United States we have a single species.

Bacunculus tenuescens Scudder.

Plate LVI, figs. 1, 2.

Bacunculus tenuescens Scudder, Cat. Orth. U. S., app., 1899, p. 95.

This species is figured on Plate I, figs. 1 and 2 of the above work, and described in the following words:

Body exceedingly slender, flavous beneath, brown (male) or green (female) above, becoming infuscated on the lower portion of the sides, forming a post-ocular stripe. Head greatly elongated, much longer than the pronotum; antennæ much shorter than the body. Entire body quite smooth with a very delicate mesial carination. Seventh and ninth abdominal segments of male subequal in length, slightly longer than the eighth and about half as long as the sixth, the seventh segment scarcely inflated, bearing beneath a deflexed subspatulate convex plate, reaching the tip of the eighth segment and no broader than it; ninth segment cylindrical, equal, truncate, bearing a pair of decurved and incurved, cylindrical but slightly clavate, blunt tipped cerci, about as long as the segment.

Length of body, male, 64.5 mm., female, 53 mm.; antennæ, male, 41 mm., female, 35 mm.; head, male, 3.25 mm., female, 3.5 mm.; thorax, male, 31.5 mm., female, 25 mm.; mesothorax, male, 16 mm., female, 13 mm.; abdomen, male, 30 mm., female, 25 mm.; fore femora, male, 18 mm., female, 15.5 mm.; middle femora, male, 14.5 mm.; female, 13.5 mm.; hind femora, male, 20 mm., female, 16 mm.; width of mesothorax at middle, male, female, 1 mm.

One male, one female. Cedar Keys, Fla., June 6; Capron, Florida.

The tip of the abdomen of the female is lost.

The female from which the above description was made is evidently immature, as the measurements do not at all agree with those of mature individuals in the collection of the U. S. National Museum. The following notes are made from a mature female collected by Hubbard and Schwarz at Cedar Keys, Florida, in the month of June:

Color uniformly light greenish-brown, probably green in life. Sixth abdominal segment slightly longer than the seventh. Supraanal plate subtriangular, mesially keeled. Cerci long and slender, about as long as the last abdominal segment. Extreme length of body from front of head to tip of cerci, 85 mm., head 4.5 mm., mesothorax 19 mm., metathorax 14.5 mm., fore femora 19 mm., middle femora 16.5 mm., hind femora 20.5 mm., cerci 4 mm.; width of meso-thorax at middle 2 mm.

A female specimen from Biscayne, Florida, from the Riley collection, which is referred to this species, is apparently much above the ordinary size, giving the following measurements: Extreme length of body 110 mm., head 5.5 mm., mesothorax 24 mm., metathorax 19.5 mm., fore femora 27.5 mm., middle femora 21 mm., hind femora 26 mm., cerci 4 mm. This specimen is but little thicker than moderate-sized individuals and shows no peculiarities indicative of a new species.

The brown color of the males of this species varies from light to quite dark, and the legs, probably also the body in some specimens, are greenish-brown.

Diapheromera Gray.

Diapheromera Gray, *Syn. Phasm.*, 1835, p. 18.

This genus has the following characters:
Head smooth in both sexes, subquadrate or subcylindrical, usually less than twice as long as broad and obliquely attached to the thorax; antennæ much more than twice as long as the anterior femora; prothorax usually less than one-fourth as long as the mesothorax; meso- and metathorax subequal in length. Body linear, especially in the male; basal segment of abdomen oblong, in male twice as long as broad. Middle femora much swollen in the male, distinctly thicker than the hind ones; those of the female scarcely swollen and not distinctly larger than the hind ones. Posterior femora armed beneath on median line near the apex with a single spine, in the male large and distinct, in the female sometimes large and distinct but usually much smaller than in the male and sometimes minute or even wholly absent. Cerci of male cylindrical, longer than the last abdominal segment and, except in *D. mesillana*, strongly incurved.

Our common northern walkingstick belongs to this genus, the species of which are distributed more widely over our country than those of any other of our genera. None of the species have been found west of the Rocky Mountains. Five species occur in the United States. They may be separated by the following table, which is for the greater part taken from a paper on this genus by Dr. Scudder:[a]

a. Male cerci strongly incurved.
    b. Ninth abdominal segment of male subequal, scarcely larger at apex than at base, the seventh segment much longer than the eighth; male cerci with a basal tooth.
        c. Inner ventro lateral carina of the posterior femora with minute serrations; meso- and metathorax unicolorous.
            d. Male cerci with a blunt tooth at inner inferior base (Plate LVIII, fig. 6); female cerci relatively stout, about half as long as the last dorsal segment ..... *femorata* Say.
        dd. Male cerci with a sharp thorn at inner inferior base (Plate LVIII, fig. 5); female cerci relatively slender, almost or quite as long as the last dorsal segment ..... *veliei* Walsh.

[a] *Psyche*, IX, 1901, pp. 187-189.

cc. Inner ventro-lateral carina of the posterior femora smooth; meso- and metathorax longitudinally marked with black beneath ..... *arizonensis*, new species.

bb. Ninth abdominal segment of male apically inflated, and here nearly half as broad again as at base, the seventh and eighth segments of subequal length; male cerci without a basal tooth ..... *carolina* Scudder.

aa. Male cerci rigidly straight ..... *mesillana* Scudder.

Diapheromera femorata Say.

Plate LVII, fig. 4; Plate LVIII, fig. 6.

Spectrum femoratum Say, *Exp. Long.*, II, 1824, p. 297; *Amer. Ent.*, III, 1828, p. 37, pl. xxvii—Leidy, *Proc. Acad. Nat. Sci. Philad.*, III, 1846, pp. 80-84.

Diapheromera femorata Harris, *Treat. Ins. Inj. Veg.*, 1840, p. 119.—Scudder, Psyche, IX, 1901, p. 188.

Phasma (Bacteria) femorata Haan, *Bijdr. kenn. Orth.*, 1842, pp. 101, 134.

Bacunculus femoratus Uhler, Harris, *Treat. Ins. Inj. Veg.*, 3d ed., 1862, p. 146.

Diapheromera sayi Gray, *Syn. Phasm.*, 1835, p. 18.

Bacteria sayi Charpenter, *Orth. descr.*, 1841-1845, pl. iv.

Bacteria (Bacunculus) sayi Burmeister, *Handb. Ent.*, II, 1838, p. 566.

Bacunculus sayi Thomas, *Trans. Ill. St. Agric. Soc.*, V, 1865, p. 441.

Bacteria linearis Gosse, *Lett. Alab.*, 1859, p. 275.

Color fuscous or green, the males more often exhibiting the latter color. Mature individuals, especially the females, are almost always fuscous during the autumn months. The middle femora of the dark colored males are distinctly banded with lighter color.

Head smooth in both sexes, subquadrate, scarcely elongate, obliquely attached to the thorax; eyes round, slightly more prominent in the male than in the female. Antennæ long and slender, about as long as the body; prothorax short, about one-fifth as long as the mesothorax, the dorsal cruciform impression distinct, especially the transverse incision; meso- and metathorax subequal in length, without median carina. Legs of male long and slender, except the middle femora, which are much swollen and distinctly thicker than the others; of the female, shorter in proportion, and the middle femora are not swollen, no thicker than the others. Fore legs unarmed, undulate and smaller at the base; hind and middle femora of the male armed beneath on the median line near the apex with a large, prominent spine; of female, similarly armed, but the spine is much smaller, often quite minute. Abdomen smooth; intermediary segment visible only from above and firmly united to the metathorax; basal segment elongate, nearly or quite twice as long as broad in the female and three times as long as broad in the male; seventh segment in the male distinctly longer than the ninth and three times as long as the eighth. Cerci of male somewhat longer than the terminal segment of the abdomen, cylindrical, oval at apex, bluntly tubercled interiorly at base, clothed with microscopic stiff hairs and strongly curved horizontally inwards, usually crossing each other at about the middle; female cerci straight, stout, acuminate, less than half as long as the terminal segment of the abdomen, and partially concealed from above by the exposed tip of the triangular supraanal plate, which, as well as the cerci, is sparsely covered with very short hairs of microscopic size.

Length of body, male, 72 mm., female, 70 mm.; mesothorax, male, 17 mm., female, 16 mm.; metathorax, male, 16 mm., female, 13.5 mm.; middle femora, male, 15.5 mm., female, 11.5 mm.; hind femora, male, 19.5 mm., female, 15 mm.; hind tibia, male, 25 mm., female, 16 mm.

The above description was drawn up from a male and female collected in copulation at Rosslyn, Virginia, on September 12, 1900. The males are quite uniform in size, but the females are quite variable, the one from which the above measurements were taken being a small specimen. A large female from Massachusetts before me gives the following measurements: Length of body, 92 mm; mesothorax, 19 mm.; metathorax, 17 mm.; middle femora, 14.5 mm.; hind femora, 18.5 mm.; hind tibia, 20 mm.

This species is our most common phasmid and occurs throughout the northern part of the country from the Rocky Mountains eastward. It is said to also occur as far south as Mexico, but is more rare in the South, being quite generally replaced there by the next species, *veliei*. Many of the southern records pertain to allied species mistaken for *femorata*.

These insects mate in the autumn and pairs are often seen in the act of copulation. The female drops the eggs at random in the woods, where they lie till the following spring before hatching. Eggs deposited on November 9 and kept indoors gave forth the young during the last week of the following March. Some eggs are slow in giving forth the nymphs and so the insect may be found in various stages of development all through the season. Some of the eggs lie through even the second winter before hatching. The young are said to pass through but two stages in the course of growth, which averages less than two months. The newly hatched nymphs are of a uniform pale yellowish-green color and measure about 5 mm. in length, ones reared at the insectary of the Division of Entomology giving the following measurements: Length of body, 8 mm., hind femora, 3.5 mm. The young are said to live on low herbage and drop to the ground when disturbed. There is but one generation annually.

This is the only one of our phasmids that is of economic importance. It has been recorded as occurring in injurious numbers on forest trees. In such cases burning over the ground in winter to kill the eggs is recommended.

Diapheromera veliei Walsh.

Plate LVIII, fig. 5.

Diapheromera velii Walsh, *Proc. Ent. Soc. Philad.*, III, 1864, pp. 409-10.—Scudder, *Psyche*, IX, 1901, p. 189.

This species may be defined as follows:

Of the same size and form as *D. femorata*, and also agreeing with it in being dimorphic in color, both brown and green forms occurring. It differs from that species in the following particulars: Head slightly more elongate; middle femora of male not usually banded with gray; seventh abdominal segment of the male no longer than the ninth, while in *femorata* it is one-fourth longer. Male cerci with a sharp spine or tooth at the base on the inner side instead of a blunt tubercle; female cerci nearly or quite as long as the apical segment of the abdomen instead of less than half as long, and they are usually more slender than in *femorata*. In general, the color of the dark form of *veliei* seems to be somewhat lighter than that of the corresponding form of *femorata*, but in this respect both species are variable.

This species is more southern in its distribution than *femorata*. It occurs east of the Rocky Mountains from Nebraska to Maryland, south to Georgia and Texas. It occurs also in Mexico. It was described from Nebraska, and Scudder reports it from a number of States within the region specified above. I have seen specimens from Virginia, Kansas, Oklahoma, Texas, and Colorado. Some of the females from Oklahoma have the spine beneath the posterior and intermediate femora entirely aborted, causing them to be separable from the females of *Bacunculus* only with great difficulty. The shape of the head and the association of the males with the females, however, made the identification quite certain.

Diapheromera arizonensis, new species.

Slenderer than *D. femorata*, uniformly light yellowish brown, with the meso- and metathorax longitudinally marked beneath with shiny black. Antennæ nearly as long as the body and concolorous with it. Thorax smooth, with a very slight median carina; mesothorax slightly longer than the metathorax; seventh segment of the abdomen distinctly longer than the ninth, somewhat constricted on the anterior third; ninth segment with the posterior margin concave, exposing the tip of the triangular supraanal plate. Cerci shaped as in *femorata* and *veliei*, with the basal tooth intermediate between those species. Legs long and slender, the middle femora relatived; less swollen than in allied species.

Length of body, 76 mm.; antennæ, about 65 mm.; mesothorax, 18 mm.; metathorax, 16.5 mm.; middle femora, 18 mm.; hind femora, 22.5 mm.

One male, Hot Springs, Arizona, June 28, 1901. Collected by Messrs. Schwarz and Barber.

Type.—No. 6612, U.S.N.M.

This species is closely allied to *femorata* and *veliei*, but can be distinguished from them by the characters given in the table and by the more slender form. The elongate seventh abdominal segment will readily separate it from *veliei*. It is quite a characteristic-looking species, though the differences that separate it from its allies are difficult to define.

Diapheromera carolina Scudder.

Diapheromera carolina Scudder, *Psyche*, IX, 1901, p. 188.

The following is the description as given by the author:

Stouter than *D. femorata*, testaceo-castaneous, glistening, the thorax with a rather broad median bronze-fuscous stripe, not reaching the median segment, and interrupted at the posterior end of the mesonotum, the fore legs greenish, the antennæ testaceous; thorax with excessively fine transverse striation. Mesothorax and metathorax (including median segment) of similar length. Seventh and eighth abdominal segments of subequal length, each faintly enlarging from base, the ninth a little shorter, apically inflated and subglobose, nearly half as broad again at apex as at base, the cerci much as in *D. femorata*, but stouter, more compressed, and without basal tooth.

Length of body, 67 mm.; head, 3 mm.; mesothorax, 13.5 mm.; fore femora, 20.5 mm.; hind femora, 19.5 mm.

One male. North Carolina. (Morrison.)

Diapheromera mesillana Scudder.

Diapheromera mesillana Scudder, *Psyche*, IX, 1901, p. 189.

The original description is here given in full.

Slenderer than *D. femorata*, uniform greenish flavous, the antennæ infuscated beyond the basal third, the thorax smooth, with an obscure median carina; subapical inferior spine of middle and hind femora rather slight. Mesothorax and metathorax (including median segment) of equal length. Seventh and ninth abdominal segments subequal in length and distinctly longer than the eighth, all equal in width and nowhere enlarged, the ninth rather feebly and angularly emarginate, exposing a small, transverse, apically arcuate, supraanal plate; cerci about as long as the ninth abdominal segment, rigidly straight, directed backward and not at all downward, slender tapering, blunt tipped, externally convex, and internally concave.

Length of body, 55 mm.; head, 3 mm.; antennæ, circa 37 mm.; mesothorax, 12.5 mm.; fore femora, 14.5 mm.; middle femora, 11 mm.; hind femora, 13.5 mm.

Two males. Between Mesilla and Las Cruces, New Mexico, June 30. (A. P. Morse.)

Megaphasma, new genus.

Head smooth, rounded, subvertical; antennæ more than twice as long as the anterior femora; prothorax one-fifth as long as the mesothorax and transversely incised; meso- and metathorax subequal in length and with a distinct, though slight, median carina. Middle and hind femora swollen in both sexes, the middle ones somewhat larger than the posterior ones in the male, and both the middle and posterior pairs in both sexes armed beneath on the median line next the apex, with a prominent spine and sometimes, at least in the female, with a row of equally large ones extending along the entire length of the femora below.

This genus is erected for that large Southern walkingstick described by Stål as *Diapheromera dentricus*. This insect exhibits characters that are certainly of generic value. The rounded, subvertical head, broad, spatulate cerci and unusually large size will readily separate it from all other of our genera. *Diapheromera* is the most nearly-allied genus, but the characters given in the table will at once separate it from that genus of much smaller insects.

In the United States we have a single species.

Megaphasma dentricus Stål.

Plate LVII, fig. 2, 2a, 2b.

Diapheromera dentricus Stål, *Rec. Orth.*, III, 1875, p. 76.—Scudder, *Psyche*, IX, 1901, p. 187; *Harpers Mag.*, LXXXVIII, 1894, p. 456, fig 1.

This species was originally described from Opelousas, Louisiana. The following description is made from specimens, male and female, in the U. S. National Museum collection:

Yellowish brown or fuscous. Head rounded, subvertically attached to the thorax. Antennæ multiarticulate,[a] more than twice as long as the anterior femora. Cruciform impression on the pronotum distinct, meso- and metathorax subequal in length and furnished above with a scarcely perceptible delicate median carina. Ninth abdominal segment slightly longer than the seventh. Legs stout, anterior ones unarmed and but half as thick as the others; posterior and middle tibiæ deeply denticulate below on the median carina, which is considerably elevated and terminated at the apex in a blunt spine, as is also the posterior ventro-lateral carinæ. The posterior and intermediate femora are large and regularly trapezoidal in form, each border below denticulate and spined on the median line with small apinules, except the terminal one, which is very large in the male. In the female all the spines are often large, but not so large as the terminal one of the male; the femora are broadest on the lower side and slightly swollen toward the base. The male femora are somewhat more rounded than those of the female. Posterior femora extending to the apex of the third abdominal segment in the female and almost to the middle of the fourth in the male; margins above coxal cavities slightly expanded and dentate. Cerci stout, in female less than one-half as long as the last abdominal segment; in male expanded apically, somewhat spatulate and directed strongly downward.

The original description, which was made from the female sex alone, gives the following measurements: Length of body 123 mm.; thorax 53 mm.; mesothorax 24 mm.; metathorax 24 mm.; abdomen 70 mm.; fore femora 27 mm.; middle femora 20 mm.; posterior femora 23 mm.; width of middle of mesothorax 5 mm.

Often the general color is reddish brown, legs lighter. A specimen in the U. S. National Museum collection has the middle and hind femora and the posterior two-thirds of the prothorax green, variegated with light gray and brown; on the femora the gray is grouped together in the form of broad, illy defined bands. Other specimens have the anterior portion of the prothorax and mesothorax, both above and below, greenish black.

---

[a] The antennal segments of a male specimen from Texas were counted and were found to number just seventy-eight. The antennæ of the specimen figured is drawn nearly twice too thick, except basally.

This insect has been recorded from Louisiana, Texas, New Mexico, and, with doubt, from Alabama. One female specimen in the U. S. National Museum is from East Joplin, Missouri, the most northern locality yet recorded for this species.

This is the largest walkingstick that occurs in the United States, a female before me measuring 145 mm., which is 5 mm. less than one in the collection of the Academy of Natural Sciences of Philadelphia. This species suggests tropical forms more than anything else in our fauna, and the large size commands attention wherever seen. Mr. Mitchell, of Victoria, Texas, informs me that they are not uncommon in the wooded bottom in that vicinity, where they occur on grape vines.

Subfamily Anisomorphinæ.

In this subfamily the antennæ are more than twice as long as the anterior femora. Tibiæ furnished with a sunken areola below next the apex; coxæ visible from above; tarsi distinctly pentamerous. Mesothorax not more than three times as long as the prothorax. Intermediary segment invisible.

We have a single genus of this subfamily in the United States.

Anisomorpha Gray.

Anisomorpha Gray, *Syn. Phasm.*, 1835, p. 18.

This genus, as represented in the United States, has the following characters:

Head not more than one and one-half as long as broad, horizontally attached to the thorax. Body broad and stout, especially in the female; prothorax furnished with distinct odoriferous glands; meso- and metathorax subequal in length. Legs stout and thick, unequal, the middle pair the shortest; abdominal segments subquadrate or transverse, especially in the female, the seventh and ninth subequal in length, intermediary segment invisible. Cerci short, rounded, similar in both sexes.

We have two closely allied species, one occurring more commonly in the extreme Southern States and the other ranging farther north. Their differences are comparative and may be tabulated as follows:

a. Female, color generally yellowish brown with conspicuous broad black dorsal and lateral stripes. Head noticeably longer than broad; body more elongate, seven to nine times as long as broad. Male, color and head as in female. Body still more elongate, about twelve times as long as broad, averaging about 45 mm. in length ..... *buprestoides* Stoll.

aa. Female, color uniformly ferruginous of various shades or inconspicuously striped with very narrow dusky dorsal and lateral stripes. Head less noticeably longer than broad. Body proportionately shorter and broader, six to six and one-half times longer than broad. Male, color same as female. Head and proportions about the same as in *buprestoides* but smaller, averaging no more than 35 mm ..... *ferruginea* Palisot.

Anisomorpha buprestoides Stoll.

Plate LIX, fig. 1.

Phasma buprestoides Stoll, *Repr. Spectr.*, 1787-1813, p. 68, pl. XXIII, fig. 87.
Anisomorpha buprestoides Gray, *Syn. Phasm.*, 1835, p. 19.—Scudder, Can. Ent., XXVII, 1895, p. 30.
Phasma (Anisomorpha) buprestoides Haan, *Bijdr. Kenn. Orth.*, 1842, p. 101.
Spectrum bivittatum Say, *Amer. Ent.*, III, 1828, pl. xxxviii.
Spectrum vittata Jaeger, *Life N. Amer. Ins.*, 1854, p. 123.

The following description of this common Southern walkingstick is made from a series of both sexes in the collection of the United States National Museum.

Color varying shades of yellowish brown, often almost fuscous, with conspicuous broad, black stripes extending from the front of the head to the tip of the abdomen, one dorsal and one on each side. These stripes, in dark-colored individuals, are often more or less confused, but in light-colored specimens they are very conspicuous and well defined. Some specimens, apparently killed soon after transformation, are paler in color and with the stripes narrow and indistinct. Legs short and stout, unequal, the middle pair the shortest, in male more slender than in the female, dark colored, except in light-colored individuals, where they are colored the same as the body; the tibiæ and femora of each pair of legs are subequal in length. Head noticeably longer than broad, horizontally attached to the thorax and subquadrate in shape, somewhat swollen anteriorly. Antennæ about three times as long as the anterior femora, the fourth segment the shortest. Prothorax mesially incised and transversely sulcate in the middle, about twice as long as broad, usually more than one-third as long as the mesothorax furnished above on each well-elevated border in front with a prominent gland, opening laterally from which is ejected a pungent spray when the insect is excited. Meso- and metathorax subequal in length, the former usually slightly the longer and on the disk sometimes furnished, especially toward the sides, with several granules, often quite acute; there is no median carina. Abdomen smooth, without carina, segments, especially the basal ones of the female, subquadrate or transverse, in the male usually somewhat longer than broad, intermediary segment invisible. In the female the seventh segment beneath forms a large scoop-shaped process, at the base of which are situated the genital organs. Cerci short, in the female no more than one-half as long as the last abdominal segment in the male almost as long as the apical segment, straight and subcylindrical in both sexes, projecting subhorizontally backward in the female and subperpendicularly downward in the male. The male usually has the tip of the abdomen curved under.

Measurements made from a mated pair from Key West, Florida, are as follows: Length of body, male 45 mm., female 61 mm.; head, male 3.5 mm., female 6 mm.; antennæ, female 40 mm.; prothorax, male 3.5 mm., female 6 mm.; mesothorax, male 7 mm., female 12 mm.; metathorax, male 6 mm., female 10 mm.; fore femora, male 9.5 mm., female 13 mm.; middle femora, male 7 mm., female 10.5 mm.; hind femora, male 9.5 mm., female 14 mm.; width of head, male 2.5 mm., female 4 mm.

This species, which is sometimes called the musk mare, seems to occur most commonly in the extreme Southern States. The U. S. National Museum contains over twenty specimens, all from Florida, except some without labels, which are probably from Mississippi. It has been recorded from various localities in the southeastern part of the United States, but the more northern records doubtlessly belong to the next species. Several young specimens referable to this species are uniformly brownish gray in color, but otherwise resemble the adults.

Anisomorpha ferruginea Palisot de Beauvois.

Plate LIX, fig. 2.

Phasma ferruginea Palisot De Beauvois, *Ins. Afr. Amer.*, 1805-1821, p. 167, pl. XIV, figs. 6, 7.
Anisomorpha ferruginea Gray, *Syn. Phasm.*, 1835, p. 18.
Phasma (Anisomorpha) ferruginea Haan, *Bijdr. Kenn. Orth.*, 1842, p. 101.

This species is very closely allied to the preceding one. The color is in general lighter than in buprestoides and usually uniform, and not conspicuously marked by black stripes as in that species, sometimes with narrow stripes, more often noticeable in the males. The head is usually less noticeably longer than broad, and the body is proportionately shorter and broader as tabulated above. The males average less in size and the habitat seems to extend farther north than that of *buprestoides*. The measurements from a pair from Tallulah, Georgia, are as follows:

Length of head, male 3 mm., female 5.5 mm.; body, male 31 mm., female 50 mm.; fore femora, male 8 mm., female 10 mm.; middle femora, male 5.5 mm., female 8.5 mm.; hind femora, male 8 mm., female 11 mm.; prothorax, male 2.5 mm., female 5 mm.; mesothorax, male 5 mm., female 9.5 mm.; metathorax, male 4 mm., female 8.5 mm.; width of head, male 2 mm., female 4.5 mm.

This species appears to extend farther north than *buprestoides*, but it also occurs in Florida. The specimens in the collection of the United States National Museum are from Florida, Louisiana, Kentucky, and Pennsylvania.

This species, as well as the preceding one, is said to be able to throw a colored fluid to a considerable distance from the well-developed scent glands, situated on the thorax.

Timeminæ, new subfamily.

This subfamily presents the following characters:

Antennæ longer than the anterior femora; tibiæ furnished beneath at the apex with a sunken areola; coxæ invisible from above; tarsi three jointed. Intermediary segment as distinct as the rest of the abdominal segments, freely articulated to the thorax and not at all connate with it as in all other of our groups.

This well-defined subfamily is proposed for the genus *Timema* of Scudder. The structure of the insects here included is different from all other of our Phasmidæ, as is shown by the legs being attached beneath the body in such a manner as to conceal the coxæ from above. The three-jointed tarsi are also peculiar to this subfamily. The three-jointed tarsi are obviously the result of a unition of the first three segments of the normal pentamerous phasmid tarus. This is indicated by the lower surface of the first segment showing obscure segmentation where the original segments have united.

We have but one genus of this interesting subfamily in the United States.

Timema Scudder.

Timema Scudder, *Can. Ent.*, XXVI, 1895, p. 30.

The characters limiting this genus are:

General form short and broad, not linear, head subquadrate, no longer than broad, as broad as the thorax. Antennæ much longer than the anterior femora, basal segment very large, three times as long as broad, enlarged apically. Prothorax quadrate, not narrowed anteriorly, no shorter than the metathorax and without distinct odoriferous glands; meso- and metathorax subequal in length. Legs short and stout; cerci of male forcipulate, irregular in shape and curving inwards, of female stout, vertically flattened and straight, in both sexes longer than the last abdominal segment.

We have a single species.

Timema californica Scudder, new species.

Plate LVII, fig. 5; Plate LVIII, figs. 7, 7a.

This species, the type of the genus, has never been described. Dr. Scudder has very kindly furnished the following description, which is here published for the first time:

Head large, thorax depressed, abdomen depressed cylindrical, expanding somewhat posteriorily, the whole body smooth, glistening a little, nearly uniform luteo-testaceous with a faint greenish tinge, the abdomen slightly lighter in tint than the thorax, the latter striped longitudinally and narrowly with brownish fuscous, most distinctly in a submarginal stripe, in which are fuscous impressed puncta. Antennæ about as long as head and thorax together. All the legs short, the hind femora about as long as the first three abdominal segments. Last abdominal segment of male somewhat expanded and tumid, the hind margin sinuato-truncate, the cerci about as the last segment, asymmetrical, tortuous, abruptly incurved, basally depressed, apically tapering to a point.

Length of body, male 14.25 mm.; female 22.5 mm.; antennæ, male 5.25 mm; female 7 mm.; mesonotum, male 1.5 mm., female 2.5 mm.; hind femora, male 3.25 mm.; female 4.5 mm. One male, one female, Santa Cruz Mountains, California. (L. Bruner.)

The U. S. National Museum contains three typical specimens of this species, two males and one female, from Santa Cruz Mountains, California, collected by Albert Keobele. The antennæ of the males are broken, but those of the female are intact and measure 14 mm. in length and are 22 jointed. It would therefore appear that the antennæ of Dr. Scudder's specimens, at least those of the female, were broken.

The trochanters of these insects are large and distinct, more so than in any other of our Phasmidæ. The head is marked by a narrow post-ocular stripe, which extends more or less distinctly across the entire length of the pronotum.

Besides these specimens from the Santa Cruz Mountains, the U. S. National Museum contains a male and a female from Los Angeles County, California, that may represent a new species, but their condition is too poor to warrant their description as such without additional and better preserved material. They differ from the typical specimens in being proportionately shorter, head more flattened vertically, without the postoculate black line, and, together with the pronotum in the male, rugose above. The female cerci are more slender, and the meso- and metathorax of both sexes seem less developed than in the specimens from Santa Cruz Mountains. The male cerci also differ in being more foliaceous. Plate LVIII, fig. 7a, shows the male cerci of the specimen from Los Angeles County, and Plate LVIII, fig. 7, the same of the Santa Cruz Mountain specimens.

This species apparently represents a step in the transition from the Phasmidæ to the Forficulidæ. The forcipal cerci of the males, ventrally attached legs, short, broad head, and especially the short, stout legs with the three jointed tarsi, indicate a relation to the ear-wigs. As Phasmids these creatures are certainly anomalies, and at a casual glance are not always readily recognized, having, in one instance at least, been mistaken for a species of Perlid larvæ.

Note.

Since this paper has been made up into pages, Mr. E. A. Schwarz collected a specimen of Phasmidæ representing a species new to our fauna. It was taken at Key West, Florida, on April 6, and, except for the discordant factor of the median segment being slightly shorter than the metathorax, seems to fall quite naturally into the Bacterid genus *Haplopus* of Gray. As the specimen is an immature female, any attempt at specific determination would be unsatisfactory. It may eventually prove to be the *Haplopus cubensis* of Saussure, but it does not seem to agree very well with the description of that species.

Explanations of Plates.

Plate LVI. (After Scudder.)

Fig. 1. *Bacunculus tenuescens* Scudder, male.
    2. *Bacunculus tenuescens* Scudder, male, side view of the tip of the abdomen.
    3. *Pseudosermyle strigata* Scudder, female.

Plate LVII.

Fig. 1. *Parabacillus coloradus* Scudder, male.
    2. *Megaphasma dentricus* Stål, male.
    2a. *Megaphasma dentricus* Stål, male, side view of head and pronotum.
    2b. *Megaphasma dentricus* Stål, male, side view of the tip of the abdomen.
    3. *Pseudosermyle arbuscula* Rehn, female, end of the abdomen.
    4. *Diapheromera femorata* Say, male, side view of head and pronotum.
    5. *Timema californica* Scudder, female.

Plate LVIII.

Fig. 1. *Parabacillus coloradus* Scudder, female (after Scudder).
    2. *Pseudosermyle stramineus* Scudder, male (after Scudder).
    3. *Pseudosermyle truncata*, new species, male, side view of the tip of the abdomen.
    3a. *Pseudosermyle truncata*, new species, female, right middle leg.
    3b. *Pseudosermyle truncata*, new species, female, tip of abdomen.
    4. *Pseudosermyle arbuscula* Rehn, female, right middle leg.
    5. *Diapheromera veliei* Walsh, male, end of abdomen.
    6. *Diapheromera femorata* Say, male, end of abdomen.
    7. *Timema californica* Scudder, male, end of abdomen.
    7a. *Timema californica* Scudder, variety, male, end of abdomen.
    8. *Pseudosermyle strigata* Scudder, female, end of abdomen.

Plate LIX.

Fig. 1. *Anisomorpha buprestoides* Stål, female.
    2. *Anisomorpha ferruginea* Palisot de Beauvois, female.

Stick Insects

Plate LVI

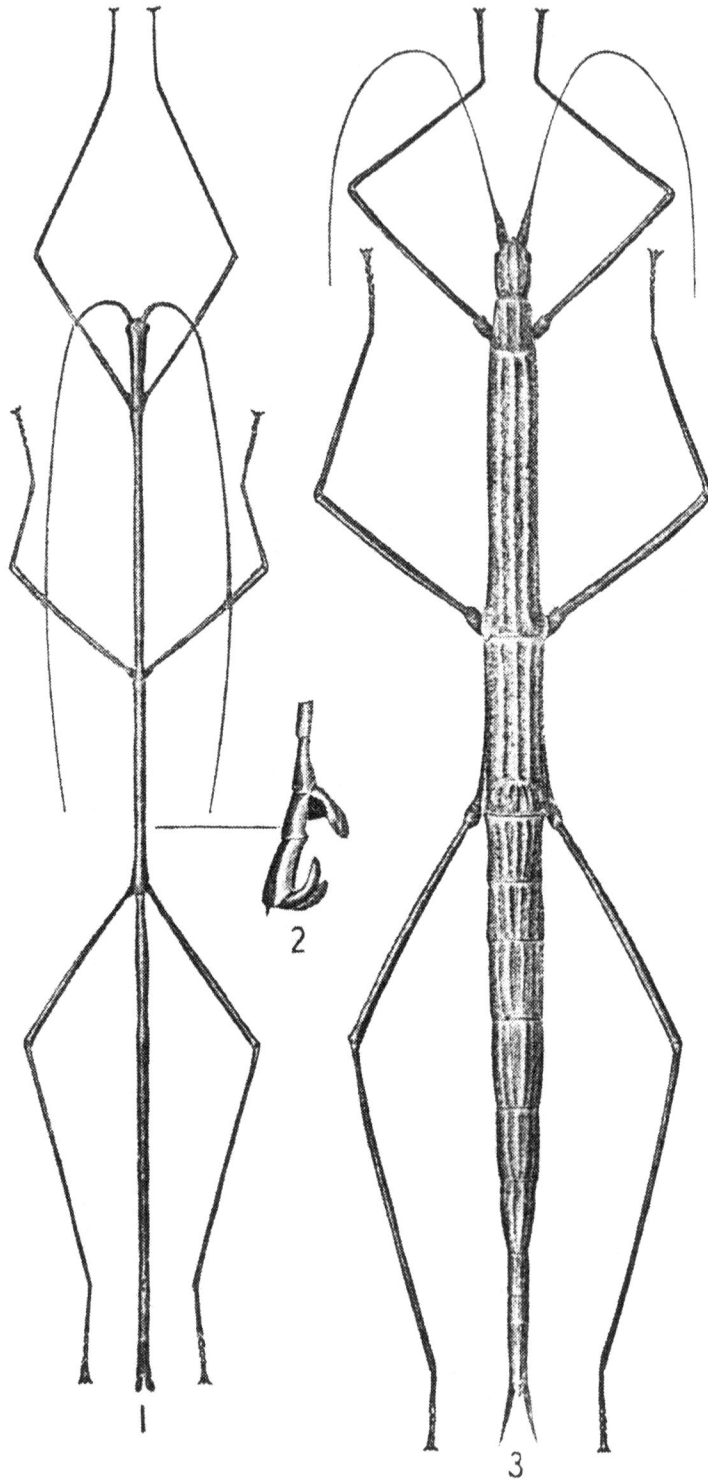

Plate LVII

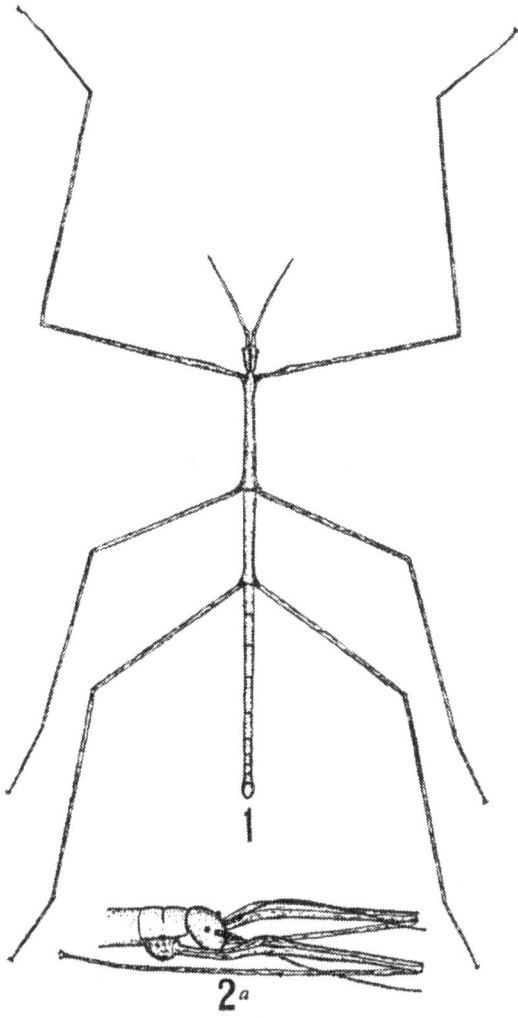

1

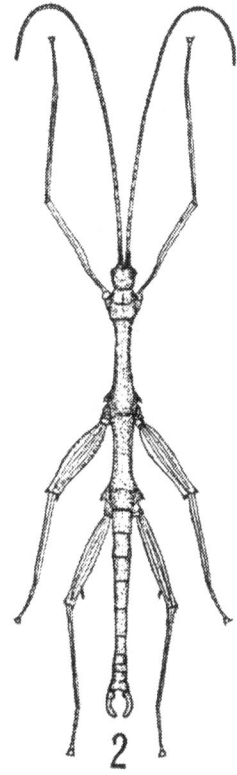

2

2ᵃ

3

2ᵇ

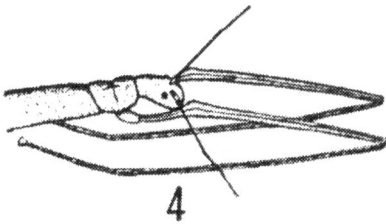

4

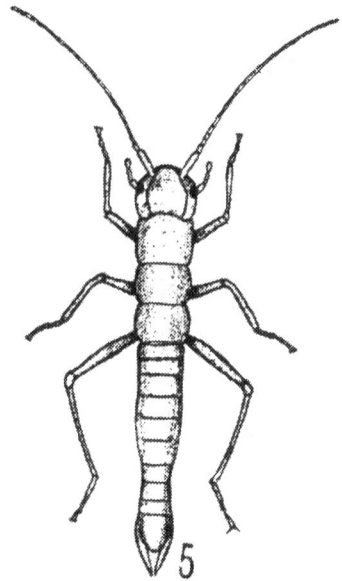

5

Plate LVIII

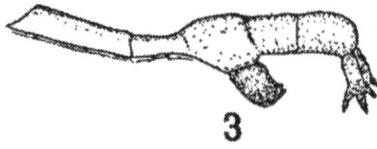

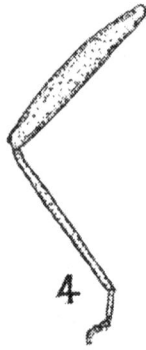

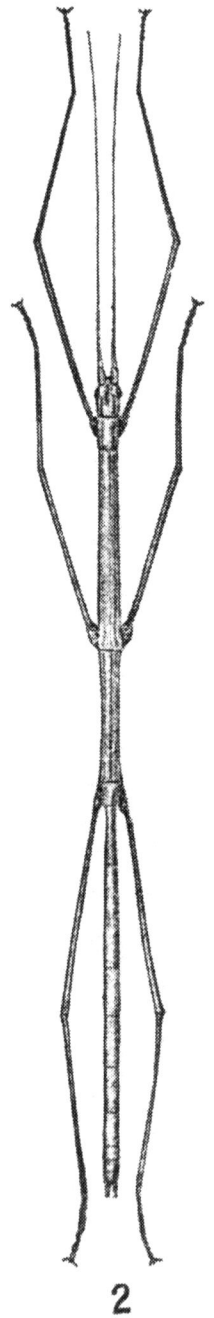

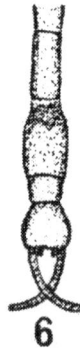

Plate LIX

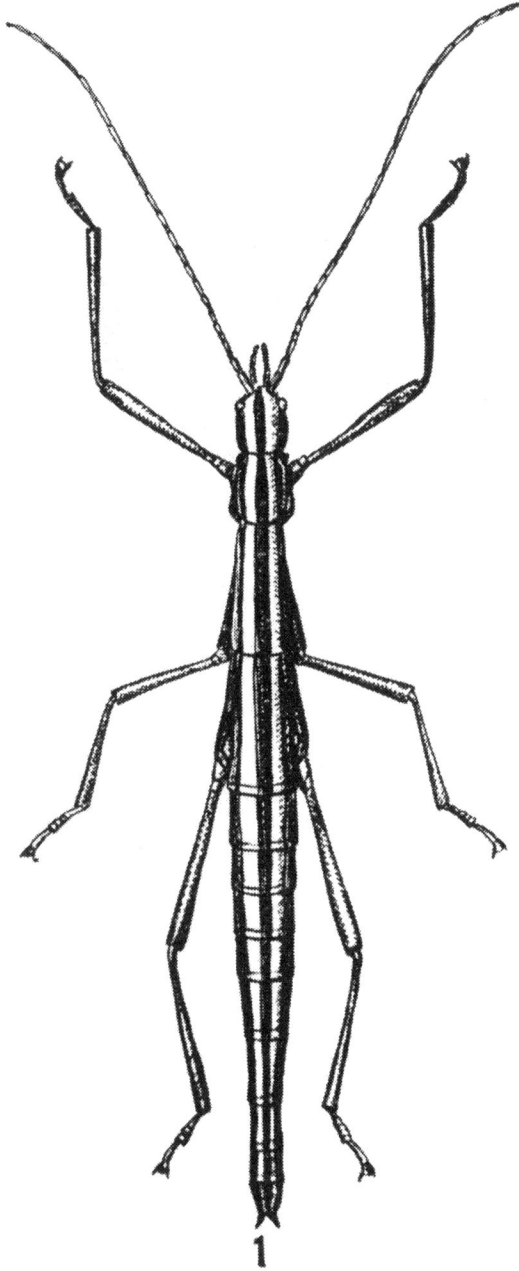

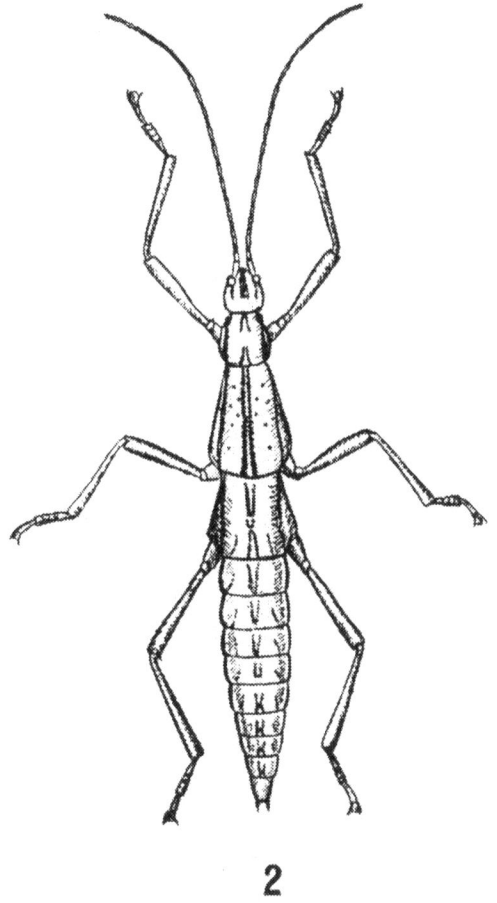

1

2

The Species of *Diapheromera* (Phasmidae) Found in the United States and Canada

Samuel H. Scudder,

Cambridge, Mass.

The common "walking stick" of the oak bushes of the northern United States, *D. femorata* (Say), was the only species known to Gray, when in 1835 he founded this genus. It was not until 1864 that a second, intimately allied, species was added by Walsh, and since 1875, when a third much larger species was described by Stål, no further additions have been made. From rather meagre material in my collection I can now add two other species, one from North Carolina, the other from New Mexico. No species appears to occur west of the continental divide. I subjoin a table for the easy separation of the species, based principally on the male sex.

Table of the United States species of *Diapheromera*.

a1. Male cerci more or less, generally conspicuously, arcuate.
　　b1. Larger and stouter form; under side of middle and hind femora distinctly spined throughout; male cerci much broader apically than at base, more or less spatulate ..... *denticrus.*
　　b2. Smaller and slenderer forms; middle and hind femora without conspicuous spines beneath, excepting the subapical spine; male cerci subequal throughout.
　　　　c1. Ninth abdominal segment of male apically inflated, and here nearly half as broad again as at base, the seventh and eighth segments of subequal length ..... *carolina.*
　　　　c2. Ninth abdominal segment of male subequal, scarcely larger at apex than at base, the seventh segment much longer than the eighth.
　　　　　　d1. Male cerci with a blunt tooth at inner inferior base; female cerci relatively stout, about half as long as last dorsal segment ..... *femorata.*
　　　　　　d2. Male cerci with a sharp thorn at inner inferior base; female cerci relatively slender, almost or quite as long as last dorsal segment ..... *veliei.*
a2. Male cerci rigidly straight ..... *mesillana.*

From: *Psyche*, Vol. 9, April, 1901, pp. 187-189.

Diapheromera denticrus.

Diapheromera denticrus Stål, Rec. Orth., iii, 76 (1875).

Originally described from Opelousas, La. My specimens all come from Texas (Belfrage), New Braunfels, Tex. (Lincecum), and the Gulf coast of Texas (Aaron), excepting a small (female from Las Cruces, N. Mex. (Cockerell). It is perhaps this species to which Gosse alludes (*Lett. Alab.*, 275) as the larger of two species found in Alabama. It varies somewhat in size, two males before me being respectively 90 and 125 mm. in length. The species is figured of half-natural length in *Harper's Magazine*, vol. lxxxviii, p. 457.

Diapheromera carolina sp. nov.

♂. Stouter than *D. femorata*, testaceo-castaneous, glistening, the thorax with a rather broad median bronze-fuscous stripe, not reaching the median segment, and interrupted at the posterior end of the mesonotum, the fore legs greenish, the antennae testaceous; thorax with excessively fine transverse striation. Mesothorax and meta-thorax (including median segment) of similar length. Seventh and eighth abdominal segments of subequal length, each faintly enlarging from base, the ninth a little shorter, apically inflated and subglobose, nearly half as broad again at apex as at base, the cerci much as in *D. femorata*, but stouter, more compressed and without basal tooth.

Length of body, 67 mm.; head, 3 min.; mesothorax, 13.5 mm.; fore femora, 20.5 mm.; middle femora, 14.5 mm.; hind femora, 19.5 mm.

1 ♂. North Carolina (Morrison).

In most features this species stands nearly intermediate between *D. denticrus* and *D. femorata*.

Diapheromera femorata.

Spectrum femoratum Say, *Exp. Long*, ii, 297 (1824); *Amer. ent.*, iii, pl. 37 (1828).

Diapheromera femorata Harr., *Treat. ins. inj. veg.*, 119 (1840, 1841).

Phasma (Bacteria) femorata de Haan, *Bijdr. kenn. Orth.*, 101, 134 (1842).

Bacunculus femoratus Uhl., Harr., *Treat. ins. inj. veg.*, 3 ed., 146 (1862).

Diapheromera sayi Gray, *Syn. Phasm.*, 18 (1835).

Bacteria sayi Charp., *Orth. descr.*, pl. 6 (1841 — 1845) .

Bacteria (Bacunculus) sayi Burm., *Handb. ent.*, ii, 566 (1838).

Bacunculus sayi Thom., *Trans. Ill. st. agric. soc.*, v, 441 (1865).

Bacteria linearis Gosse, *Lett. Alab.*, 275 (1859).

Originally described from the "United States," Niagara and the Missouri River being specified. I have seen specimens from Prout's Neck, Me., Vermont, vic. Boston, Massachusetts, Prescott, Ont. (Billings), New York, Niagara Falls, Maryland (Uhler), Virginia, Illinois, Manitoba, Jefferson, Dallas Co. and Denison, Iowa (Allen), St. Louis, Mo., Dallas, Tex. (Boll) and Ringgold Barracks, Tex. (Schott). It has also been reported, but perhaps sometimes by mistake for the next species, from Montreal (Caulfield), New Hampshire (Scudder), New Jersey (Say, Smith), Pennsylvania (de Haan), Wisconsin (Walsh and Riley), Minnesota (Lugger), Kansas and Nebraska (Bruner), Kentucky (Garman), Indiana (Blatchley), South Carolina (de Haan), Tennessee (de Haan, Saussure), Alabama (Gosse), New Mexico and Mexico (Haldeman).

The species has been frequently figured.

Diapheromera veliei.

Diapheromera velii Walsh, *Proc. ent. soc. Philad.*, iii, 409-410 (1864).

Originally described from Nebraska, and since then reported only from that state and Illinois. I have seen specimens from Maryland (Uhler), Virginia (Wirt Robinson), Georgia (Morrison), Ohio, Southern Illinois (Thomas), Manitoba, Dallas Co. and Jefferson, Iowa (Allen), Lincoln, Valentine and Sand Hills, Nebr. (Bruner), Platte River, Nebr. (Hayden), Barber Co., Kans. (Bruner), Dallas, Tex. (Boll), Ringgold Barracks, Tex. (Schott), Pecos River (Capt. Pope), Albuquerque, N. Mex. (Bruner), Sancelito, Mex. (Palmer), San Pedro and Montelovez, Coahuila, Mex. (Palmer), and Venis Mecas and Sierra San Miguelito, San Luis Potosi, Mex. (Palmer).

Diapheromera mesillana sp. nov.

♂. Slenderer than *D. femorata*, uniform greenish flavous, the antennae infuscated beyond the basal third, the thorax smooth, with an obscure median carina; subapical inferior spine of middle and hind femora rather slight. Mesothorax and metathorax (including median segment) of equal length. Seventh and ninth abdominal segments subequal in length and distinctly longer than the eighth, all equal in width and nowhere enlarged, the ninth rather feebly and angularly emarginate, exposing a small, transverse, apically arcuate, supraanal plate; cerci about as long as the ninth abdominal segment, rigidly straight, directed backward and not at all downward, slender, tapering, blunt tipped. externally convex, and internally concave.

Length of body. 55 mm.; head, 3 mm.; antennae, circa 37 mm.; mesothorax, 12.5 mm.; fore femora, 14.5 mm.; middle femora, 11 mm.; hind femora, 13.5 mm.

2 ♂. Between Mesilla and Las Cruces, N. Mex., June 30 (A. P. Morse).

Two Orthoptera Hitherto Unrecorded from the United States

Andrew Nelson Caudell,

Of the Department of Agriculture.

Through the kindness of Mr. C. Schaeffer, of Brooklyn, New York, I have had an opportunity of studying a small but interesting collection of Orthoptera from the Southern States, made by himself and others during the past year. The greater portion of the collection was made at Brownsville, Texas, and by agreement the results of the examination of that material is to appear in the Science Bulletin of the Brooklyn Institute of Arts and Science. This prohibits the discussion at present of several most interesting additions to our fauna. The following two species, however, not being from Brownsville, form no part of that report and are here recorded for the first time from the United States:

Haploplus evadne Westwood.

Haploplus evadne Westwood, Cat. Phasm., 1859, p. 85, pl. XVIII, fig. 6, male.

One mature female (fig. I) and one large nymph, also a female, were taken at Loggerhead Key, Dry Tortugas, Florida. The label bears no date nor reference to the collector.

This is the first record of the occurrence in the United States of any winged Phasmid, though a young male larva of what I now suppose to be of this species was mentioned in my recent paper on the Phasmidæ of the United States.[a] The large nymph exhibits characters intermediate between those of the small male specimen mentioned above and this mature female. Hence my inference that they all belong to the same species. If I am correct in this, as I now believe I am, the young *evadne* is seen to have the intermediary segment subequal with the metanotum and the legs bear small lobe-like expansions on the posterior and intermediate femora and on all the tibiæ. As the insect approaches maturity these expansions become obliterated on the anterior and posterior tibiæ. The young are also less acutely spined than the

[a] *Proc. U. S. Nat. Mus.*, XXVI, 1903, p. 884.

Extract From: *Proceedings U.S. National Museum*, Vol. XXVII, No. 1378, pp. 949-952.

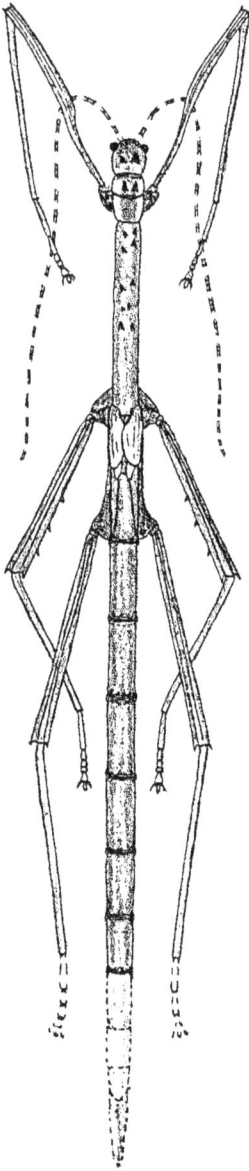

Fig. 1—*Haplopus evadne.*
Female (enlarged).

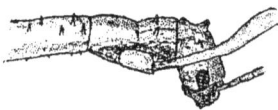

Fig. 2—Head of *Haplopus
evadne* (enlarged).

adult. The intermediary segment of the adult female as well as the nymphs is scarcely longer than the metanotum. The long-winged male insect as figured by Westwood seems also to have the intermediary segment subequal with the metanotum.

The adult female, which has never been described, is shining brown above, yellowish below, the margins of the pronotum and elytra and the center of the dorsal surface of the intermediary segment longitudinally marked with chalky-white, probably a variable character. The head (Fig. 2) has the usual horn-like tubercles, the right one fully twice as large as the one on the left. Behind these main tubercles is a pair of smaller ones, likewise dissimilar in size. The pronotum is transversely divided mesially by a deep sulcus and the anterior lobe is divided longitudinally by a narrow sulcus and bears a pair of stout black-tipped sharp spine-like tubercles. The mesonotum bears ten irregularly placed, black-tipped spines or sharp tubercles. The elytra are about as long as the metanotum, the wings about the same length, though they project a millimeter beyond the tip of the elytra, being placed farther back. The abdominal segments are about three times as long as broad and are apically furnished with a slight crescent-shaped transverse blunt carina. The tip of the abdomen and the antennæ are gone but are drawn in dotted lines from the large nymph as a model. The legs are slightly lighter colored above than the body, below concolorous with the ventral portion of the body, unarmed except that the posterior and intermediate femora are armed below on the outer two-thirds with a few large black-tipped spines, the tip of the tibiæ below also furnished with an elevated longitudinal ridge.

Length. 80+ mm.; pronotum, 4.75 mm.; mesonotum, 19.5 mm.; metanotum, 6 mm.; intermediary segment, 6.5 mm.; anterior femora, 19 mm.; intermediate femora, 15.5 mm.; posterior femora,

21 mm.; width of head, 3.5 mm.; pronotum, 3.5 mm.; mesonotum 2.5 mm.; first abdominal segment, 3 mm.

The large female nymph is dark opaque brown in color, lighter below. Head armed as in the adult as are also the pro- and mesonotum, though the spines or tubercles are here quite small. Anterior legs unarmed, though the fore tibiæ of the small male specimen have a small compressed expansion near each end above, as have also all the tibiæ in that specimen. In the large female nymph these expansions are mantained only on the middle pair where there is, in both nymphs, also a small longitudinal expansion near the base below. Middle and posterior femora furnished above with a pair of parallel lobes near the apex and armed below with spines as in the adult, except smaller. The measurements are as follows:

Length, 69 mm.; antennæ, 24 mm.; pronotum, 3 mm.; mesonotum 14 mm.; metanotum, 4.5 mm.; intermediary segment, 4.5 mm.; oviscapt, beyond the tip of the abdomen, 5.5 mm.; posterior femora, 13 mm.; intermediate femora, 10 mm.; anterior femora, 12 mm.; width of head, 3 mm.; pronotum, 3 mm.; middle of mesonotum, 2.75 mm.; of metanotum, 3 mm.; of first abdominal segment, 2.5 mm.

The right hind leg of this specimen has been broken off and regenerated, being therefore smaller then the other, the femora measuring but 9 mm. in length.

This species was described from Santo Domingo, West Indies, and is an unusually interesting addition to our fauna by reason of its being the only winged representative of the family occurring within our borders. The long-winged males are objects of note and suggest tropical forms. The asymmetrical horn-like tubercles of the head seem to be a constant character of the genus. Why one of these tubercles, usually the one on the right, should be longer or larger than its fellow is, so far as I know, unexplained.

Aplopus mayeri,* New Species

A. N. Caudell
Washington, D. C.

The Phasmid described and figured by the writer as *Haplopus evadne* of Westwood (*Proc. U. S. Nat. Mus.,* xxvii, 950, 1904) is not that species, the male having been found to be brachypterous. A number of specimens of both sexes were taken in Florida, Dry Tortugas, Loggerhead Key, by Dr. A. G. Mayer. The specimen figured at the above reference is really a male and not a female as there stated. The restored tip of the abdomen however very well represents that of the true female as represented by specimens in the present collection. The female agrees in structure with the male except that the form is more robust and the pronotum and mesonotum are not so smooth and are more thickly spinose, the spines, however, smaller than those of the male. The antennæ of both sexes are about the length represented in the restoration in the figure, the basal segment quite strongly depressed, especially at the base, and considerably thicker than the succeeding ones, the entire antenna gradually tapering to a fine point. The elytra are generally tumid centrally. The males usually, but not always, have the abdominal segments laterally marked longitudinally with white and the margination of the elytra seems quite constant in that sex. As suggested in the former article, the chalky markings of the body are not constant. The end of the male abdomen is very moderately swollen, the seventh and eighth segments subequal, the ninth very slightly shorter, subquadrate, apically subtruncate, mesially very obscurely emarginate; the operculum reaching the apex of the eighth segment. The cerci are very stout, slightly recurved, cylindrical, bluntly terminated organs about as long as the ninth abdominal segment and directed backward, a little downward and scarcely inward. The intermediate and posterior femora of both sexes are usually armed for their entire length beneath on the median line with from five to seven black spines, the apical two moved forward to the anterior carina and opposite them, on the hinder margin, is a single small spine; all the femoræ have the

---

* *Aplopus* was used prior to Gray's work by Megerle von Muehlfeld but seems to not have been used in a valid sense. Thus Gray's name is not invalidated by it. *Aplopus* being the original spelling, should be used, not the emendation *Haplopus* of Burmeister.

From: *Journal of the NY Entomological Society,* Vol. 13, No. 2, 1905, pp. 83-85.

geniculations spinose on both sides, those of the anterior pair the least developed. The anterior femora are armed below on the apical third with a couple of very small spines.

The measurements of a typical pair are as follows: Entire length male, 90 mm., female, including the oviscapt 125 mm.; antennæ, male, 53 mm., female, 45 mm.; mesonotum, male, 20 mm., female, 26 mm.; metanotum, male, 6 mm., female, 6 mm.; intermediary segment, male, 7 mm., female, 8 mm.; elytra, male, 7 mm., female, 8.5 mm.; anterior femora, male, 20 mm., female, 20 mm.; intermediate femora, male, 16 mm., female, 17 mm.; posterior femora, male, 21 mm., female, 22 mm; oviscapt, female, beyond the tip of the abdomen, 12 mm.; median width, mesonotum, male, 3 mm., female, 5.5 mm.; second abdominal segment, male, 2.75 mm., female, 5.5 mm.

Types in the Museum of the Brooklyn Institute of Arts and Sciences, Brooklyn N. Y., and cotypes in the National Museum, Washington, D. C.

In many particulars this species seems near *Aplopus micropterus* but the shorter wings and other less noticeable characters seem to separate them. It is also closely allied to *A. scabricollis* Gray, as stated in a letter from Mr. W. F. Kirby, to whom specimens were submitted; but that is a larger species with a considerably longer oviscapt in the female. The location of this species in the genus *Aplopus* is merely tentative, the brachypterous males excluding it from this genus unless the male of micropterus, the type, is proved to be also brachypterous. In that case the species with macropterous males would necessarily take another generic name.

Regarding *Diapheromera veliei* Walsh and *Manomera blatchleyi* Caudell (Orth.: Phasmidae).

A. N. Caudell of the Bureau of Entomology.
U. S. Department of Agriculture. Washington, D. C.

The type material of *Diapheromera veliei* Walsh consisted of one female specimen from Illinois, taken in a place overgrown by weeds beneath the boughs of two isolated ash trees, and one pair from Nebraska taken by Dr. Velie in a place overgrown by weeds but with no trees within a long distance of it. The description drawn from these three specimens appears to apply to *Manomera blatchleyi* so far as concerns the female, but the characters ascribed to the male apply to the true *veliei*. The slender acute basal spine of the cerci of the male described by Walsh certainly pertain to *veliei* rather than to *blatchleyi* and, besides, if it had been the male of *blatchleyi* Walsh had before him he would very surely have mentioned the but slightly swollen intermediate femora as a character decidedly at variance with those of *D. femorata*, the species with which he compared this new species. That he did specifically notice the middle femora is evident from the fact that he mentions their lacking the brown banding of *femorata*. Thus it appears very certain that, while the female from Illinois was quite surely a specimen of *M. blatchleyi*, the male from Nebraska, probably also the Nebraska female, was the true veliei. That the male is to be rightly considered as the specific type is evident from the fact that the male is morphologically the more important in this group and that this construction is according to good sense and in compliance with Par 73h of the Entomological Code of Nomenclature.

Diapheromera veliei may be distinguished from *Manomera blatchleyi* by the comparatively shorter and anteriorly broader head of both sexes, by the strongly swollen intermediate femora of the male and by the posterior femora of both male and female being furnished beneath with a prominent subapical spine, in *Manomera* this spine being either entirely absent or very small. The last dorsal segment of the abdomen of the female is longer in *blatchleyi* than in *veliei*, being about 4 mm. in the former and 3 mm. in the latter; the cerci of the female *Manomera* are also decidedly longer than in either *Diapheromera veliei* or *femorata*, the actual length in adult individuals before me being 3.75 mm. in blatchleyi, 2 mm. in length and 1.25 mm. in femorata. Additional characters for the separation of the males of *veliei*

From: *Entomological News*, Vol. xxix, July, 1918, pp. 258-260.

and *blatchleyi* are found in the inner basal projections of the cerci, these being slender and apically acute in *veliei*, while in *blatchleyi* they are blunter and stouter, less so, however, than in *D. femorata*.

Diapheromera veliei is apparently not at all a common species and probably does not occur in Illinois, or rarely so.

Material in the National Museum comes from the following localities; San Diego, Texas, May 15th, one male, Schwarz; Victoria, Texas, August 24th one male, W. E. Hinds; 40 miles South of Alice, Texas, June 15th, 1904, one mated pair, Barber; Stillwater, Oklahoma, one male, Caudell; Garden City, Kansas, July 27th, 1891, one female; Lakin, Kansas, July 27th, 1891, one male; Pipestone, Minnesota, August 4th, 1911, one male. The locality labels on the Kansas specimens are not perfectly legible and, as the dates are the same, it is possible that they are from the same source.

As represented by the above listed material this species is seen to extend across the Middle States from Texas to Minnesota. The exact local habitat of none of these specimens is known except of the mated pair from 40 miles south of Alice, Texas; these were taken by Mr. Barber on weeds or shrubs on the prairie some distance from any woodland. This agrees with the habitat of the type.

Manomera blatchleyi is represented in the National Museum by material from Iowa, Indiana, Illinois, Kansas, Oklahoma, Maryland, Virginia, New York and New Jersey. The Atlantic Coast material is composed of female specimens only, but they appear to agree specifically with specimens from the type locality. The Middle West specimens, so far as known, were taken in open field or prairie regions. Of the Atlantic Coast specimens I took one in the woods on a stone and Mr. Barber took one on a post by the Club House on Plummer's Island, Maryland. These are the only ones of which I know the exact local habitat, but my good friend, Wm. T. Davis, of Staten Island, New York, who has taken these insects in numbers, assures me that this is not a tree species. The following quotation is from a recent letter from him on this question. "I have collected a great many females of the *Manomera* that occurs about New York, and have seen a great many more that I let stay in the low vegetation, so that they might not be exterminated. I have always found the insects on golden rods, Asters and such like plants, and can assure you that it isn't a tree species." This conforms with the known habitat of more western material and seems to make rather sure the determination of these eastern specimens as *blatchleyi*. It is certainly singular that among the somewhat ample material of Atlantic Coast specimens found in various eastern collections not a single male is to be found. Can it be that this indicates parthenogenesis?

The Walking-Sticks

W. S. Blatchley

This family of non-saltatorial Orthoptera comprises the insects commonly known as walking-sticks. The North American species have the body elongate, very slender, subcylindrical; head free, nearly horizontal, usually subquadrate; antennæ long, rather stout; eyes small, ocelli often absent; pronotum very short; abdomen elongate, composed of ten segments, the basal one usually closely united with the metathorax, often invisible; tegmina and wings absent (except in the genus *Aplopus*), the location of the wings generally indicated by a stationary wing-like pad, bearing a gland; legs very long and slender, of nearly equal size; tarsi in our eastern genera, 5-jointed, terminated by two claws between which is a large pad (arolium); ovipositor concealed by the subgenital plate; cerci not jointed.

Our species of Phasmidæ are remarkable for their resemblance to twigs of different plants, while some of the tropical species are so modified as to resemble leaves, frequently bearing so close a resemblance to the foliage as to deceive a keen observer. Their movements are, in general, very slow, though the males can run with some rapidity when in pursuit of the opposite sex. They feed during their entire lives upon leaves, being especially fond of those of oak and wild cherry. The eggs are dropped loosely and singly upon the ground by the mother, where they remain through the winter thus tiding the insect over the cold season. The outer case or shell of the egg is hard and often sculptured, and those of our common species resemble seeds or small beans. The young, when hatched, trust to chance and their peculiar shape to escape those higher animal forms which are ever ready to prey upon every moving object which promises them a bit of sustenance. The largest living insects are walking-sticks, found in Borneo and other East India Islands, two of the wingless forms having the body 33 cm. or 13 inches in length.

That the Phasmidæ have the power of reproducing their lost or broken legs has been shown by Scudder. Such restored limbs are much smaller and have but three or four tarsal joints,[27] the usual fourth joint being absent. If the leg is removed in front of the trochanto-femoral joint it is never reproduced.

The family is in the main, a tropical one, and is feebly represented in the United States, where but five of the 16 recognized subfamilies are known to occur. Three of

[27] *Proc. Bost. Soc. Nat. Hist.*, XII, 1868, 138.

From: *Orthoptera of Northeastern America*, 1920, Nature Publishing, Indianapolis.

these subfamilies are represented in the Eastern United States by six genera and eleven species. The following literature treats especially of the North American representatives of the family: Riley, 1879; Scudder, 1895, 1901; Caudell, 1903a, 1913, 1918; Brunner, 1907; Severin, 1911, 1911a, 1913; R. & H., 1916; Somes, 1916.

Key to Eastern Subfamilies of Phasmidæ.

a. Mesothorax four or more times as long as prothorax; hind and middle tibiæ not deeply emarginate beneath at apex.
  b. Tegmina and wings absent; median segment not or barely longer than broad; head unarmed above. I. BACUNCULINÆ, p. 131.
  bb. Adults with short tegmina and wings; median segment longer than broad; head armed above with two short horns. II. PHIBALOSOMINÆ, p. 143.
aa. Mesothorax never more than three times as long as prothorax; hind and middle tibiæ broadly and deeply emarginate beneath at apex, thus forming a cavity to receive the base of the tarsi when bent upon them. III. ANISOMORPHINÆ, p. 144.

Subfamily I. BACUNCULINÆ.

This subfamily comprises the longest and most slender of our North American walking-sticks. They have the mesothorax usually five or more times as long as prothorax; antennæ in our eastern genera more than twice as long as the front femora; tibiæ without a sunken areola beneath the apex; tarsi five-jointed. Seven of the United States genera belong to this subfamily. Of these representatives of four have been recorded from the area covered by this work.

Key to Eastern Genera of Bacunculinæ.

a. Head subquadrate or subcylindrical, usually distinctly longer than broad, attached obliquely or horizontally; small or medium sized species, rarely over 95 mm. in length; hind femora without a row of spines beneath; cerci of male not spatulate.
  b. Hind femora of both sexes armed beneath with a subapical spine, prominent in male, smaller in female; middle femora of male usually distinctly thicker than the hind ones; head subquadrate, but slightly longer than broad. I. *Diapheromera*.

bb. Hind femora unarmed beneath; middle femora of male not or but slightly thicker than the hind ones.

    c. Middle femora armed beneath with a distinct subapical spine; head subcylindrical, twice or more as long as broad. II. *Manomera*.

    cc. Middle femora not spined beneath. III. *Heteronemia*.

aa. Head short, ovate, scarcely longer than broad, attached subvertically; very large species, length 115 or more mm.; hind femora, at least in female, with a median row of strong spines beneath; cerci of male broadly spatulate. IV. *Megaphasma*.

I. *Diapheromera* Gray, 1835, 18. (Gr., "unequal + thigh.")

Body long, slender, subcylindrical; head smooth, obliquely attached to thorax; antennæ inserted in front of eyes; pronotum about as long as head, less than one-fourth the length of mesonotum, the latter longer than any other segment; metanotum about three-fourths the length of mesonotum; basal segment of abdomen oblong, in male twice as long as broad. Legs very long and slender, middle femora of male much swollen, armed, like those of hind pair on under side near apex, with an acute spine, most prominent in male. Cerci of male long, terete and incurved; those of female short, straight. The species of this genus are widely distributed over the United States east of the Rocky Mountains, three of the seven recognized having been recorded from east of the Mississippi.

Key to Eastern Species of *Diapheromera*.

a. Seventh segment of abdomen distinctly longer than eighth in both sexes (Fig. 54, a); base and apex of ninth abdominal segment of male subequal in width; meso- and metanotum without median black dorsal stripe.

    b. Cerci of male with a blunt basal tooth or tubercle; cerci of female about half as long as the last dorsal segment (Fig. 54, b.) 52. *femorata*.

    bb. Cerci of male with an acute and slender basal tooth; cerci of male more slender, almost or quite as long as the last dorsal segment (Fig. 54, d.) 53. *veliei*.

aa. Seventh and eighth segments of abdomen subequal in length; apex of ninth abdominal segment of male inflated, nearly half as broad again as base; cerci of male without a basal tooth or tubercle; meso- and metanotum with a broad blackish dorsal stripe. 54. *carolina*.

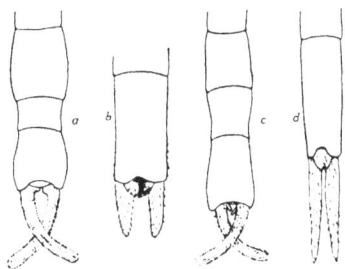

Fig. 54. Apical portions of abdomen of Phasmidæ, showing relative length of segments, cerci, etc.; a, of *Diaphero-mera femorata* Say, male, b, female; c, of *Manomera blatchleyi* Caud., male, d, female (After Hart.)

52. *Diapheromera femorata* (Say), 1824a, 297. Common Walking-stick.

Color variable, being either gray, brown or greenish-brown; body of male usually greenish-brown, sometimes almost wholly green; head yellowish with three vague lengthwise fuscous stripes; front legs and tibiæ of the others usually green; middle femora often banded: with dark gray; female duller, usually grayish-brown, often with paler specks and mottlings on head and back. Head smooth in both sexes, subquadrate; eyes round, more prominent in male; antennæ very slender, about as long as body. Abdomen smooth, basal segment about twice as long as broad in female, three times as long as broad in male, seventh segment in male three times as long as eighth. Cerci of male cylindrical, oval at apex, clothed with short stiff hairs, strongly curved inward and usually crossing near middle; of female, straight stout, rather blunt, pubescent. The male is easily distinguished by the shorter and more slender body, longer legs and antennæ; narrower and less dilated front femora, swollen middle femora and by the greater stoutness of the subapical spines beneath the middle and hind femora. Length of body, ♂, 68—84, ♀, 70—101; of antennæ, ♂, 58—65, ♀, 45—57; of mesothorax, ♂, 17—18, ♀, 16—20; of meta-thorax, ♂, 15—16, ♀, 13.5—18; of hind femora, ♂, 19.5—21, ♀, 15—19 mm. (Fig. 55.)

This walking-stick is quite a common insect throughout Indiana, though the average observer will probably see but one or two of them a year. They reach maturity in August, and may then often we found upon the leaves of oak or wild cherry, especially on isolated trees along fence rows. One of my students at Terre Haute once brought in on October 15, a hundred or more which he had gotten from a wild cherry tree on whose leaves they had

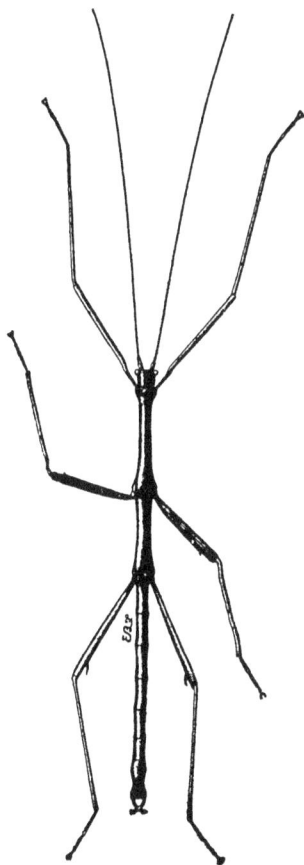

Fig. 55. *Diapheromera femorata* (Say.) Male.

been feeding. It moves very slowly and has a habit of remaining motionless and apparently dead for a considerable length of time. On such occasions it usually stretches itself out from a twig, with its front legs and antennæ extended, and can then scarcely be distinguished from a prolongation or branch of the twig. Many people who see them thus for the first time and afterwards watch them moving slowly away, can scarcely be persuaded that they are not real twigs, gifted in some mysterious manner with life and motion. On September 18, 1918, they were found in numbers in a grove of the black locust in Putnam County, 40 or more specimens being secured in a few minutes. They were usually found mating on the boles of the locust and when approached and touched would drop to the ground and there remain motionless.

D. femorata is the most common and widely distributed Phasmid in the United States, ranging from Maine to the Rocky Mountains, north to central Ontario and Selkirk, Manitoba, and south and southwest at least to northern Florida, northern Texas and the Organ Mountains, New Mexico. In Florida it has been recorded from Monticello by Davis (1915) and several specimens labeled "Gainesville, Aug. 15" are in the collection of the Florida Experiment Station. R. & H. (1916, 124) record it from Virginia, North and South Carolina, and from numerous stations in Georgia, and state that a male from Albany, Ga., is 84.5 mm. in length, and that the material from the four states mentioned "was all taken in the undergrowth of pine and oak woods." A female at hand from near Mobile, Ala., 101 mm. in length, has one of the hind legs aborted, the length of the femur being but 19 and of the tibia 11 mm. as against 24 and 27 mm. for the same segments of the opposite leg. The basal joint of the tarsus is less than one-third that of the corresponding normal one and only two additional joints are present.

This is the only North American walking-stick abundant enough to be of economic importance. In feeding they eat the edges of a leaf, preferably those of an oak or wild cherry, usually straddling it with their legs, and in an hour will devour a piece an inch long by a third of an inch wide. Riley (1879) records that on occasions they are so numerous as to do much damage to oak, hickory, locust and other trees. In Yates Co., New York, he once found them very abundant in a woodland of 50 acres, which they had attacked in numbers two and four years previously. He states that:

> "By the middle of August the bulk of the pests were going through their last moult, and by the end of autumn they had stripped most of the trees, showing, however, a decided preference for the black, red and rock-chestnut oaks, over the white oaks and hickories, which they affect but little until after the first mentioned trees are stripped. The underbrush was also effectually cleaned of its foliage, and the insects hung from and clung to the bare twigs and branches in great clusters. They settled to roost on the witch-hazel, but

did not defoliate it until the other trees mentioned were pretty bare. Sumach and thorn were also little affected, while peach and apple in an adjoining orchard were untouched. Whenever they had entirely stripped the trees and shrubs they moved in bodies to fresh pastures, crowding upon one another and covering the ground, the fence rails, and everything about them so that it was impossible for a person to enter the woods without being covered by them. The timber affected could be recognized by its seared and leafless appearance from a great distance, and upon entering the woods the ear was greeted by a peculiar seething noise, resulting from the motion of the innumerable jaws at work on the leaves. Their depredations first began to attract attention soon after wheat harvest, and were most noticeable in September. The injury to the trees done in 1874 and 1876 was manifest in the death of most of the black oaks, and, according to the owner's observations, trees die in three years after the first attack."

The eggs, of which each female lays about 100, are a little less than 3 mm. in length, long oval in shape and of a polished black color with a whitish stripe on one side. They resemble a small, plump bean or seed of other leguminous plant. They are simply dropped loosely upon the ground from whatever height the female may happen to be, and says Riley: "During the latter part of autumn where the insects are common, one hears a constant pattering, not unlike drops of rain, which results from the abundant dropping of these eggs, which in places are so thick among and under the dead leaves that they may be scraped up in great quantities. The eggs remain upon the ground all through the winter and hatch for the most part during the month of May. Some of them, however, continue hatching much later, so that all through the summer and even into the fall, young individuals may be found. When first hatched the young measure 4.5 mm. and with their feelers and legs outstretched, near double that length. They are invariably, during early life, of a pale yellowish-green color. The insect changes very little in appearance from birth to maturity except so far as color is concerned, and moults but twice. Growth is rapid, averaging, under favorable circumstances, about six weeks from birth to adult. With age the green color gives way to various shades of gray and brown. In this way we find great correspondence with its surroundings. While the vegetation is green, the walking-sticks are green also; when the foliage turns in autumn, they change color correspondingly, and when the foliage is stripped they so closely resemble, both in appearance and color, the twigs upon which they rest—the habit of stretching out the front legs and feelers greatly enhancing the resemblance—that when they are few in number it is difficult to recognize them. A few green specimens, more particularly of the males, may always be found, even among the mature individuals."

It will be noted that Riley, in the above account, which was the first one attempting to give in detail the life history of *D. femorata*, states that the young "moult but twice." Our knowledge of the life history of other Orthoptera would tend to show that this was an error and Severin has proven it to be so by rearing 100 examples of the species under conditions as normal as possible. He states (1911) that "23 per cent. moulted four times, 76 per cent. five times and only one per cent. six times." He adds that since the insect usually eats parts, or all of its cast-off skin it is possible that Riley overlooked some of the moults on this account. He also states that those specimens "which moulted four times reached sexual maturity on an average in 50 days, while those which moulted five times required 57.5 days, on an average before beginning the egg-laying period. * * * The eggs, after passing out of the vaginal orifice, may be retained for a number of hours within the peculiar 'external uterus' formed by the ovipositor."

The thick-thighed walking-stick appears to be abundant in any certain locality only every other year. This is in part due to an increase of the insect's natural enemies on those years in which they are most abundant. These enemies are several species of true bugs (Heteroptera), crows and other birds. The main reason for the greater number of walking-sticks in alternate years is, however, thought to be due to the fact that the larger proportion of the eggs, especially those laid late in the autumn, take two years in hatching. If at any time the insect threatens to become injurious in woodlands, it can be held in check by burning the leaves on the ground in the winter season, thus destroying the hibernating eggs.

53. *Diapheromera veliei* Walsh, 1864, 410.
Prairie Walking-stick.

Form, size and color much as in *D. femorata*, the middle femora of male not usually banded with gray as in that species. Head slightly more elongate. Male with seventh abdominal segment no longer than ninth, in femorata one-third longer; eighth segment two-thirds as long as seventh; cerci with a very slender, sharp curved spine on inner side near base, instead of a blunt tubercle as in femorata. Female with emargination at apex of ninth abdominal segment deep, broadly rounded, in femorata more shallow, triangular, with apex acute; subapical spine beneath the middle and hind femora often very small. Length of body, ♂, 61, ♀, 74; of mesonotum, ♂, 14, ♀, 16; of metanotum, ♂ and ♀, 12; of hind femora, ♂ and ♀, 18 mm.

Walsh's male type of this walking-stick was from Nebraska, and one of his female cotypes from Illinois. Its main distribution is west and southwest of the Mississippi, extending from Staples and Pipestone, Minn., to Colorado, Texas and Mexico. East of that river it has been recorded from New York, New Jersey, Maryland, Virginia, Georgia and Illinois, but Caudell has shown (1918) that the majority of these records are probably based on individuals of his *Manomera blatchleyi*, a species very closely resembling *D. veliei*. The eastern limits of the range of *veliei* cannot, therefore be given with certainty, but it has been taken by Somes at Memphis in the northeastern corner of Missouri and at Elmira in eastern Iowa, and therefore very probably occurs in Illinois and other states bordering the Mississippi. Somes (1916) states that *veliei* averages smaller than *femorata*, especially in the males, and these also tend to brighter coloration, being often quite distinctly marked with two light colored lateral stripes, the pleura being light colored in life, though after drying the color is less distinct. It frequents tall grasses and low brush rather than trees and tall shrubs, being often found on such plants as *Andropogon scoparius* Mx., *Lespedeza capitata*, Mx. and *Salix humilis* Marsh."

54. *Diapheromera carolina* Scudder, 1901, 188.
Carolina Walking-stick.

"Stouter than *D. femorata*, testaceo-castaneous, glistening; thorax with a rather broad median bronze-fuscous stripe, not reaching the median segment, and interrupted at posterior end of mesonotum; fore legs greenish, antennæ testaceous; thorax with excessively fine transverse striation. Mesothorax and metathorax (including median segment) of similar length. Seventh and eighth abdominal segments of subequal length, each faintly enlarging from base, the ninth a little shorter, apically inflated and subglobose, nearly half as broad again at apex as at base, the cerci much as in *D. femorata*, but stouter, more compressed and without basal tooth. Length of body, ♂, 67; head, 3; mesothorax, 13.5; fore femora, 20.5; hind femora, 19.5 mm." (Scudder.)

The above is the original description of the unique male type of this well marked Phasmid which was collected in North Carolina by Morrison. An examination of it at Cambridge shows that it has the cerci rather strongly incurved and flattened, being fully twice as thick vertically as horizontally, with the apical half subspatulate within; ninth segment of abdomen globose, scarcely longer than wide; seventh and eighth segments subequal, each slightly broader than long and a little shorter than the ninth. The only specimen known, other than the type, is a male taken by Mrs. A. T. Slosson at Lake Toxaway, N. C., and now in the Davis collection. It agrees fully with Scudder's description as emended above and there can be no doubt of its specific standing. The shining dark dorsal stripe, narrow on pronotum and much wider on meso- and metanotum, is a striking character. The sides of the seventh and eighth abdominal segments also bear a curved black stripe, and the subapical spines of under surface of middle and hind femora are shining black.

II. *Manomera* Rehn & Hebard, 1907, 283. (Gr., "thin" + "thighs.")

Very closely allied to *Diapheromera*. Head more slender, smooth, swollen in front, twice or more as long as broad, attached horizontally to the thorax; antennæ about two and a half times as long as the front femora; middle femora armed beneath with slender subapical spine, hind femora unarmed; cerci of male stout, cylindrical, pubescent, decurved and incurved, sometimes crossing near middle and armed on the inner side at base with a spine or tubercle (Fig. 54, c); cerci of female slender, lanceolate, about as long as the ninth abdominal segment (Fig. 54, d.).

This genus is characterized very briefly by its authors thus: "From *Diapheromera*, *Manomera* can be separated in the male by the slender head, absence of caudal femoral spines, uninflated median femora and more elongate abdominal appendages." Now the middle femora of the male of *M. blatchleyi* are distinctly inflated, and the cerci of the male of no species of *Manomera* are more elongate than those of *D. femorata*, while the long female cerci are paralleled in that sex of *D. veliei*. This leaves only the more slender head and the absence of spines on hind femora as the valid characters separating the two genera. Since these femoral spines are often absent in the females of *Diapheromera* it will be readily seen that *Manomera* has a very precarious standing. The species at present ascribed to the genus may be separated as follows:

Key to the Species of the Genus *Manomera*

a. Middle femora of male not or scarcely thicker than the hind ones; head slender, more than twice as long as broad.
　b. Seventh, eighth and ninth abdominal segments of male together one-half longer than sixth; ninth segment cylindrical, distinctly longer than wide, male, longer than prothorax, female; cerci of male with a slender sharp tooth at base. (Fig. 56, a.) 55. *tenuescens.*
　bb. Seventh, eighth and ninth abdominal segments of male together no longer than the sixth; ninth segment but slightly longer than wide, enlarged at apex, male, equal in length to prothorax, female; cerci of male with a swollen, blunt, oblique basal tooth. (Fig. 56, b.) 56. *brachypyga.*

aa. Middle femora of male distinctly thicker than the hind ones; head shorter, stouter, about twice as long as broad; cerci with a blunt tooth at base. (Fig. 54, c.) 57. *blatchleyi.*

55. *Manomera tenuescens* (Scudder), 1900, 95.
Slender-bodied Walking-stick.

Male very slender, elongate; female much stouter and longer. Male brown, female green above, both brownish-yellow beneath; sides of male usually with a fuscous stripe, bordered below with yellow, the legs in part greenish. Head slender, one-third longer than pronotum. Male with seventh and ninth abdominal segments subequal in length, each slightly longer than the eighth and about one-half as long as sixth; subgenital operculum slender, strongly spatulate, reaching the tip of the eighth segment. Female with ninth segment slightly longer than seventh, its apex truncate; cerci very slender, strongly tapering, as long as the ninth segment, their margins minutely serrate. Length of body, ♂, 63—67, ♀, 85— 110; of head, ♂, 3.2—3.5, ♀, 3.5—5.5; of mesothorax, ♂, 16—17, ♀, 19—24; of metathorax, ♂, 12—13, ♀, 14.5—19.5; of hind femora, ♂, 18—20, ♀, 24—26, mm.

A Southern species whose known range is from Selma and Winter Park, North Carolina to Southern Florida. Numerous nymphs have been taken about Dunedin in February and March. They are pale grass-green and were swept from huckleberry and other low shrubs in open pine woods. Scudder's types were from Cedar Keys and Capron, Fla., and it has been recorded from numerous localities from Jacksonville

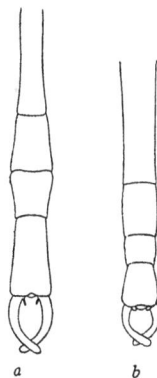

Fig. 56. Apical portions of abdomen of males of *Manomera*.
a. *M. tenuescens*; b. *M. brachypyga*. x 3. (After R. & H.)

and Live Oak in the north, to Homestead and Punta Gorda in the south. Adults are found from April to November on wire grass, saw palmetto and other undergrowth in open pine woods, rarely on vegetation in low damp places. *Manomera orthostylus* Caudell (1913, 612) has been shown by R. & H. (1916, 125) to be a synonym of *M. tenuescens*, having been based on a male in the instar preceding maturity, the cerci of the male in the nymph stages being straight, pilose and delicate in structure.

56. *Manomera brachypyga* Rehn & Hebard, 1914c, 384.
Short-rumped walking-stick.

Very similar to *M. tenuescens* agreeing in general form, color and structure, but differing in the much shorter seventh, eighth and ninth abdominal segments and the form of the apex of the male abdomen, as described in the key and shown in Fig. 56. The female differs from that sex of *tenuescens* in having the sixth dorsal segment considerably longer than the seventh and eighth, the ninth segment equal in length to thorax and the subgenital plate rounded or subtruncate, with caudal margin very little produced. Length of body, ♂, 69.6—88.5, ♀, 92.6; of mesothorax, ♂, 15.8—21.4, ♀, 21; of hind femora, ♂, 20—25.3, ♀, 23.8 mm.

Originally described from Homestead and Detroit, Florida, July 10—12; San Pablo, Aug. 13, and Miami (female and 11 nymphs), March 28. Since recorded from Marco, LaBelle, La Grange and Charlotte Harbor, Fla. Like *M. tenuescens*, it occurs mainly on the undergrowth of pine woods. Davis (1914) states that at La Grange, Sept. 9-12, with the aid of a lantern he found both *M. tenuescens* and *brachypyga* at night, when they were active and walking about on the low vegetation in the pine woods.

57. *Manomera blatchleyi* (Caudell), 1905c, 212.
Blatchley's Walking-stick.

Form shorter and proportionally slightly stouter than in tenuescens. Color the same as that of *D. veliei* the males usually somewhat darker than those of that species and with a pale lateral stripe extending back to hind femora. Head subcylindrical, feebly enlarged in front. Pronotum narrower and but slightly shorter than head. Length of mesonotum four-fifths that of metanotum and median segment combined. Seventh and eighth abdominal segments of male subequal in length, each slightly shorter than ninth, the latter in female feebly and broadly emarginate, the supra-anal plate small, triangular, carinate above. Cerci of male cylindrical, scarcely at all tapering, decurved and incurved as in *D. femorata*, the subbasal tooth on the inner margin very short, blunt; cerci of female slender, straight, tapering, as long as the ninth segment (Fig. 54, d.) Legs stouter proportionally than those of *tenuescens*; middle femora of male very finely serrate beneath and armed near apex with a stout, blunt, nearly horizontal spine; those of female slender, the spine short, straight. Length of body, ♂, 58, ♀, 67; of head, ♂, 3, ♀, 4; of mesonotum, ♂, 13, ♀, 15—16; of metanotum, ♂ and ♀, 12; of hind femora, ♂, 20, ♀, 18—20; of cerci, ♀, 3.7 mm.

The types of this walking-stick in the U. S. National Museum were taken by me near Bass Lake, Starke Co., Ind., Aug. 20, 1902, and no additional specimens have since been personally collected. It doubtless occurs, however, throughout the northern half, perhaps over the entire State. A female is at hand from Cedar Point, Ohio, and Kostir (1914, 371) states that numerous females but no males were taken at that place. Hart (1907, 259), recorded it as occurring on rank prairie vegetation throughout Illinois, and also from Geneva, Wis. Gerhard has sent me a male and two females taken at Argo, Ill., July 27, and has collected others at Palos Park and Fourth Lake, Ill. Somes (1916) records *M. blatchleyi* from Iowa and Missouri, the sexes occurring in about equal numbers. Elsewhere the males seem to have been very scarce.

As noted above under *D. veliei*, many if not all the eastern records of that species probably refer to *M. blatchleyi*, the females especially of the two forms being very difficult of separation. Davis (Ms.) states that he now considers the species occurring about New York City, and formerly thought to be *D. veliei*, as *M. blatchleyi*, but that no males have as yet been taken on either Long or Staten Islands, although the females are fairly common on golden-rod, asters and associated plants. Morse (1919, 16) records an adult female and nymph of *blatchleyi* from Greenwich, Conn. The known range of *blatchleyi* therefore extends from Kansas and Oklahoma to Virginia and Connecticut.

Under the generic heading I have referred to the close relationship between the genera *Diapheromera* and *Manomera*. The species *blatchleyi* seems to be a sort of connecting link between the two. The rather short head and thick middle thighs of male would refer it to the former and the unarmed hind femora to the latter genus.

III. *Heteronemia* Gray, 1835, 13. (Gr., "different" + "race.")

Head of male unarmed, of female with two longitudinal ridges between the eyes; first abdominal segment longer than wide; hind femora of female subequal in length to that of the four basal abdominal segments combined, of male much longer than those segments; all the femora unarmed; cerci of male of similar shape and proportions as those of *Diapheromera*.

Two species of this genus were described by Brunner (1907, 336), both of which were in part from localities within the area covered by this paper. Caudell (1913, 613) states that they "are very probably synonyms of other species, but until the types are seen it is not deemed advisable to so place them." The females were separated by Brunner as follows:

Key to Eastern Species of *Heteronemia*

a. Second and third segments of abdomen scarcely longer than broad: cerci short. 58. *lævissimus*.

aa. Second and third segments of abdomen twice as long as broad; cerci long, lanceolate. 59. *texanus*.

58. *Heteronemia lævissimus* Brunner 1907, 338.
Smooth backed Walking-stick.

"♀.—Body wholly smooth. Head not longer than pronotum. Front femora equal to mesonotum. Second and third abdominal segments subequal, as long as wide. Anal segment semicylindrical, emarginate. Cerci short, terete; operculum obtuse; ovipositor free. Length of body, 60; of mesonotum, 15; of metanotum, 12.5; of front femora, 15; of hind femora, 14 mm." (Brunner.)

Brunner's types of this species were from St. Louis and "Lacus, Ontario." Caudell suggests that the type may have been a young female of *Diapheromera femorata*.

59. *Heteronemia texanus* Brunner, 1907, 333.
Texas Walking-stick.

"Head elongate, longer than pronotum. Femora short, the middle ones subincrassate, scarcely longer than metanotum. Anal segment of male strongly fornicate. Cerci curved. Ninth ventral segment very short. Subgenital plate large, hood-shaped. Abdomen of female smooth. Cerci long, terete, acuminate. Operculum lanceolate, acuminate, not reaching the tip of ninth segment. Length of body, ♂, 47, ♀, 65—84; of mesonotum, ♂, 10, ♀, 14—18; of front femora, ♂, 12, ♀, 17; of hind femora, ♀, 15—20.5 mm." (Brunner.)

This species was described from Texas and New York.

IV. *Megaphasma* Caudell, 1903a, 878. (Gr., "large" + "apparition.")

Walking-sticks of very large size having the head short, smooth, rounded, subvertical; antennæ more than twice as long as front femora; pronotum about one-fourth the length of mesonotum and with a deep median transverse impression; meso- and metanotum subequal in length, both with a fine median carina; middle and hind femora swollen in both sexes, the middle ones thicker than hind ones in male, both armed with a prominent subapical spine beneath. Cerci stout, those of male somewhat spatulate, decurved, their tips meeting but not crossing; of female less than half the length of last abdominal segment. The type of the genus and only known species is

60. *Megaphasma dentricus* (Stål), 1875, 76.
Giant Walking-stick.

Form elongate, robust as compared with that of preceding species; the female much the more so. Brownish-yellow or fuscous with legs paler, body and legs of male often in part green, sometimes maculate or banded with gray. Pronotum about as long as head, with broad, deep median transverse impression and a much finer longitudinal one. Seventh and eighth abdominal segments subequal in length, each shorter than ninth. Front legs much longer and more slender than either of the other pairs; middle and hind femora in both sexes thick, 4-sided, broadest beneath, their surface rough, the carine granulate or finely dentate, the median line below finely toothed in male, more strongly so in female. Length of body. ♂, 117, ♀, 123—150; of pronotum, ♂ and ♀, 5.5; of mesonotum, ♂, 22, ♀, 24; of front femora, ♂, 29, ♀, 27; of hind femora, ♂, 26, ♀, 23 mm.

Stål's type of this giant walking-stick was a female from Opelousas, La. It has since been recorded from Alabama, Iowa, Missouri, Texas and New Mexico, and Caudell (Ms.) states that a female taken on a porch near Louisville, Ky., in 1911 is now in the U. S. National Museum. Somes (1916) states that it is not uncommon in the Ozark region of Missouri and has been taken by him as far north as Hamburg and Clarinda, Iowa. It is found, he says, "on shrubs and trees and does not apparently differ greatly in habits from the well-known *Diapheromera femorata*." Near Victoria, Texas, *M. dentricus* is said to be rather common on wild grape vines in the wooded bottom lands.

This is the largest Phasmid known from the United States, a female in the Philadelphia collection measuring 150 mm. in length. In size it is approached, however, by the females of *Aplopus mayeri*, one of which, in the Davis collection measures 118 mm., while R. & H. record others as reaching a length of 127.5 mm. excluding the oviscapt.

Subfamily II. PHIBALOSOMINÆ.

This subfamily is represented in extreme southern Florida by a single species belonging to the following genus:

I. *Aplopus* Gray, 1835, 34. (Gr., "single" + "foot.")

Elongate, robust species having the head short, subvertical, armed above with two short unequal horns or spines, the right one the larger; antennæ rather stout, setaceous, slightly more than half the length of body, male, one-fourth shorter, female; mesonotum more than twice as long as metanotum; tegmina and wings present in the form of short oval or oblong pads; legs slender, not very elongate; middle and hind femora armed beneath with several short, sharp spines and terminating at knees in a pair of similar spines.

Fifteen species of the genus were recognized by Kirby (1904, 363), all of them from the West Indies, Central and South America. The following species has been since described:

61. *Aplopus mayeri* Caudell, 1905b, 83.
Mayer's Walking-stick.

Male greenish-yellow, the tegmina and wings darker; female fuscous-brown, the head, pronotum, sides of metanotum and femora and terminal abdominal segments more or less blotched with chalky white; males with sides of tegmina and abdominal segments usually marked lengthwise with white. Pronotum subquadrate, deeply impressed transversely, the front portion with a faint longitudinal impression and a pair of short black-tipped spines, hind one with a pair of similar but smaller spines in female; mesonotum of male with eight or ten, of female with 20 or more, scattered similar spines. Tegmina very short, oval, strongly veined, their tips obliquely rounded; wings oblong, projecting 2 or 3 mm. beyond the tegmina. Front legs more slender, and but slightly longer than middle ones, their femora with basal third strongly narrowed and more or less curved; middle and hind femora of female with their dorsal carinæ crested near apex. Apex of male abdomen moderately enlarged, the seventh and eighth segments subequal; ninth slightly shorter, subquadrate; the seventh nearly as long as the next two in female. Cerci of male stout, cylindrical, blunt, decurved, a little shorter than the ninth segment. Length of body, ♂, 83—93, ♀, 114—127; of antennæ, ♂, 53, ♀, 45; of mesonotum, ♂, 20, ♀, 26—28; of metanotum,

♂, 6, ♀, 8 of tegmina, ♂, 7, ♀, 8.5; of front femora, ♂ and ♀, 20; of hind femora, ♂, 21, ♀, 22 mm.

This is the only winged Phasmid known from the United States. The first specimens were taken at Loggerhead Key, Dry Tortugas, Fla., and were recorded, described and figured by Caudell (1904) as *Haplopus evadne* Westwood, a Santo Domingo species. A number of additional specimens, taken later on the same island by Dr. A. G. Mayer, were afterward submitted to the same authority, who concluded that his first identification was wrong, and described them (loc. cit.) under the name they now bear. In 1912, R. & H. visited Loggerhead Key and secured a number of specimens, finding them only on bushes of the bay cedar, *Suriana maritima* L. They record (1914c, 387) the species also from Bird Key and Garden Keys of the Tortugas groups, and from Key West and Long Key, July 3-13. It is also known from Key Largo and Everglade, Fla., a specimen from the latter point, taken by Davis, being the only one known from the mainland of the State. The large size and bizarre appearance of this Phasmid suggest its tropical origin, and it is very probable that in time it will be found to inhabit some of the adjacent West India Islands, while in Florida it will probably be found only in the subtropical area of the extreme southern portion.

Subfamily III. ANISOMORPHINÆ.

Rather short, robust species having the antennæ more than twice as long as front femora; mesonotum not more than three times as long as pronotum; intermediary segment invisible; coxae visible from above; tibiæ deeply and widely notched at apex below, thus forming a "sunken areola" which receives the base of tarsi when the latter are reflexed. To this subfamily, as at present restricted, belongs in our fauna only the single genus:

I. *Anisomorpha* Gray, 1835, 18. (Gr., "unequal" + "form.")

Body broad and stout, especially so in female; head horizontally attached to the thorax, unarmed, not more than one and a half times as long as broad. Pronotum furnished with distinct odoriferous glands; mesonotum nearly one-fourth longer than metanotum; legs unarmed, stout, thick, unequal, the middle pair the shortest; abdominal segments, especially those of female, subquadrate or transverse, the seventh and ninth subequal in length; cerci of both sexes short, stout, cylindrical, pubescent.

Five species are known, all from the Western Continent, two of them occurring in our territory. When disturbed or picked up, they have the power of exuding from glands beneath the prothorax a vapor from the male and a white milky fluid from the female. This is spurted out through a pore near the front angles of the pronotum and possesses a peculiar, though somewhat pleasing odor, which has been likened to that of the common everlasting, *Gnaphalium obtusifolium* L. The secretion is doubtless used as a defense against certain enemies, being probably very distasteful, and perhaps harmful, to birds and rapacious insects. Scudder (1876g) has noted this secretion, and concludes that the Phasmidæ with their slender form and sluggish movements have especial need of such a weapon as these glands furnish.

Key to North American Species of *Anisomorpha*

a. Larger, male averaging 45, female about 65 mm. in length; black dorsal and lateral stripes broad, conspicuous, head distinctly longer than broad. 62. *buprestoides.*

aa. Smaller, male averaging not more than 35, female about 55 mm.; dorsal and lateral dark stripes narrow, inconspicuous; head but slightly longer than broad. 63. *ferruginea.*

62. *Anisomorpha buprestoides* (Stoll), 1813, 68.
Larger Striped Walking-stick.

Male brownish-yellow, female usually more or less fuscous, both with a broad blackish stripe extending along the back from front of head to tip of abdomen, and another each side; legs dark brown, often paler in male. Head somewhat swollen in front, about one-third longer than broad; antennæ about three times as long as front femora. Pronotum nearly twice as long as broad, marked lengthwise and crosswise by a feeble median impressed line, and bearing each side near the front angle a circular pore, connected with a hidden gland. Metanotum usually furnished with several rounded black granules along the sides of its front half. Seventh segment of female bearing beneath an elongate scoop-shaped process which conceals the genital organs; male with a similar shorter triangular process. Cerci of male deflexed strongly downward; of female projected horizontally backward and extending slightly beyond the apex of ninth segment. Length of body, ♂, 39—47, ♀, 61—77; of head, ♂, 3.5—4, ♀, 6; of pronotum, ♂, 3.5—4, ♀, 6—6.5; of mesonotum, ♂, 7—9, ♀, 12—16 of metanotum, ♂, 6—7.5, ♀, 10—12; of hind femora, ♂, 9.5—10, ♀, 14—17.5 mm.

Gainesville, Sanford, Dunedin, Cape Sable and Key West, Fla., Nov. 4—March 29 (*W. S. B.*); several pairs taken, usually in copulation, the female stretched straight out along the stems of weeds or coarse grasses. At Dunedin one pair was taken December 12 on Hog Island, three miles across from the mainland. Recorded from numerous localities between Jacksonville and Pensacola on the north and Miami and Key West. It occurs more abundantly in moist situations, often beneath the loose bark of pine logs and stumps or between or beneath boards. From December to April about Dunedin, the brownish-gray nymphs are frequently swept from dwarf huckleberry and other undergrowth in open pine woods.

Davis (1914) states that: "This fat and lubberly insect, which is always ready to squirt a charge of acrid, condensed-milklike fluid at the collector, was in evidence at all the places visited. While it has been my experience in various parts of Florida to find more nymphs of this species in the spring, yet adults may be found at any season, and each female usually has attached to herself one of the diminutive males. At night the insects become much more active."

This stout-bodied walking-stick often called the "musk-mare," is found only in the southern states, ranging from South Carolina through Georgia and Florida, and west at least to Agricultural College, Miss., two specimens from that place having been given me by the late Dr. L. M. Underwood.

63. *Anisomorpha ferruginea* (Beauvois), 1805, 167.
Lesser Striped Walking-stick.

Fuscous or ferruginous, with inconspicuous, narrow, dusky, dorsal and lateral stripes; these in the female less distinct, often obsolete on a portion of the abdomen; antennæ dull reddish-brown; under side of body dull clay yellow, brownish when dried; legs reddish-brown, head but little longer than broad. Tubercles on sides of mesonotum more distinct. Body of female six to six and a half times longer than broad; of male, about twelve times as long as broad. Ninth segment of male abdomen much more deeply notched at apex than in buprestoides. Length of body, ♂, 30—36, ♀, 50—56; of head, ♂, 3, ♀, 5.5; of antennæ, ♂, 22, ♀, 34; of mesonotum, ♂, 5—6, ♀, 9—10; of metanotum, ♂, 4—5, ♀, 8—9.5; of hind femora, ♂, 9, ♀, 12 mm. (Fig. 57.)

This walking-stick has been taken in Indiana only near Wyandotte, Crawford Co., Grand Chain, Posey Co., and Medora, Jackson Co., having been found in large numbers in all three localities. The first ones noted were in Crawford Co. on June 28, 1902, when the young about an inch and a half long were found beneath loose flakes of bark on oak and other trees. In the first week in September I again visited the locality and found scores of pairs of them, all mating, beneath the loose bark of old oak snags and stumps. A half dozen or more pairs were often found within an area of a foot or two square, the large, heavy bodied female bearing her diminutive liege lord upon her back. None of the specimens noted were feeding, though they probably live upon the leaves of oak and other trees. The species was later found in numbers in Posey and Jackson Counties, and probably occurs in most of the counties bordering the Ohio River. It is but one of many forms of insect and plant life which have their most northern habitat in the southern third of Indiana.

The range of *A. ferruginea* is given by R. & H. (1916, 127) as extending from "just north of the Ohio River, south over the Mississippi to the Gulf States, west to extreme southeastern Nebraska and eastward through the Appalachians in Virginia and in the high portions of the Carolinas and Georgia." It is known from Union Co., Ill., and a specimen in the U. S. National Museum collection is from Arcadia, La. Caudell's Florida record (1903a) is now known to have been based on a specimen of *buprestoides*.

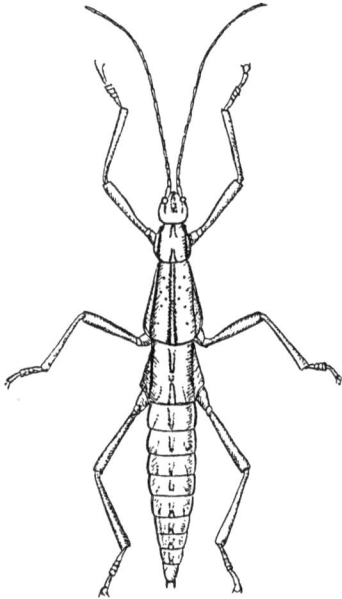

Fig. 57. Female. Natural Size. (After Caudell.)

A New Walking-Stick Insect from Eastern North America

Wm. T. Davis,

Staten Island, N. Y.

In the low-lying meadows, and occasionally elsewhere on Staten Island, Long Island, as well as in other localities along the Atlantic coast, there is a walking-stick insect to be found on the golden-rods and associated plants that has interested entomologists for some time. It has passed under the name of *Manomera blatchleyi* (Caudell), but as no males have been recorded, much uncertainty has existed regarding the specific name.

Bacunculus blatchleyi Caudell was described in the *Journal, New York Entomological Society*, Vol. 13, p. 212, 1905, from a male collected in Starke County, Indiana, and according to Mr. Blatchley in his *Orthoptera of North-Eastern America*, has also been found in Missouri, Iowa, Wisconsin, Ohio, and Illinois. Through the kindness of William J. Gerhard, I long ago received a male and female of this species collected in September at Palos Park, Ill., and in 1922 he sent me an additional female from Palos Park; five females from Argo, Ill., as well as several males from both of these localities.

Comparing the seven females with the forty-six females collected on Staten Island and Long Island, as well as those from other localities along the Atlantic coast, it was noted that they differed in the shape of the head, length of legs and cerci; also in the shape of the sub-genital plate. In the original description is the statement: "Cerci of female rounded and as long as the terminal segment of the abdomen."

On the plate accompanying this article the first four figures represent eastern specimens, while the last four are from photographs of a like number of females sent to me by Mr. Gerhard, which appear to represent the true *blatchleyi*, Fig. 8 having measurements about as given in the original description. The differences shown by these figures are, we think, sufficient to constitute at least a geographic race, and very likely if the male of the eastern form is found, the differences will be still more apparent.

From: *Journal of the NY Entomological Society*, Vol. 31, 1923, pp. 52-55.

Manomera blatchleyi atlantica, new race.

Plate X, Figs. 1 to 4.

Resembles *blatchleyi* as described by Caudell and by Blatchley (loc. cit.), except that the head in *atlantica* is broader across the eyes and tapers gradually toward the posterior margin, whereas in typical *blatchleyi* the sides of the head are much more nearly parallel. Specimens of the same length, when compared, have the legs in the eastern examples longer and the cerci shorter, those from Illinois. The cerci are much shorter than the last abdominal segment in *atlantica*, whereas in *blatchleyi* they are more nearly of the same length. These differences are shown on the accompanying plate. The subgenital plate in *atlantica* has the extremity, as a rule, more evenly rounded than in *blatchleyi*, where it is often quite pointed.

Length of head in female type 3.5; pronotum 3.25; mesonotum 15; metanotum, 12; fore femora 18; middle femora 14; hind femora 19; cerci 3 mm.

Type female, Clove Valley, Staten Island, .N. Y., September 9, 1893. Davis collection.

In addition to the type, three other mature females have been collected on Staten Island, at Richmond Valley, Sept. 23, 1883; Mariners' Harbor, Sept. 26, 1903, and one on August 7 without definite locality. Numerous female nymphs have been found in the Clove Valley, at Watchogue and near Richmond, in the months of June, July and August. On Long Island no less than forty-two females have been collected; many more were found but allowed to escape. The greatest number (31) have come from a piece of low-lying ground at Maspeth, where Mr. C. E. Olsen located a flourishing colony in 1912. Here, near the habitations of man, and apparently free from many natural enemies, they were quite numerous. Very often in an hour or two, we could find a dozen or more, usually on *Solidago rugosa*, as well as on other species of golden-rod and associated plants. When additional specimens were needed in 1922, Mr. Frederick M. Schott collected twenty-one females on the afternoon of September 23, and let a few others go. Mr. Olsen, Mr. Schott and I have looked particularly for the male in this locality at several seasons of the year, both by day and night but thus far without success. Many of the specimens found are green. but they may be grayish, brownish, or even purplish in color. Elsewhere on Long Island females have been collected at Brooklyn, Flushing (E. L. Bell, Dr. W. H. Wiegmann and W. T. Davis), Roslyn, Setauket (G. P. Engelhardt), Sea Cliff, Wading River, River Head, Amityville (Edw. D. Harris), and Blue Point. The dates of capture for mature specimens range from July 30, 1919 (Wading River), to Oct. 1, 1918 (Setauket).

From elsewhere the writer has specimens as follows: New Haven, Conn., Sept. 4, 1911 (C. E. Olsen); Crotona Park, N. Y. City, Oct. 9, 1904 (Frank E. Watson); Paterson. N. J., Aug.; Plainfield, N. J., Oct 20, 1916 (W. De W. Miller); Keyport, N. J. (no date); Erma, Cape May Co., N. J., August, 1912, 10 females; Dyke, Va., July 18, 1913 (Davis), and Vienna, Va., Aug., 1918 (H. G. Barber).

The only other species of walking-stick insect found in the north-eastern states is *Diapheromera femorata* (Say). It has not been collected on Staten Island, but on Shelter Island (Long Island) it was quite common a number of years ago according to Mr. Adolph W. Callisen. In the fall of 1922 Mr. Roy Latham found a number at Orient, Long Island. Elsewhere on the neighboring mainland, it is often quite common feeding on a number of trees and bushes, but it is not as a rule found on herbaceous plants, as is *Manomera atlantica*.

Explanation of Plate.

Fig. 1. *Manomera blatchleyi atlantica*. Type. Clove Valley, Staten Island.

Fig. 2. *Manomera blatchleyi atlantica*. Richmond Valley, Staten Island.

Fig. 3. *Manomera blatchleyi atlantica*. Maspeth, Long Island.

Fig. 4. *Manomera blatchleyi atlantica*. Vienna, Virginia.

Figs. 5-8. *Manomera blatchleyi*. Argo, Illinois.

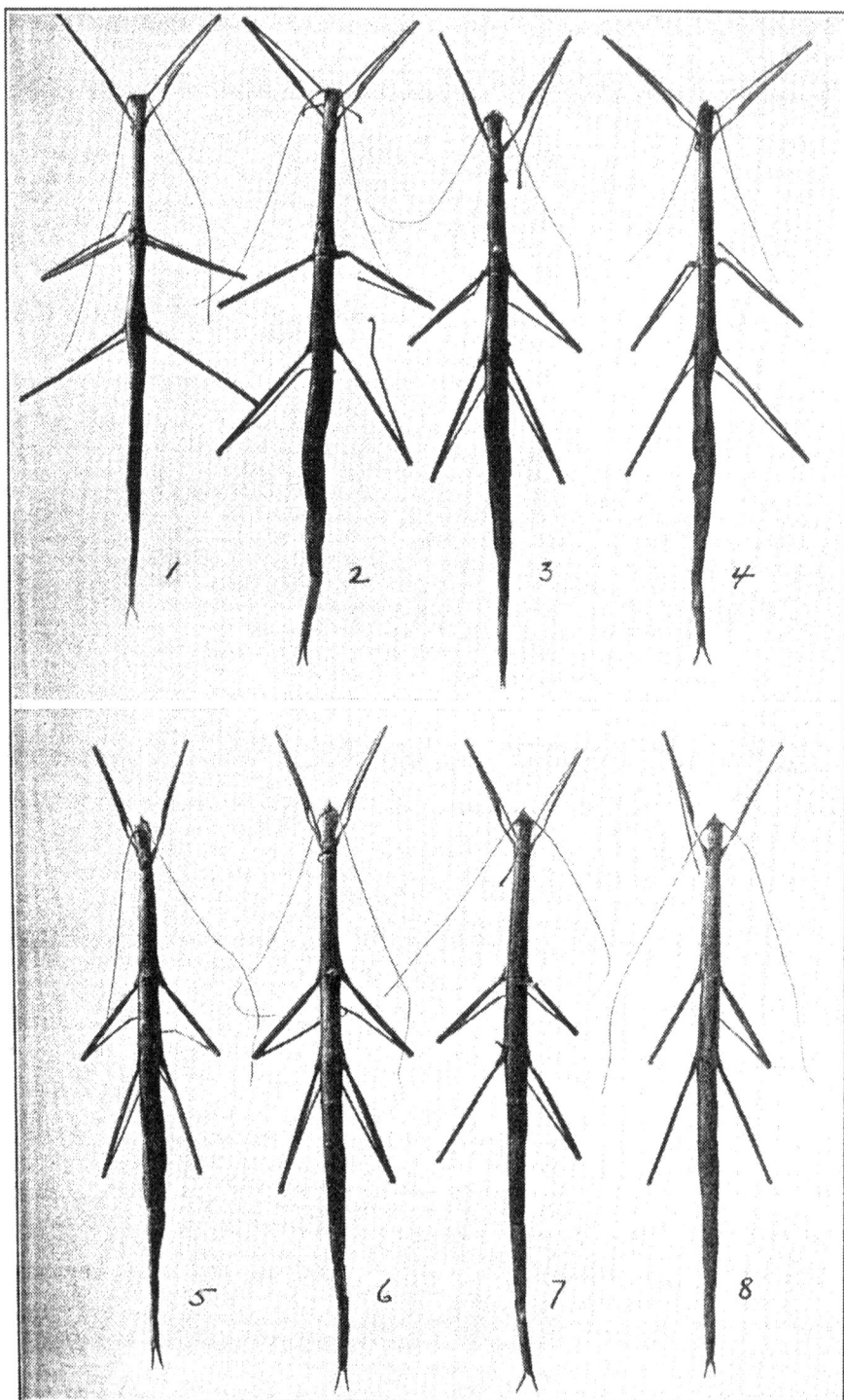

The Races of *Diapheromera veliei*
(Orthoptera, Phasmidae, Heteronemiinae)

Morgan Hebard,

Philadelphia, Pennsylvania.

Recently in our studies of the Orthoptera of Kansas we found that *Diapheromera veliei* Walsh, occurred in its typical form over that entire State, its maximum abundance being reached in the central Great Plains. It is apparently less hardy than *Diapheromera femorata* (Say) as its known northern limits are Lake Hendricks, South Dakota, and Julesburg, Colorado, while toward the foot of the Rocky Mountains in Colorado (except probably in its southern portion) it disappears, this probably due there to the greater elevation and consequently more boreal environment of the plains.

To the south we have it typical as far as Stillwater, Oklahoma, Dalhart, Texas, and Vaughn, New Mexico, and it reaches westward over the lower divides of the Rockies as far as Albuquerque, in the latter State. Further south in Texas and New Mexico, however, we find it supplanted by a geographic race and study of the literature convinces us that that race must bear the name *Diapheromera veliei mesillana* Scudder. The following data lead to this conclusion.

Diapheromera veliei mesillana Scudder.

1901. *Diapheromera mesillana* Scudder, *Psyche*, IX, p. 189. [[Juv.] ♂; between Mesilla and Las Cruces, New Mexico.]

1907. *B* [*acunculus*] *texanus* Brunner, *Insektenfam. der Phasmiden*, p. 333. [♂, ♀; Texas.[1]]

Scudder described *mesillana* from immature males and, though difficult to associate specifically, we have sufficient such material to be satisfied that the species represented is the same as that here discussed from large series of adults. In the Rio Grande valley of New Mexico this is the only species of this type present.

---

[1] The specimen recorded from New York was either mislabeled or represents a distinct species.

From: *Journal of the NY Entomological Society*, Vol. 31, 1923, pp. 52-55.

Brunner's description of *Bacunculus texanus* is very unsatisfactory. Probably immature material (at least in part), in which femoral spines are often lacking, led to the generic assignment, as there is no Heteronemiid found in the United States in which the adults have both median and caudal femora unarmed. Selecting Texas as type locality of *texanus*, we find that the description fits best the present insect of the forms which occur in that State and we therefore place that name as a synonym. With the wealth of material which was available in preparing "*Die Insektenfamilie der Phasmiden*" it is very regrettable that the work throughout is so very superficial and inaccurate.

This race differs from typical *veliei* in having the male poculum very broadly lipped, while in the female sex the femoral apices are usually strikingly suffused with black. The head averages broader, but this is apparently not constant, and the female cerci average considerably shorter. Though in all central Texan material the female femoral apices are conspicuously black, this marking is wholly absent in a female before us from Vaughn, New Mexico and in one from El Paso, Texas. It is, however, very decided in a female from Pecos, Texas and in one from Lake Valley, Sierra County, New Mexico. Absence of such marking, never found in typical veliei, may indicate that such an individual has developed in different plants or bushes than are usually selected by the present insect.

Intergradation with *veliei veliei* is shown by the following material. A large series from Midland, Texas, has the male proculum as in typical *veliei*; the females have the femoral apices narrowly suffused with black and the cerci very elongate, even more elongate than the average for *veliei veliei*, in which more individual variation in this feature is shown than in *veliei mesillana*. A large series from Melena, Chaves County, New Mexico, is similar except that the female cerci are slightly shorter, though much longer than in *veliei mesillana*.

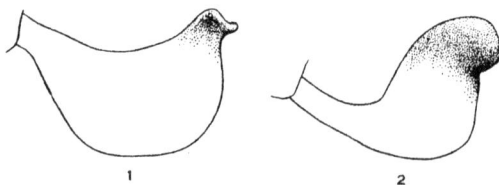

Fig. 1. *Diapheromera veliei veliei* Walsh. Lateral view of male poculum. Syracuse, Kansas. (Much enlarged.)

Fig. 2. *Diapheromera veliei mesillana* Scudder. Lateral view of male poculum. Foothills of Ord Mountains, Brewster County, Texas. (Much enlarged.)

The range of the present race extends from Lake Valley and Deming, New Mexico, east to Robstown and Cisco, Texas. It was reported from San Diego, Alice and Victoria, Texas, as *veliei* by Caudell in 1918.[2] It is one of the most abundant and generally distributed Phasmids in central Texas, where it is particularly encountered on the low mesquite trees which there are thickly scattered over the plains. Its area of intergradation with *veliei veliei* apparently extends from central-northern east New Mexico eastward.

[2] *Ent. News*, XXIX, p. 25

Studies in Orthoptera which Occur in North America
North of the Mexican Boundary

Morgan Hebard

IV. Synonymy and a New Species of the Genus *Diapheromera*,
(Phasmidae, Heteronemiinae)

Diapheromera Gray

In 1909 Rehn and Hebard erected the subgenus *Ceratites* to include their species *covilleae*, distinguished from *Diapheromera* by having two occipital horns, and that year Rehn added *tamaulipensis* from northeastern Mexico. In 1912, finding that the generic name *Ceratites* was preoccupied, Rehn and Hebard proposed *Rhabdoceratites*. Seventeen years later Strand proposed *Ceratita*[1] not realizing that Rehn and Hebard had renamed their *Ceratites*, thus adding another name to this synonymy. The author recognized this entity as of generic rank in 1932 and added the Mexican *beckeri* (Kaup), 1871.

Study of the available series and the new species described below shows that decided variation in the occipital horns occurs, while the male type of *tamaulipensis* lacks these and it is quite possible that they are regularly absent in that sex of that species. Further characters of generic value apparently do not exist and we believe that it is best to place *Rhabdoceratites* as a synonym of *Diapheromera*, though the species there assigned form a group well distinguished from any of those to which the species of the eastern half of the United States belong.

Diapheromera torquata new species   (Pl. XX, figs. 1, 2, 3)

This is a small and graceful species apparently peculiar to the Chisos Mountains in the Big Bend region of the Rio Grande in western Texas. Nearest relationship is to *D. erythropleura* Hebard from the state of Sinaloa, Mexico. Males are quickly distinguished by the unusual position of the poculum, which is twisted into an almost vertical position, protecting the concealed genitalia dextrad, while other plates are produced to protect them over the remaining area. Moreover the simple male cerci are distinguished by having no specialization whatever proximo-internally, in this feature agreeing only with *erythropleura* of the previously described species.

[1] *Arch. Naturgesch.*, 92, p. 46, (1926).

From: *Transactions of the American Entomological Society*, Vol. 60, 1934, pp. 281-293+.

A half grown female shows two very small angular projections on the head slightly above and back of the eyes which are definitely longitudinal. Half grown male immatures of this insect and of *tamaulipensis*[2] are difficult to distinguish agreeing in the absence of occipital horns and in general proportions, the poculum in this stage of *torquata* being in normal ventral position but projecting to beyond a median point on the ninth tergite, whereas in *tamaulipensis* it only slightly surpasses the intersection of the eighth and ninth tergites.

Type.—♂; Lost Mine Peak, Chisos Mountains, Texas, at 5800 feet. September 6, 1912. (Rehn and Hebard). [Hebard Collection, Type No. 1245].

Size small, form decidedly slender for the genus. Surface smooth and shining. Head no longer than pronotum but considerably longer than wide, lacking occipital horns. Seventh tergite moderately enlarged in distal two-thirds, its disto-ventral angles produced, acute angulate, its dorsal length distinctly less than the combined length of the eighth and ninth tergites. Eighth tergite transverse, about half as long as ninth. Ninth (ultimate) tergite strongly convex dorsad, widening slightly to a subapical point and there as wide as long, caudal margin in dorso-caudal aspect broadly rounded rectangulate emarginate, leaving the apex of the minute supra-anal plate exposed. Cerci simple, unarmed, moderately elongate, curving moderately inward, with internal surface flattened and apex rounded. Poculum springing from eighth sternite dextrad, small, rounded spoon-shaped, twisted into an almost vertical dextral position; eighth sternite produced in two rounded adjacent elongate plates the convex surfaces of which conceal the genitalia ventro-sinistrad, sinistrad and sinistro-dorsad and act as a convex lid to the poculum. Cephalic femur slightly longer than combined length of head, pronotum and mesonotum. Median femur much heavier but not enlarged to the degree usual in males of most of the other species of the genus. Median femur with a large sigmoid distal spine of the medio-longitudinal ventral carina,[3] beneath which this carina shows a decided convex elevation. Caudal femur similarly but less strongly specialized. Median tibia with medio-longitudinal carina of ventral surface with minute denticles, this and the lateral carinae each terminated distad in a tuft of spiniform hairs; caudal tibia similar but with denticulations very small and weak.

In the immature females discussed above the limbs are shorter, the median femora not enlarged, the femoral spine very small and the tibiae have no denticulation. The seventh tergite is slightly longer than the ninth, the eighth tergite slightly longer than broad and distinctly longer than the short, straight cerci. In the adult female these proportions may show some difference.

[2] Immature material representing both sexes of *tamaulipensis* from Sanderson, Texas, is before us.

[3] Similar in *erythropleura*. Though the tooth rests inside the tibia when the limbs are folded it does not spring from the ventro-internal margin in either species, though such was incorrectly stated in the description of that species.

Head brownish ochraceous-buff, occiput with a very broad weak longitudinal band of saccardos umber and moderately broad postocular bands of the same. Pronotum brownish ochraceous-buff with a medio-longitudinal band of verona brown. Mesothorax, metathorax, abdomen to apical portion and limbs shining cinnamon brown (more reddish); lateral margins of mesonotum and metanotum dull light ochraceous tawny; distal portion of abdomen clay color. Antennae clay color tinged with olivaceous.

The immatures are all light green, apparently uniformly colored in life.

The measurements of the extremes are here given for the adult males. Length of body 51.3 to 55.4, length of mesonotum 12.3 to 14.2, median width of mesonotum 1.2 to 1.2, length of metnotum (including median segment) 11.7 to 12.3, length of median segment 1.8 to 1.8, dorsal length of seventh tergite 2 to 2, length of cephalic femur 16.7 to 18, length of caudal femur 17.3 to 19 mm.

Specimens examined: 10; 5 males and 5 immature individuals.

Texas: Canyon behind Pulliam Bluff, Chisos Mountains, 4600 to 5000 feet, IX, 7, 1912, (Rehn and Hebard; on low Acacia among weeds and in shrubbery, Zone of Oaks), 1 ♂, *paratype*, 3 juv. ♂, 2 juv. ♀. Lost Mine Peak, Chisos Mountains, 5800 feet, IX, 6, 1912, (Rehn and Hebard; on slopes covered with high grass and much oak brush), 4 ♂, *type* and *paratypes*.

V. The Pachymorphinae of the United States (Phasmidae)

Parabacillus Caudell
1903. *Parabacillus* Caudell, *Proc. U. S. Nat. Mus.*, XXVI, p. 865.
Monotypic genotype: *Parabacillus coloradus* (Scudder).

In 1893[4] Scudder very briefly described two species which he referred to *Bacillus*. Both were presented by females only; the first, *coloradus*, from an elevation of 5500 in Colorado, the second, *carinatus*, from "Arizona" and "Mexico." Caudell described a third species, *Bacillus palmeri*,[5] based on a female from Durango, Mexico, in 1902. In his revision of the Phasmidae of the United States in 1903 he considered that only a single species, subject to considerable individual variation was present in this country, *carinatus* for some time having been placed as a synonym of *coloradus*.

Very large series now before us show beyond question the presence in the United States of two species, very similar in the females but easily distinguished in the males. Both species lack the sparse and fine tuberculation of the body described by Scudder for

---

[4] *Psyche*, VI, p. 372.

[5] *Ent. News*, XIII, p. 274.

his *carinatus*, but Mexican females before us[6] all show that feature. As a result we can not help believing that the specimen of *carinatus* labelled "Arizona" actually came from Mexico.

Three species are here distinguished, as follows:

A. Female (male unknown) with dorsal surface of body sparsely and finely tuberculate. Mesosternum and metasternum with a decided medio-longitudinal carina except at their lobes. Penultimate (ninth) abdominal tergite (preceding supra-anal plate) nearly one and one-half times as long as the preceding (eighth) tergite. Jalisco, Mexico.   *Parabacillus carinatus* (Scudder)

AA. Both sexes with dorsal surface of body entirely lacking tuberculation.[7] Female mesosternum and metasternum with a weak medio-longitudinal carina cephalad which soon becomes obsolete. Female penultimate (ninth) abdominal tergite (preceding supra-anal plate) normally proportionately shorter, one and one-quarter times to only slightly longer than the preceding (eighth) tergite.

B. Male with penultimate (ninth) abdominal tergite no longer than its greatest width. Poculum with suture between eighth and ninth sternites (which form it) distinct, apex reaching base of cerci and convex, not emarginate. Southern Utah, Nevada, all but extreme eastern and the Plateau of Arizona, Oregon and California.   *Parabacillus hesperus* new species

BB. Male with penultimate (ninth) abdominal tergite fully twice as long as its greatest width. Poculum with suture between eighth and ninth sternites (which form it) obsolete apex reaching only opposite base of ninth tergite and strongly emarginate. Southwestern South Dakota, western Nebraska, Kansas, Oklahoma and Texas, southeastern Wyoming, all of Colorado and New Mexico and eastern Utah and the Plateau of and extreme eastern Arizona.
Parabacillus coloradus (Scudder)

---

[6] Guadalajara, Jalisco, VII, 16 and 22, 1903, (J. F. McClendon), 3 ♀, recorded by Rehn as *palmeri*, *Proc. Acad. Nat. Sci. Phila.*, 1904, p. 516. Zapotlanejo, Jalisco, VII, 31, 1903, (J. F. McClendon), 1 ♀.

[7] Very rarely a female occurs with very feeble tuberculation indicated on the cephalic portion of the mesonotum only (one—Clovis, New Mexico; one—Paradise, Arizona).

In considering *carinatus* we believe, from the large Arizonan series before us in which not a single case of general dorsal tuberculation is shown, that Scudder's "Arizona" female was probably incorrectly labelled and that it, like the female upon which that name is based, probably came from Mexico. We therefore here select as type of *carinatus* the female labelled "Mexico" in the collection of the Museum of Comparative Zoology.

The proper association of Caudell's *palmeri*, based on a female from Durango, Mexico, can not be made with any certainty until more material, and particularly males, can be studied. Caudell writes that it is not tuberculate and so it may represent one of the species occurring in the United States. If that is the case it is more likely to prove to be a synonym of *coloradus*, as the penultimate (ninth) abdominal tergite measures 2 mm. and the eighth tergite 1 1/3 mm. The elongate limbs given by Caudell as the major feature to distinguish *palmeri* from *coloradus* are shown by our series to have no diagnostic value whatever in the genus.

In the United States the males of the two species which occur there are easily separated and this is usually true for females where both sexes occur. In the north, however, where parthenogenesis is universal in both, it is a difficult problem to determine where the eastern species finds its western limits and the western species takes its place. This is particularly true for the Arizona Plateau where the mingling of Great Plains and western species is so decided that we assign our material from that region to *coloradus* with considerable uncertainty.

Parabacillus hesperus new species   (Pl. XX, figs. 5, 6)

This interesting new species has been consistently confused in past literature with *P. coloradus* (Scudder), all previous records of *coloradus* from Arizona, Oregon and California being referable to *hesperus*.

As noted above males are easily separated by the penultimate tergite and poculum, but females are much more difficult to distinguish, having in *hesperus* the ninth tergite as a rule only slightly longer than the eight but this feature being subject to individual variation in both species.

The present insect is known north to the Wah Wah Range, Utah; Caliente, Nevada, and the Steens Mountains and Boardman, Oregon; west to the Pacific (but absent over much of the area west of the Sierras); south to the Mexican boundary, and east to the Huachuca Mountains, Arizona, and Leeds and Bellevue, Utah.

Type.—♂; south slopes of Atascosa Peak, Pajaritos Mountains, Arizona. Elevation 5500 to 6100 feet. September 21 and 22, 1924. (Rehn and Hebard). [Hebard Collection, Type No. 1259].

A medium small and extremely slender walking-stick. Antennae short, less than three times length of the elongate head. Surface smooth, without tubercles, a prominent medio-longitudinal carina on mesonotum and metanotum and with coarse low sub-marginal longitudinal carinae on each side; mesosternum and metasternum with a medio-longitudinal carina indicated only very briefly at cephalic end. Median segment symmetrically trapezoidal, as long as proximal width, greatest width caudad. Ninth (penultimate) tergite only very slightly longer than wide, with a fine medio-longitudinal carina, its surfaces laterad convex. Supra-anal plate not visible from above. Cercus incurved, apex rounded, a rounded lobe proximo-internally with surface facing mesad flat and apposed to the corresponding surface of the opposite cercal lobe. Poculum elongate, convex, formed by the eighth and ninth sternites, suture between these sternites distinct, spical portion narrowing to the broadly rounded apex which reaches as far as the base of the cerci. Limbs very slender, unarmed; femora with genicular lobes angulate.

Allotype.— ♀; same data as type but taken September 21, 1922. [Hebard Collection].

Considerably longer than male and more robust, though exceedingly attenuate. Antennae proportionally shorter, only a little longer than head. Body smooth, without tubercles, carinae similar but traces of lateral carinae proximad on mesosternum and metasternum, abdomen showing traces of a number of longitudinal carinae. Median segment markedly broader than long. Seventh tergite slightly shorter than combined length of eighth and ninth, eighth tergite very slightly shorter than ninth. Supra-anal plate very small, triangular, with a medio-longitudinal carina. Cerci straight, elongate, distinctly longer than ninth tergite. Operculum moderately elongate, flattened, with triangular apex, beyond which the exposed ovipositor valves reach to the base of the cerci.

Individuals are as a rule straw color, but some specimens vary from light red brown (rare) to mummy brown (frequent only in rare series). A striking broad medio-longitudinal band of brown is present on head and thorax but becomes weaker on the abdomen in most of the males, this being obsolete or weak on the abdomen in most females. A narrow post-ocular band of brown is usually present on the head, being decided in intensive specimens, but often well defined even in extremely recessive individuals.

The size variation is great, as shown by the following measurements (in millimeters).

♂	Length of body	Length of mesonotum	Length of cephalic femur	Length of ninth tergite
Carr Canyon, Huachuca Mts., Arizona	50.5	11.4	22.2	1.13
Lower Madera Canyon, Santa Rita Mts., Arizona	52.8-54.8	12.7-13	23.8-25.6	1.2-1.23

South slope Atascosa Peak, Arizona	50.7-53.8	12-12.8	24.7-26	1.2-1.3
Ajo, Arizona	46.8	10.6	22.7	1.23
Goffs, California	46.3-52.8	11.3-11.8	20.3-25	1.27-1.34
Cactus Flat, San Bernardino Mts., California	41.	9.	16.6	1.06

♀

Bellevue, Utah	50.7	11.	17.2	1.06
Lee Canyon, Spring Mts., Nevada	56.3	12	19.7	1.3
Lower Madera Canyon, Santa Rita Mts., Arizona	68.7	14.4	24.4	1.34
South slope Atascosa Peak, Arizona	74.3-80	16.4-17.2	27.7-27.8	1.4-1.5
Sycamore Canyon, Baboquivari Mts., Arizona	66.7-78.2	15.7-16.3	24.5-28.2	1.5-1.63
Dewey, Arizona	47.7	10.3	17.9	1.42
Goffs, California	61.4	13.2	21.3	1.56
Paradise Valley, Tehachapi Mts., California	50.7	10.6	16.7	1.25
Descanso, California	60.7	12.8	21.8	1.42

A warmer environment clearly brings about greater size and attenuation in this species. No males are known from northern Arizona, Utah, Nevada, Oregon, or north of Goffs in California. The insect is evidently parthenogenic in the northern portions of its range. We have already noted the difficulty in determining the eastern limits of *hesperus* in that region.

Specimens Examined: 151; 37 males, 79 females and 35 immature individuals.

Utah: One and a half miles north of Bellevue, 4100 feet, IX, 11, 1926, (Rehn; beaten from yellow grass), 2 ♀. One mile south of Leeds, 3600 feet, IX, 6, 1926, (Hebard; beaten from composite, "Rabbit Brush"), 2 ♀. Pink sand hills between Three Lakes and Virgin River, 5750 feet, IX, 1, 1926, (Rehn; beating), 1 ♀. Base of Hurricane ledge above Hurricane, 3700 feet, IX, 4, 1926, (Hebard; resting sprawled out on top of a small composite, "Rabbit Weed"), 1 ♀. Road summit, Wah Wah Range, 6600 feet, VIII, 24, 1926, (Rehn; in fine dry grasses), 1 ♀. Road pass, Beaver Dam Mountains, VII, 31, 1930, (E. R. Tinkham), 1 juv. ♀.

Nevada: Caliente, 5200 feet, IX, 3, 1909, (Rehn and Hebard; in dry grasses on mountain side), 1 teneral ♀. Lee Canyon, Spring Mountain Range, 4000 feet, VIII, 18 and 22, 1919, (Rehn and Hebard; occasional in tufts of slender yellow grass, zone of Tree Yucca), 3 ♀ (one teneral), 9 large juv. ♀.

Arizona: Rock House Canyon, Dos Cabezos Mountains, 4300 feet, X, 14, 1910, (Rehn and Hebard; in bunch grass among *Dasylirion* and junipers), 1 ♂. Carr Canyon, Huachuca Mountains, IX, 23 and X, 8, 1904, (C. R. Biederman), 1 ♂, 1 ♀, recorded by Rehn as *coloradus.* Huachuca Mountains, VIII, 1, 1927, (R. H. Beamer), 1 ♂, [Univ. of Kansas]. Elgin, IX, 1, 1927, (J. C. Bradley), 1 juv. ♀, [Cornell Univ.]. Upper Madera Canyon, Santa Rita Mountains, IX, 24 and 25, 1924, (Rehn; in grass on open south slope at 5100 feet; Hebard, one in tuft of fine grass in opening of oak forest at 6200 feet), 1 ♂, 3 ♀. Lower Madera Canyon, Santa Rita Mountains, 4600 to 4900 feet, (Rehn; in tufts of fine grass on open hillside), 2 ♂, 1 ♀. Santa Rita Mountains, VI, 12, 1933 and VII, 17, 1932, (R. H. Beamer), 3 ♂, 1 ♀, 2 juv., [Univ. of Kansas]. Patagonia Mountains, IX, 22, 1922 (Hebard; climbing on automobile), 1 ♀. Oracle, IX, 8, 1931, (E. R. Tinkham; in zone of oaks), 1 ♀. Tucson, X, 12, 1910, (Rehn and Hebard; beaten from creosote bush), 1 ♀, (very dark); XII, 1926 (G. F. Woods), 1 ♂. Tumamoc Hill, Tucson Mountains, 2400 to 3092 feet, X, 3 and 4, 1910, (Rehn and Hebard; plentiful in dry fine yellow grasses), 6 ♂, 16 ♀, 1 juv. ♂, 3 juv. ♀, (eleven very dark, evidently beaten from desert bushes). Snyder's Hill, 2500, X, 11, 1910, (Rehn and Hebard; one beaten from dry grass, one attracted to light at night), 2 ♂. Sahuaro plain west of Robles Pass, Tucson Mountains, X, 5, 1910, (Rehn and Hebard), 3 ♂. Cat Mountain, Robles Pass, Tucson Mountains, 3000 feet, IX, 27, 1924, (Hebard; very scarce in tufts of fine dry yellow grass), 2 ♀. Palo Alto Rancho, Altar Valley, 3000 feet, X, 6, 1910 (Rehn and Hebard), 1 ♀. Sycamore Canyon, Baboquivari Mountains, 3700 to 4200 feet, X, 6 to 9, 1910, (Rehn and Hebard; in dry grasses, fairly common on canyon slopes, few on alluvial fan), 15 ♀, 3 juv. ♂. Schaeffer Canyon, Baboquivari Mountains, 5500 feet, IX, 19, 1924, (Rehn and Hebard), 1 ♀. Baboquivari Mountains, VII, 19, 1932, (R. H. Beamer), 1 ♀, [Univ. of Kansas]. South slope of Atascosa Peak, Pajaritos Mountains, 5500 to 6100 feet, IX, 21 and 22, 1922 and 1924 (Rehn and Hebard; in grasses, few in 1922, more numerous in

1924), 5 ♂, 4 ♀, *type, allotype, paratypes.* Hilltop north of Montana Mine, Tumacacori Mountains, 4900 to 5000 feet, IX, 21, 1924, (Rehn and Hebard; moderately common in tufts of dry fine yellow grass with immature individuals of *Achurum sumichrasti*), 1 ♂, 3 ♀ *paratypes.* Growler Valley south of Growler Pass, 1200 feet, IX, 19, 1922, (Hebard; beaten from desert vegetation in wash), 1 large juv. ♂. Valley of the Ajo, six miles north of Ajo, 1600 feet, IX, 18, 1922, (Rehn and Hebard), 3 ♂. Ajo, 1800 feet, IX, 18, 1922, (Rehn and Hebard, in creosote bush and a small gray-leaved desert brush), 3 ♂. Base of Vermilion Cliffs, eleven miles north of Pipe Springs, 5100 feet, IX, 4, 1926, (W. W. Farrar), 1 ♀. Avondale, 1000 feet, IV, 1 to 15, 1927, (O. C. Poling, 1 ♀. Fortuna, Gila Mountains, 800 feet, IX, 12, 1924, (Hebard; in a tuft of yellow weedy plant on hillside above camp), 1 juv. ♀.

Oregon: Wild Horse Canyon, Steens Mountains, 4400 feet, IX, 1, 1928, (Rehn; beaten from "Six weeks grass"), 2 ♀. Boardman, X, 5, 1922, 1 ♀, recorded by Fulton as *coloradus.*

California: Needles, 600 feet, VIII, 4, 1919, (Rehn; beaten from creosote bush), 1 ♀. Goffs, 2600 feet, VIII, 5, 1919, (Rehn and Hebard; from desert plants on plain, particularly in tufts of tall dry yellow grass), 2 ♂, 2 ♀, 1 juv. ♂. Bagdad, 750 feet, VIII, 6, 1919, (Rehn; beaten from very small desert plant), 1 ♀. Barstow, 2400 feet, VIII, 7, 1919, (Hebard; resting on creosote bush on hillside), 1 ♀. Little Lake, VIII, 6, 1931, (E. R. Tinkham), 1 small juv. ♀. Paradise Valley, Tehachapi Mountains, VIII, 7, 1931, (E. R. Tinkham), 1 ♀. Cactus Flat, San Bernardino Mountains, 5900 feet, VIII, 31, 1919, (Rehn; beating), 1 ♂, 1 juv. ♂. Mill Creek, San Bernardino Mountains, 4200 feet, VIII, 30, 1919, (Rehn and Hebard), 1 small juv. ♂. Palm Springs, VI, 8, 1930, (Timberlake), 1 ♂. Pasadena, (F. Grinnell Jr.), 1 juv., recorded as *coloradus* by Rehn, [A. N. S. P.]. Nellie, VIII, 9 to 22, 1917, (E. P. Hewlett), 7 juv. ♀. Wagon pass eight miles east of Jacumba, 3700 feet, IX, 15, 1922, (Rehn and Hebard), 1 small M. Resort, Laguna Mountains, 6100 feet, IX, 14, 1922, (Rehn; in dry yellow grasses under pines and oaks), 1 ♀. Descanso, 3400 feet, IX, 13, 1922, (Rehn; in short dry yellow grass), 3 ♀. Dulzura, 1500 feet, IX, 12, 1922, (Rehn; from chaparral on low gravelly hills), 1 ♀.

Parabacillus coloradus (Scudder)   (Pl. XX, figs. 7, 8, 9)
1903. *B[acillus] coloradus* Scudder, Psyche, VI, p. 372. [~; [Plains of eastern] Colorado at 5500 feet.]

This species has been correctly recorded a number of times from the Great Plains and New Mexico, but all records in the literature from west of the Rocky Mountains are referable to *P. hesperus* here described.

The species is known north to Wilson Mesa, Sierra La Sal, Utah; Glenwood Springs and Fort Collins, Colorado; Pine Bluffs, Wyoming, and Capa and Chamberlain, South Dakota: east to that locality; Badger and Kimball, Nebraska; Syracuse, Kansas; Logan, Oklahoma, and Canadian and Sanderson, Texas: south to the Mexican boundary: west to Osborn, Arizona and in that state to the north over the entire Arizona Plateau as far as the Hualapai Mountains, and Wilson Mesa, Sierra La Sal, Utah.

Like in *hesperus*, very decided size variation occurs, the measurements of the extremes before us being as follows.

♂	Length of body	Length of pronotum	Length of cephalic femur	Length of ninth tergite
Dalhart, Texas	43.8-48.	8.6-10.7	18.-22.2	1.8-2.05
Pulliam Bluff, Chisos Mts., Texas	48.3-53.7	10.4-11.3	19.9-21.8	1.9-2.2
Raton, New Mexico	37.-40.3	7.7-8.4	15.-16.2	1.75-1.9
Roswell, New Mexico	44.1-49.8	10.1-11.	18.8-19.3	2.-2.05
Cloudcroft, Sacramento Mts., New Mexico	34.2	7.4	13.8	1.75
Denton Well, New Mexico	47.-48.3	10.2-11.8	20.7-21.8	1.9-1.9

♀				
Capa, South Dakota	50.	10.9	17.2	1.35
Badger, Nebraska	52.2	10.9	18.4	1.7
Dalhart, Texas	55.1	12.8	17.8	1.7
Pulliam Bluff, Chisos Mts., Texas	61.	13.1	21.	1.75
Raton, New Mexico	47.8	10.3	15.4	1.7
Clovis, New Mexico	62.6	13.8	20.	1.9
Paradise, Arizona	65.-72.2	15.-15.7	23.-26.7	1.4-1.7

As is true for *hesperus*, the series from the northern portions of the species distributions and at high elevations to the south (Raton and Cloudcroft, New Mexico) average decidedly smaller and stockier than those from the warmer portions of its range. To the north both species are also parthenogenetic and not a male of *coloradus* is known from north of New Mexico, Texas and Oklahoma, but strangely enough such is not the case at high elevations in boreal surroundings to the south.

The coloration of this insect is very like that of *hesperus*. Fewer dark specimens occur, however, and none of our series are as mottled with limbs closely and finely annulate as is the case in rare individuals of that species from Arizona.

In addition to considerable material previously recorded we have before us the following 172 specimens; 75 males, 74 females and 23 immature individuals.

Nebraska: Badger, VIII, 5, 1901, (L. Bruner), 1 ♀. North Platte, VII, 28, 1910, (Rehn and Hebard; in grasses near sand hills), 1 juv. ♀. Sidney, VII, 30, 1910, (Rehn and Hebard; from bunch grasses in gully), 3 ♀.

Wyoming: Pine Bluffs, (L. Bruner), 1 ♀.

Colorado: La Junta, VII, 22 and 23, 1919, (Rehn and Hebard; rare in low plants on plains), 1 juv. ♀. Las Animas County, IX, 22, 1927, (L. D. Anderson), 1 ♂, [Univ. of Kansas]. Glenwood Springs, 6100 feet, IX, 9, 1909, Rehn and Hebard; from sage brush on summit of first ridge), 1 ♀.

Oklahoma: Guymon, VIII, 15 and 16, 1921, (Rehn; in medium high grass and weeds), 3 ♂, 1 ♀ (female deep rose pink in life).

Texas: Canadian, VIII, 20, 1921, (Rehn; beaten from heavy grasses, weeds and sage brush on hills), 1 ♀. Dalhart, VIII, 17, 1921, (Rehn; numerous in high grasses), 23 ♂, 10 ♀, 1 juv. ♀. Lubbock, VIII, 21, 1921, (Hebard; in heavy weeds), 2 ♂, 7 ♀. Sanderson, VIII, 25, 1912, (Rehn and Hebard; in low grasses and plants), 1 small juv. ♀. Marathon, VIII, 20, 1919, (Rehn), 1 ♂; VIII, 26 and 27, 1912, (Rehn and Hebard), 2 ♂. Garden Spring, Brewster County, IX, 2, 1912, (Rehn and Hebard), 1 juv. ♀. Moss Well, Chisos Mountains, 4600 to 4800 feet, IX, 5 to 8, 1912, (Rehn and Hebard; only two seen), 1 ♀, 1 juv. ♀. Canyon behind Pulliam Bluff, Chisos Mountains, 4600 to 5000 feet, IX, 7, 1912, (Rehn and Hebard; moderately common at lower elevations in dry grasses), 17 ♂, 1 ♀, 2 juv. ♀. Marfa, IX, 1, 1912, (Rehn and Hebard), 1 ♂. Foothills west of Ord Mountains, Brewster County, 1928, (O. C. Poling), 3 ♀. Pine Mountain, Davis Mountains, 6300 to 7000 feet, VIII, 29, 1912, (Rehn and Hebard; moderate numbers in grasses especially in pasture at 7000 feet), 1 ♂, 2 ♀, 1 juv. ♀. Livermore Peak, Davis Mountains, 8200 feet, VIII, 30, 1912, (Rehn and Hebard; in grasses of meadow), 1 ♀. Franklin Mountains, 3800 to 5500 feet, IX, 15 and 16, 1912, (Rehn and Hebard), 5 ♀, 1 juv. ♀.

New Mexico: Raton, 6600 feet, VIII, 4, 1921, (Rehn; numerous in tall grass on rolling plains), 10 ♂, 4 ♀, 1 juv. ♀. Clifton House, 6400 feet, VIII, 4, 1921, (Rehn; beaten from tall grass in swale), 1 ♂. Wagon Mound, 6200 feet, VIII, 6, 1921, (Rehn; beaten from grasses and composites), 4 ♂, 1 ♀., 1 juv. ♂. Tucumcari, 4194 feet, VIII, 14, 1921, (Rehn; beaten from grass), 1 ♀. Clovis, 4218 feet, VIII, 22, 1921, (Rehn and Hebard; occasional in heavy taller patches of grass on plains), 9 ♀. Cameo, 4124 feet, VIII, 22, 1921, (Hebard; few in grasses of grass covered sand dune), 1 ♂. Melana, 3500 feet, VIII, 24, 1921, (Rehn; beaten from grasses), 1 ♀. Roswell, 4000 feet, VIII, 23,

1921, (Rehn and Hebard; beaten from composites on hill), 2 ♂. Carlsbad, 3300 feet, VIII, 25, 1921, (Rehn; beaten from composite), 1 ♂. Tesuque Creek, west slope of Lake Peak, Sangre del Cristo Range, 7900 feet, VII, 27, 1919, (Rehn and Hebard), 1 small juv. ♀. Jemez Mountains, 6400 feet, VIII, 25 and 28, 1916, (John Woodgate), 2 ♀, [A. N. S. P.]. Jemez Hot Springs, (John Woodgate); VII, 21, 1913, 1 juv. ♀; IX, 8 to 20, 1914, 2 ♀. Above Well Country Camp, east slope of Sandia Mountains, 8000 feet, VIII, 16, 1921, (Hebard; beaten from composites in zone of pines), 1 juv. ♀. Socorro County, VIII, 18, 1927, (L. D. Anderson), 1 ♂, [Univ. of Kansas]. Fort Wingate, VIII, 6 and 9, 1910, (John Woodgate), 2 ♀. Hachita Grande Peak, 6800 feet, IX, 27, 1922, (Hebard; in grass on steep pinyon covered slopes), 1 small juv. ♂. Canyon WNW of Hachita Grande Peak, IX, 27, 1922, (Rehn and Hebard), 1 ♀. Denton Well, Playa Valley, 4200 feet, IX, 27, 1922, (Rehn and Hebard; in rich grass), 3 ♂.

Utah: Wilson Mesa, Sierra La Sal, 6200 feet, VII, 19 to 26, 1920, (H. Skinner), 1 ♀., [A. N. S. P.].

Arizona: Paradise, VIII, 22 to IX, 1, 1915, (O. C. Poling), 4 ♀. South end of Perillas Mountains, 4500 feet, IX, 24, 1922, (Rehn and Hebard), 1 small juv. ♀. Osborn, 4700 feet, IX, 23, 1922, (Hebard; in grasses on plain), 1 juv. ♀. Bill Williams Mountain, IX, 15 to 30, 1917, (O. C. Poling), 2 ♀. Coconino County, VIII, 13, 1927, (R. H. Beamer), 1 ♀. Dewey, IX, 8, 1917, (O. C. Poling), 1 ♀. Prescott, VIII, 14, 1917, (J. A. Kusche), 1 juv. ♀. Mount Trydal, 7300 feet, VIII, 27 and 28, 1917, (J. A. Kusche), 1 juv. ♀. Senator, VIII, 12, 1917, (J. A. Kusche), 2 juv. ♀. Kingman, VIII, 2, 1919, (Hebard; beaten from "rabbit weed" (a low composite)), 1 juv. ♀. Wheeler Canyon, Hualapai Mountains, V, 30, 1920, (O. C. Poling), 1 ♀. Hualapai Mountains, VII, 25, 1920, (O. C. Poling), 1 ♀.

Explanation of Plate XX

(Figures much enlarged.)

Fig. 1.—*Diapheromera torquata* new species. ♂. Type. Lost Mine Peak, Chisos Mountains, Texas. Dorsal view of distal portion of abdomen.

Fig. 2.—*Diapheromera torquata* new species. ♂. Type. Lost Mine Peak, Chisos Mountains, Texas. Lateral (sinistral) view of distal portion of abdomen.

Fig. 3.—*Diapheromera torquata* new species. ♂. Type. Lost Mine Peak, Chisos Mountains, Texas. Dextral view of poculum.

Fig. 4.—*Diapheromera torquata* new species. ♂. Type. Lost Mine Peak, Chisos Mountains, Texas, Sinistral view of poculum.

Fig. 5.—*Parabacillus hesperus* new species. ♂. Type. Atascosa Peak, Pajaritos Mountains, Arizona. Dorsal view of distal portion of abdomen.

Fig. 6.—*Parabacillus hesperus* new species. ♂. Goffs, California. Dorsal view of distal portion of abdomen.

Fig. 7.—*Parabacillus coloradus* Scudder. ♂. Las Animas County, Colorado. Dorsal view of distal portion of abdomen.

Fig. 8.—*Parabacillus coloradus* Scudder. ♂. Canyon behind Pulliam Bluff, Chisos Mountains, Texas. Dorsal view of distal portion of abdomen.

Fig. 9.—*Parabacillus coloradus* Scudder. ♂. Denton Well, Playa Valley, New Mexico. Dorsal view of distal portion of abdomen.

The several figures of the distal portion of the male abdomen for the two species of *Parabacillus* are given to show that, although decided variation in attenuation of individuals of each species occurs, the great specific difference in proportions of the penultimate tergite does not vary. Figure 5 is of a very attenuate specimen of *hesperus*, figure 6 of an unusually robust specimen of the same species. Figures 7 and 8 are of normal specimens of *coloradus* but the penultimate tergite in 8 has curled inward disto-ventrad more than is usual (possibly in drying), while figure 9 is of an exceptionally attenuate specimen of the same species.

Plate XX

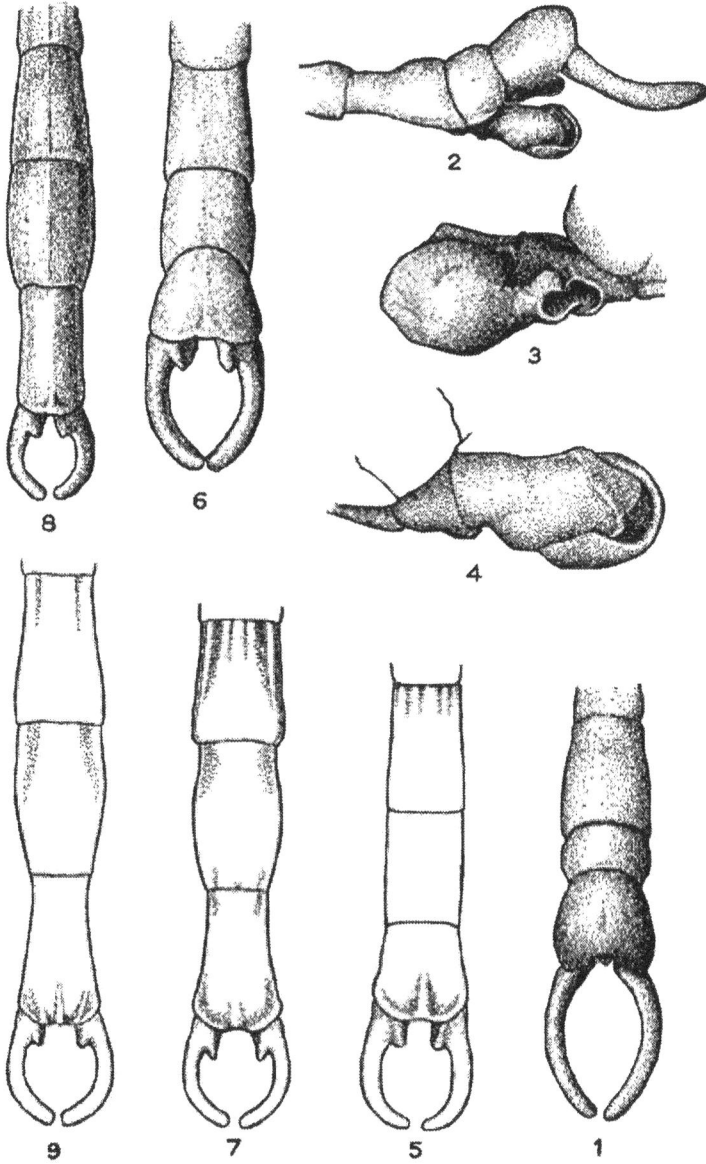

Studies in Orthoptera Which Occur in North America North of the Mexican Boundary

Morgan Hebard

In 1934 the present series of papers was begun[1] in order to place in the literature the still undescribed species and races which I realized existed in this region and to establish certain synonymy. The list of Orthoptera is now well advanced, but there is still considerable to be done before publication would seem advisable.

VII. Notes and a New Species of *Timema*, and a New Race of *Diapheromera velii*, (Phasmidae)

The recent receipt of a specimen of *Timema* from the mountains of southeastern Arizona comes as a decided surprise, as the genus was previously known only from the forested high mountains of California west to the Pacific Coast.

My prior attempt to bring order out of the confusion surrounding *Diapheromera velii* was seriously marred by failure to assign properly the immatures which had been described as *mesillana*. Study of additional material leads me to place that name as a synonym and the southwestern race which I had recognized must not only be described but its distribution must be corrected.

Timema Scudder

Since I revised this genus[2] an additional species has been added.[3] The four species now recognized may be distinguished as follows:

---

[1] All of these have appeared in the present publication as follows: LIX p. 363, I on *Psychomastax*, p. 371, II on *Cyphoderris*; LX, p. 31, III on the Decticinae, p. 281, IV on *Diapheromera*, p. 284, V on the Pachymorphinae; 1936, LXII, p. 231, VI on *Arethaea*.

[2] *Ent. News*, XXXI, pp. 126 to 132, figs. 1 and 2, (1920).

[3] Strohecker, *Ent. News*, XLVII, pp. 267 and 268, figs. 1 and 2, (1936). In figure 1 the minute tooth proximed on the internal margin of the male sinistral cercus is not shown on the shaft as it should be, being apparently misplaced and shown dextrad and very much too large.

From: *Transactions of the American Entomological Society*, Vol. 63, 1937, pp. 347-354.

Males

1. Dextral cercus simple. (Sinistral cercus with a minute proximo-internal tooth and a broad medio-internal flange with inner margin convex to the minute acute apex.) Southern Sierra Nevada Mountains, California ..... *podura* Strohecker
    Dextral cercus with a disto-internal flange 2
2. Sinistral cercus (with a minute proximo-internal tooth) slender, with a disto-internal flange which is similar to but smaller than that of dextral cercus. Coastal California south to Monterey County and the Sierra Nevada Mountains south to the Kings River ..... *californicum* Scudder
    Sinistral cercus much heavier, with flange not distal 3
3. Sinistral cercus without a minute proximo-internal tooth, with a proximo-internal flange which is large and acute-angulate produced and directed meso-caudad. Sierra Madre, (probably San Bernardino) and San Jacinto Mountains, California ..... *chumash* Hebard
    Sinistral cercus with a minute proximo-internal tooth, with a medio-internal flange which is narrow with its inner margin straight to the minute acute apex. Santa Rita Mountains, Arizona ..... *ritensis* new species

Females

1. Penultimate tergite produced with distal margin not bilobate 2
    Penultimate tergite produced with distal margin feebly bilobate (thus showing moderate angulate-emargination mesad) ..... *californicum* Scudder
2. Distal margin of this production truncate ..... *podura* Strohecker
    Distal margin of this production convex ..... *chumash* Hebard

The female of *ritensis* is not known. Whether the dorsal surface is tuberculate or smooth appears to have no diagnostic value, though such tuberculation is a striking feature in all of the males of the genus before me.

All of our series of *californicum* were dull green in life (except possibly some of those in which immersion in alcohol has destroyed their original ground color, as is also the condition of the "Los Angeles County" series of *chumash*), but among these the female from Carmel in Monterey County and to a less degree the male from that locality and the female from Paradise Valley on the King's River, show submarginal markings of dark brown. All of the specimens of *podura* and *ritensis* are light buffy brown suffused and marked with blackish brown, showing some ochraceous-tawny.

The proper sequence of the species would appear to be: *californicum* (Scudder), *ritensis* new species, *podura* Strohecker and *chumash* Hebard.

Little is yet known of the life history and habits of the species of this unusually distinctive genus. Once individuals were secured in considerable numbers by beating fir trees; one was swept from *Ceanothus* sp. Individuals have been taken from sea level up to 9432 feet.

Only the following unrecorded material has been received since 1920.

Timema californicum Scudder

Ross, Marin County, California, IV, 28, 1918, (J. C. Bradley), 3 ♂, 2 ♀, [Cornell Univ. and Hebard Cln.].

Timema chumash Hebard

San Jacinto Mountains, California, VI, 30, 1933, (R. H. Beamer), 1 ♂, 3 ♀, [Univ. of Kansas and Hebard Cln.]

Timema ritensis new species (Pl. XXI, fig. 1.)

This insect is nearest *podura* Strohecker of the southern Sierra Nevada Mountains in California. It is easily distinguished by the features given in the present key.

Type.—♂; Old Baldy, Santa Rita Mountains, Arizona. Elevation 9432 feet. July 6, 1936. (R. A. Flock; dead on steps of lookout cabin).[4] [Hebard Collection, Type no. 1317].

Size moderately large for this genus of very small walking-sticks; form robust, averaging more so even than in the most robust previously known species, *chumush*. Dorsal surface glossy, without trace of tuberculation. Cephalic margin of pronotum with lateral concavities, behind swollen postocular areas of head, very broad and shallow, more so than in podura and much less conspicuous than in *californicum* and *chumash*. Apterous. Penultimate tergite much as in the other species; rounded rectangulate production above base of dextral cercus with inner portion of dorsal

---

[4] I believe that, like the other species of *Timema*, this insect appears adult in the Spring. As the summit of this mountain is a bald with much eroded granite where small clumps of oak about a foot high grow, I further believe that it will be found among the latter unless the present specimen had been accidently carried up from the forest below.

surface thickly toothed. Supra-anal plate minute, rounded shield-shaped, situated just sinistrad of a median line. Dextral cercus an elongate moderately heavy cylindricad and evenly incurved shaft with internal surface flattened and produced at apex in a small rounded lamella. Sinistral cercus fairly broad, slightly incurved with apex rounded, dorsal surface flattened; a minute tooth present at base on inner side; the inner margin lamellate produced mesad, this gradually widening to its acute apex but narrow throughout. Sinistrad of the dextral cercus and occupying over half the area between the cercal bases is a large process which almost immediately becomes lamellate, is briefly produced directly caudad and then is bent strongly sinistrad, its margins in that large section almost straight, feebly divergent and rounding into the transverse apex, the dextral of these minutely toothed, this process longer than the dextral cercus. Above the base of this process is a short heavy rounded process. Subgenital plate with surface moderately convex, then moderately concave to the finely thickened evenly convex distal margin. Styles absent. Limbs heavy for the genus.

Measurements.—Length of body 12.7, length of pronotum 2., width of pronotum 3.7, length of caudal tibia 4. mm.

Coloration.—Generally light buffy brown. Antennae ochraceous-tawny, lateral margins of pronotum largely of this color and flecks of the same on margins of all tergites. Head with flecks and cheeks entirely blackish brown, this continued as a broad dorso-lateral band narrowing on abdomen and interrupted by symmetrically placed flecks of light buffy brown. Another symmetrically arranged rows of blackish brown flecks on abdomen and some marbling of the same on entire dorsum. Limbs and ventral surface very light buffy brown marbled and finely tessellate (the latter particularly on abdomen) with dark brown.

Diapheromera velli eucnemis new subspecies.
(Pl. XXII, figs. 1 and 2.)

1931. *Diapheromera veliei mesillana* Hebard in part not *mesillana* (Scudder), *Ent. News*, LXII, p. 65, fig. 2, (Lateral view of male poculum.) [Robstown, Texas[5].]

When studying the species of this genus which are present in Kansas, I found in 1931 that the literature for some of the western forms was chaotic and attempted to separate what appeared then to be a southwestern race of *velii* as *mesillana*.[6] Study

[5] The only locality quoted where *velli eucnemis*, though discussed and figured, occurs typical.

[6] At that time *Bacunculus texanus* Brunner was placed as a synonym in error. I can now state, from more complete evidence, that it is instead a synonym of *persimilis* Caudell.

not only of our entire collections but also of important material belonging to the National Museum and the Museum of Comparative Zoology now enables me to state that *mesillana* must be placed as a synonym of velii velii (the original material was immature, but adult material from the vicinity of Mesilla, New Mexico, I have reason to believe, will be found to be representative though probably slightly atypic of that race).

Though the race here described occurs in southwestern Texas, I find that *velii velii* occurs down the Rio Grande as far as El Paso (though atypic there) while to the north of the range of *velii eucnemis* a considerable area is occupied by an intergrading condition, agreeing with *velii velii* in the shape of the male poculum and female cerci but with *velii eucnemis* in size and in females in the coloration of the femoral apices.

Type.—♂; Marathon, Texas. Elevation 3900 feet. September 12 and 13, 1912. (Rehn and Hebard). [Hebard Collection, Type no. 1311].

Agrees closely with typical *velii velii* except in the larger size and proportionately decidedly larger and more bilobate (in caudal aspect) lip of the poculum.[7] Size large, form slightly but definitely more robust compared with related species of the genus. Head shorter than pronotum, its length about equal to the width at and (including) the small protuberant eyes, lacking occipital horns. Seventh tergite moderately enlarged except in short proximal portion, its disto-ventral angles produced and acute angulate, its dorsal length about one-fifth greater than that of the ninth tergite; eighth tergite moderately transverse, slightly more than half as long as ninth tergite. Cercus simple, with a very minute sharp proximointernal spine, shaft moderately elongate, curving evenly inward, enlarging very faintly distad to the rounded apex. Poculum as in *velii velii*, symmetrical though bent slightly sinistrad, differing in that nearly dorsal half of the distal portion is formed by the large lip, which curves dorso-caudad and the dorsal (distal) margin of which is bilobate in caudal aspect, the median portion of that margin showing a feebly obtuse-angulate rounded emargination. The genitalia embraced by the poculum are seen to be covered by a chitinous plate, convex dorsad and with a prominent node projecting sinistrad. Cephalic femora approximately equal in length to combined length of pronotum and mesonotum, slender and curving past head proximad. Median femora decidedly thickened, with surface longitudinally grooved and bluntly carinate, the ventral median carina armed with a very heavy swollen subapical ventro-external tooth but not elevated beneath this tooth. Caudal femora similar but decidedly less strongly specialized with homologous tooth very much longer and more slender.

---

[7] Females, as discussed below, show two other striking differences.

Tibiae with ventral carina (but particularly of the median pair) microscopically denticulate becoming hirsute more and more decidedly distad.

Allotype.— ♀; same data as type. [Hebard Collection].

Agrees closely with this sex of typical *velii velii* except in the larger size, much shorter cerci and brief blackish suffusions of the femoral apices. More robust than male (and averaging larger), but with femora proportionately shorter, much simpler and disto-external ventral tooth of median and caudal pair much smaller and less conspicuous. Head longer than pronotum, its length greater than its width at (and including) the eyes, which latter are very slightly less prominent than in the male. Seventh tergite simple, intermediate in length between the simple eighth and ninth tergites. Cercus small, simple, cylindrical, tapering to its rounded apex, projecting beyond the supra-anal plate slightly more than twice its width there. Operculum reaching to apex of eighth tergite, its distal margin obtuse-angulate produced mesad. Cephalic femur much shorter than in male, approximately equal to combined length of mesonotum and one-half that of pronotum, proximad more curved and beyond more lamellate. Median femur only slightly thickened and with ventro-external subapical tooth much smaller than in male. Caudal femur not thickened and with homologous tooth very small and inconspicuous.

Coloration.—Male generally brownish buff, the head with a faint suffused post-ocular line. Cephalic femora and median tibiae light green to near apices and a few antennal joints beyond the first tinged with green. Spines of median and caudal femora blackish brown.

Female generally brownish buff, the suffused postocular line more conspicuous, greenish becoming light green and broader on pronotum, mesonotum, metanotum, median segment and first abdominal tergite, the other tergites entirely this color. A buffy line which separates the dorsal from the ventral segments becomes weak caudad. Limbs brownish buff, cephalic femora strongly and median femora feebly green proximad, all femora with apices briefly but conspicuously blackish brown.

This sex also develops a very dark gray or strongly grizzled light and dark gray color phase in which the dark apical areas of the femora are naturally less conspicuous.

Large immature females show no trace of the apical femoral coloration, so I feel that this is the least important of the apparently striking features which distinguish the race. Conversely the lipping of the male poculum is important, being indicated down to quite small instars of immaturity.

It is probable that the normal color phase is usual in individuals living in mesquite, weeds and grasses, which are certainly the types of environment in which this walking-stick occurs in greatest numbers, while the very much scarcer gray phases probably live in the gray leafless desert brush of the region.

Measurements (in millimeters)

♂	Length of body	Length of mesonotum	Median width of mesonotum	Length of mesonotum (including median segment)	Length of median segment	Length of caudal femur	Dorsal length of seventh tergite
Corpus Christi, Tex.	70.	14.9	1.7	14.4	2.1	17.7	1.9
Benavides, Tex (16)	59.8-80.3	13.8-17.8	1.6-1.9	12.9-16.8	1.8-2.4	18.8-23.2	1.7-2.3
Marathon, Tex. (22)	65.-88.2	14.7-20.2	1.4-2.	13.7-19.8	1.9-2.6	19.7-24.8	1.8-2.4

♀	Length of body	Length of mesonotum	Median width of mesonotum	Length of mesonotum (including median segment)	Length of median segment	Length of caudal femur	Cercus exceeds supra-anal plate by—
Benavides, Tex (4)	72.7-85.	15.8-19.	3.1-3.2	12.9-15.3	2.-2.1	16.8-19.3	1.-1.4
Marathon, Tex. (19)	77.8-93.8	15.9-19.9	3.2-3.4	15.9-17.4	2.1-2.8	17.3-19.7	1.1-1.8
Denton Well, New Mexico	81.3	17.3	3.	14.8	2.3	17.8	1.1

Males of *D. tamaulipensis* Rehn are superficially very similar but may be readily separated by the very different poculum. They also appear definitely more slender, but rare males of *velii eucnemis* are much more slender than is usual in this race.

Series before me of atypic *velii velii* which differ from that race and converge toward *velii eucnemis* in averaging fully as large as the latter, with female femora black tipped, are from Ballinger, Big Spring, Metz, Barstow and Pecos, Texas. Such a tendency, but in color only and that weaker, is shown by material from the malpais near Carrizozo and the White Sands in the Tularosa Valley, New Mexico. Down the Rio Grande, however, *velii velii* has apparently extended its distribution far southward, females before me from El Paso, Texas, being apparently typical of that race.

Specimens examined: 117; 56 males, 31 females and 30 immature individuals.

TEXAS: Corpus Christi, VII, 29, 1912, (M. Hebard; in plants and grasses near beach), 1 ♂, 1 ♀ (female dark gray, atypic in having longer cerci, which extend beyond supra-anal plate 2.2 mm.). Robstown, VIII, 9, 1912, (M. Hebard; immatures common on Mesquite), 1 medium juv. ♂, 2 medium juv. ♀, (pair light green, one female mottled dark gray) Lyford, VIII, 6 and 7, 1912, (Rehn and Hebard; in low weed in field), 1 ♀. Jim Wells County, VII, 24, 1928, (R. H. Beamer), 1 ♂. Brooks County, VII, 25, 1928, (R. H. Beamer), 1 ♂, [Univ. of Kansas]. Brownsville, VI, (C. F. Wickham), 1 ♂, [A.N.S.P.]. Benavides, VIII, 9 and 10, 1912, (Rehn and Hebard; on Mesquite), 16 ♂, 4 ♀, small to medium juv. ♂, 1 medium juv. ♀. Cotulla, V, 11, 1906, (F. C. Pratt), 1 ♂, [U.S.N.M.]. Laredo, VIII, to 10 and 12, 1912, (Rehn and Hebard), 3 ♂, 2 small and medium juv. ♀, 1 medium juv. ♀. Uvalde, VI, 18 to 20, (C. F. Wickham), 1 ♂, 1 ♀; VIII, 21 and 22, 1912, (Rehn and Hebard; on hill slopes on low sensitive-leaved mimosa), 1 ♂, 1 ♀, 3 small juv. ♂. Carrizo Springs, X, 1 to 10, 1884, 1 ♂, 1 ♀. Del Rio, VIII, 22 and 23, 1912, (Rehn and Hebard), 3 small juv. ♂. Marathon, VIII, 20, 1919, (J. A. G. Rehn), 3 ♂, paratypes, 1 medium juv. ♂; 3900 feet, IX, 12 and 13, 1912, (Rehn and Hebard; very local but very common in high grasses in damp spot on plain), 22 ♂, 19 ♀, type, allotype, paratypes, 1 large juv. ♂, 2 medium large juv. ♀ (one female uniform gray, two immature females mottled gray). Hackberry Creek, IX, 2, 1912, (Rehn and Hebard), 1 large juv. ♂. Garden Spring, IX, 2 and 11, 1912, (Rehn and Hebard), 1 large juv. ♂. Two miles north of Bone Spring, IX, 9, 1912, (Rehn and Hebard), 1 ♀, 1 large juv. ♀ (the latter mottled gray). Neville Spring, IX, 5 and 8, 1912, (Rehn and Hebard), 1 medium juv. ♀ (mottled gray). Chisos Mountains, VII, 1911, (H. A. Wenzel), 1 ♂, [A.N.S.P.]. Western foothills of Ord Mountains, 1928, (O. C. Poling), 1 ♂, 1 ♀ (female dark gray). Sierra Blanca, 4700 feet, IX, 14, 1912, (M. Hebard; in green yellow-flowered bush), 1 ♂.

New Mexico: Lake Valley, (from Cope Collection), 1 ♀ (dark gray), [A.N.S.P.]. Deming, 4300 feet, VII, 18, 1907, (Rehn and Hebard), 1 medium juv. ♂, 5 medium to small juv. ♀ (largest female gray). Denton Well in Playa Valley, 4200 feet, IX, 27, 1922, (M. Hebard; in Mesquite), 1 ♀.

A Study on the Structure of the Egg of the Walking-Stick, *Diapheromera femorata* Say; and the Biological Significance of the Resemblance of Phasmid Eggs to Seeds.*

Henry H. P. Severin,
University of Wisconsin.

A detailed description of the eggs of the walking-stick is essential because in the systematic work on the Phasmidae, the eggs are said to be a very valuable auxiliary means of identification, since their form, "für die Genera charakteristisch ist." (Brunner von Wattenwyl †). Kaup (8) even remarks, "Vielleicht wird man später die Arten durch die Eier schneller unterscheiden lernen als durch die Thiere selbst!"

Measurements of Eggs: Heymons (6) found with Bacillus rossi that the size of the eggs is not constant. "Es sind mir Eier zugekommen, wahrscheinlich die letzten, welche das Weibchen abgesetzt hat, die höchstens die Hälfte der üblichen Grösse besassen, trotzdem waren sie aber normal gebaut und es sind aus ihnen ebenfalls Larven ausgeschlüpft." In *Diapheromera femorata* a considerable variability in the dimensions of the eggs is also present but the smaller eggs were not necessarily the last ones which the female lays,—they may appear among the first or at any time during the egg-laying.

The size of the eggs varies between the following dimensions:

Length	20-29 mm.
Depth, from dorsal to ventral surface	11-18 mm.
Width or thickness from side to side	9-14 mm.

The majority of eggs varied between the following dimensions:

Length	25-29 mm.
Depth	15-17 mm.
Width	12-13 mm.

* Submitted as a part fulfillment of the thesis requirements for the degree of Ph. D. at the University of Wisconsin.

† Paper not accessible. Quoted from v. Brunn's (2) paper.

From: *Annals of the Entomological Society of America*, Vol. 111, No. 2, June 1910, pp. 83-92.

Shape and Color of Egg: The eggs resemble very small beans with some variation in shape; some are ellipsoid, others ovoid and still others nearly spherical in form. Their color is usually a glossy black, except on the slightly more convex side which is white; instead of the black, however, there may be light shades of gray or light chocolate-brown. Out of a thousand eggs, twelve showed the light shades of gray and only three, the light chocolate-brown color.

When the operculum is removed the egg, in this region, is obliquely truncate and surrounded by an elliptical or oval rim. On the inner margin of this rim rested the operculum. The rim is provided with a circle of yellow, chitinous, bristle-like projections. In most eggs the white color of the slightly more convex side is continued around the base of the rim as a white line.

Operculum: The operculum (Fig. 1, *op*) fits perfectly within the rim of the egg capsule (Fig. 1, *ri*) and is usually set free when the egg is broken. If the operculum is cleared, mounted and examined under the microscope a ragged membrane is discernible at its margin (Fig. 3, *vi*). This is the torn, so-called "shell membrane" to which the operculum was attached.

Sharp (16) who has described a number of Phasmid eggs, has probably overlooked the fact, that the operculum is attached to the so-called "shell membrane." He writes, the operculum "is present in all known eggs of the Phasmidae; it is a lid that fits very accurately to the truncate anterior extremity of the egg; its margin is surrounded by a margin of the capsule, and it is owing to the perfect fit between the two that the operculum retains its position." Müller (13), however, in the case of *Phasma ferula* claims that, "Am Rande des Ausschnitts springt die innere Schalenhaut etwas vor, ein Rudiment der Verbindung der Schale mit dem Deckelchen. Die innere Haut des Deckelchens und die innere Haut der Schale sind also an dem unverletzten Ei ein Continuum." Leuckart (10) who has worked on the structure of the eggs of two species of Phasmids belonging to different genera also finds that, "Durch Hülfe dieser Schalenhaut wird der Deckel, der sonst vollkommen isolirt ist, in seiner Lage erhalten und befestigt."

A number of zoologists who have worked on the structure of the eggs of the Phasmidae claim that a "shell membrane" exists within the inner surface of the chorion. Müller (13) writes "Die innere Fläche der Schale wird von einer sehr dünnen häutigen Lamella, *der Schalenhaut*, überkleidet, die sich nur in kurzen Stücken von der Schale selbst wegnehmen lässt." Leuckart (10) agrees with Müller that a "shell membrane" lines the inner surface of the chorion. "Dazu kommt als Bekleidung der innern Chorion-fläche noch eine eigne dünne 'Schalenhaut,' die schon von J. Müller aufgefunden ist, also wahrscheinlich unter den Phasmoden eine ziemlich allgemeine Verbreitung hat, obgleich sie den übrigen Insekteneiern abgeht." In the eggs of *Diapheromera femorata* the so-called "shell membrane" is the innermost layer of the chorion, which peels off in small fragments in the eggs that are in the early stages of development, but in the later stages, as Leuckart (10) has observed, "Bei *Cyphocrania* lässt sich diese Haut ohne grosse Schwierigkeiten in continuo abheben—bis auf die Narbe, an der dieselbe fest mit dem Chorion verwachsen ist und ein weisses Aussehen hat." To Leuckart's observation may be added, in the case of the eggs of *Diapheromera femorata*, that a firm attachment also exists at the rim between the so-called "shell membrane" and the next outer layer of the chorion.

A microscopical examination of the operculum from the outer surface shows a resemblance to the framework of a dome, which is shut off at the base by a slightly concave floor of chitin. The framework consists of brownish, irregularly-flattened, chitonous rods. All of these rods arise from an elliptical or oval brownish rim of chitin (Fig. 3, *br*) which is in continuation with the similarly colored upper surface of the floor of the dome (Fig. 4, *c*). Some of the rods anastomose, enclosing a large, more or less, central space at the top of the dome (Fig. 3, *c*) and a varying number of irregular areas (Fig. 3, *d*) which are not constant in number in the different opercula. Those rods which do not extend to the top of the dome project free into the irregular spaces (Fig. 3, *p*).

Various authors have called attention, in different Phasmidae, to the resemblance in the histological structure of the egg capsule to the structure of certain plant tissue. Murray (14) finds, "a most striking resemblance to a piece of honey comb" in the structure of the egg capsule of *Phyllium Scythe*. According to Joly (7) who has worked on the structure of the egg of *Phyllium crurifolium* "ce tissu présente la plus grande analogie avec celui du liège, c'est-à-dire qu'il est formé de cellules irrégulières (carrées, pentagonales, sexagonales) très petites et très serrées. La couche extérieure qui recouvre cette coque, est beaucoup plus épaisse et, comme nous l'avons dit, elle ressemble à l'ecorce rugueuse du Chêne-liège, dont elle a la légèreté. Nouvelle et curieuse analogie de notre insecte avec le règne végétal: analogie qui devient plus complète encore, quand on songe que l'oeuf du *Phyllium* est muni d'un opercule qui s'ouvre lors de l'éclosion, à la manière d'une pyxide." Brongniart* who has examined the eggs of *Phyllium pulchrifolium* also compares the external envelope to that of cork. According to Henneguy (5) who has also worked on the histological structure of the egg-capsule of *Phyllium crurifolium*, "L'ensemble de la couche externe présente une grande analogie de structure avec la partie libérienne d'une écorce de dicotylédone traversée par les rayons médullaires."

A cross section through the operculum of the egg of *Diapheromera femorata* shows that the space between the floor and top of the dome is partially filled with chitinous deposits, which, according to a vegetable histologist, resembles somewhat the

* Paper not accessible. Quoted from Henneguy's (5) paper.

thin walled parenchyma of plant tissue, except that no middle lamella was discernible (Fig. 4, *a*). Müller (13) describes the chitinous deposition as "ein zelliges Gewebe aus deutlich sechseckigen oben offenen Zellen bilden. Dies scheint einer besonderen Beachtung werth, da die Ercheinung eines regelmässigen zelligen Gewebes in der Organisationsstufe der Insecten gewiss die seltenste ist." It would be rash to speculate as to the formation of this chitinous deposition since the manner in which the operculum is formed is obscure. Sharp (16) suggests two methods: "first, autotomy of the pole of the egg; second, adhesion of the mass of matter from the adjacent nutrient chamber, to form as it were a very imperfect second egg."

"Hilar area, cicatricula or Narbe" of Egg: On the outer surface of the exochorion, of the slightly more convex side of the egg is an elliptical region resembling somewhat the hilum of a seed. Sharp (16) calls this region the "hilar area," Müller (13) the "cicatricula" or "Narbe," Leuckart (10) and Heymons (6) also use the term "Narbe." The margin of this "hilar area" is slightly elevated and buff-colored (Figs. 1 and 8, *m*).

At the posterior end, this margin narrows enclosing a semicircle (Figs. 1 and 8, *s*) within which lies the micropylar orifice (Figs. 1 and 8, *o*). The margin of this semicircular area is in continuation with a ridge which extends towards the posterior pole of the egg. The buff-colored ridge joins a triangular extension of the black region of the egg (Fig. 1, *r*) and gradually disappears as it passes posteriorly into the surrounding black surface. Within the slightly elevated buff-colored margin is a white convex region which terminates at the posterior end in the micropylar orifice, where the white color gives way to black (Figs. 1 and 8, *o*).

Mycropylar Apparatus: Müller (13) did not understand how eggs of insects with a hard chorion were fertilized and he takes an extreme view as to the way this phenomenon takes place in the eggs of the Phasmidae. "Bei den Phasmen hat die Samenkapsel ausser ihrer einen Oeffnung nach aussen keinen besondern Ausführungsgang. Aber der Eingang der zweihörnigen Samenkapsel liegt gerade über dem länglichen Ausgang des Eiergangs. Der Samen tritt also aus der Eingangsöffnung der Kapsel unmittelbar in der Mündung des Eierganges ein, um sofort zu den Eierleitern und Trompeten zu gelangen."

"Wir haben aber bewiesen, das eine Befruchtung der Phasmeneier nicht anders, als vor ihrer Ausbildung und namentlich vor der Ausbildung der Schale, möglich sey."

The micropylar apparatus is very remarkable and differs from any of those which Leuckart (10) has described for so many insect eggs. As already mentioned the micropylar orifice is found at the posterior end of the convex area, just within the space enclosed by the semicircular chitinous thickening of the margin. This opening leads into a small canal, the micropylar canal, which passes a short distance towards the anterior pole of the egg. The micropylar canal is elliptical in cross section and surrounded by extremely thick chitin (Fig. 5, *g*). When the inner surface of the "hilar area" in the region of the micropylar apparatus is examined under a microscope, an invagination of the inner surface of the chorion is readily seen; at the bottom of this inpushing is the opening of the micropylar canal (Figs. 6 and 8, *i*). If the vitelline membrane in this region is now examined under a binocular, one finds that a small, obliquely-inclined, membranous tube has been torn away from the opening of the canal (Fig. 2, *t*). A glance at Fig. 7, *v*, shows the opening of this membranous tube, the vitelline membrane micropyle, into the vitelline membrane. The sperm thus enters the micropylar orifice, passes through the micropylar canal, then through the membranous tube and out of the vitelline membrane mycropyle to reach the egg.

Müller's (13) supposition that the sperm passes from the seminal receptacle, through the common oviduct, then into the oviducts to the ovarian tubule and fertilizes the egg before the chorion is formed is entirely erroneous. Leuckart (10) from observations on Gomphocerus found that the micropyles, "nicht von Anfang an dem Chorion zukommen, sondern erst nach der Ablagerung desselben durch Resorption ihren Ursprung nehmen * * * * . Eine Bestätigung dieser Beobachtung finde ich darin, dass ich nicht selten (wie u. a. bie Borborus, Tetanocera und velwandten Fliegen) Eierstockseier antraf, deren Micropylapparat noch ohen Oeffnung war, sonst aber bereits vollkommen entwickelt schien."

"Vor der Ablagerung des Chorions habe ich an der Dotterhaut niemals eine Micropyle wahrgenommen * * * * . Wohl aber habe ich Fälle beobachtet, in denen bei Anwesenheit der Chorion-micropyle die Dotterhaut noch ohne Loch zu sein schien." In all probability the eggs of the walking-stick are fertilized as they pass below the opening of the seminal receptacle.

The Biological Significance of the Resemblance of the Phasmid Eggs to Seeds: A number of naturalists have called attention to the striking resemblance of the Phasmid egg to a seed. In some cases, the egg resembles the seed of the natural food plant of the insect.

In seventeen species of Phasmids obtained from Lifu and New Britain, Sharp (16) has described the eggs of a number of these. In regard to the resemblance of the eggs to seeds he writes: "The climax of the peculiarities is found in the extremely perfect structure of their eggs and the resemblance of these eggs to seeds. The egg of the Phasmid has not only a general resemblance in size, shape, colour, and external texture to a seed, but the anatomical characters of certain seeds are reproduced on the external surface, there being a hilar area, a hilar scar, and a capitulum corresponding to the micropylar caruncle of such seeds as those of the Castor-oil plant (*Ricinus communis*). The hilar area on the inner surface of the capsule is, in shape, like the embryo of a plant. Moreover, naturalists who have examined these eggs declare that the minute structure of this curious egg-capsule cannot be distinguished histologically from plant-structure."

Among the leaf-insects the resemblance of the eggs to seeds is especially marked. Nab* as early as 1854 has compared the egg of one of these leaf-insects to the seed of the "Belle-de-Nuit (*Mirabilis Jalapa*)." Henneguy (5) in the case of the egg of *Phyllium crurifolium* claims that "Sa forme est celle d'un akène d'Ombellifère, et représente, par example, la moitié d'un jeune diakène de *Conium maculatum*. L'oeuf diffère de l'akène d'Ombellifère en ce que son opercule régulièrement conique, est situé au centre de sa face supérieure, tandis que le style conoïde de l'akène est aplati sur la face commissurale." Morton (12) in this same species writes that the "egg has been confused with a seed of *Mirabilis* and *Coniom*!"

According to Stockhard (18) the walking-stick, *Aplopus mayeri*, is found only on its food plant, *Suriana maritima*. "While one may find a close resemblance in size and color between the eggs of *Aplopus* and the seed of *Suriana*, both of which fall from the branches to the ground, where they are obscured among the débris" yet the eggs differ from the seeds considerably in shape.

The eggs of *Diapheromera femorata* were shown to a number of botanists, and with one exception, all mistook them for seeds. The botanist who did not fall into this error broke the egg before giving his opinion. When asked as to what seed the egg resembled all failed to recall any particular one. A leguminous seed, such as a small bean, was suggested, but none could be found in the natural habitat of *Diapheromera*, that resembled its egg in size and color.

If these botanists are unable to distinguish the egg of a walking-stick from a seed, can a grain-eating bird distinguish between the two? If a bird were to feed on the seeds of the *Suriana maritima* which resemble the eggs of *Aplopus mayeri* in size and color, could the bird discriminate between the two, on account of a difference in shape?

Goldi (4) in the case of the eggs of two Brazilian walking-sticks raises the question as to how far this imitation is useful in the protection of these eggs. Grain-eating birds may eat the egg but general insectivorous birds would probably mistake it for a seed and leave it untouched. The protective dress of the egg may be only a relative protection in which new dangers are involved. He next raises the argument that these eggs on account of the resemblance to some Brazilian seeds, deceive, so he believes, the egg-parasites.

This would imply that through the sense of sight the egg-parasite would overlook the eggs on account of their resemblance to some Brazilian seeds. It is open to serious question whether the egg-parasites are guided to the eggs of their host through the sense of sight alone, if at all. One illustration will suffice. We (15) have found that *Trichogramma pretiosa* parasitizes the eggs of *Cimbex americana*, and

---

* Quoted from Henneguy's (5) paper.

yet the egg-parasite cannot see the eggs of its hosts as *Cimbex* deposits its eggs in a receptacle within a willow leaf. In all probability, the sense of smell plays an important role in guiding the egg-parasites to the eggs of their hosts.

A careful survey of the literature shows that the eggs of Phasmids are subjected to the attack of a number of enemies. According to King (9) the eggs of *Anisomorpha buprestoides* "are victimized in a similar manner by a minute species of Ichneumon fly, one of which has fortunately been obtained; it is probably one of the Chalcididae: all the transformations take place within the egg; and when fully developed the perfect Ichneumon fly emerges therefrom."

Bates (1) "observed that the author of the note was probably in error in attributing the name of *Anisomorpha buprestoides* to the species in question, which seemed to be a true Phasma."

Smith (17) "remarked upon the peculiarity of all the transformations of the Chalcidite parasite taking place within the egg of the Phasma; such a mode of development was novel, if true, but he suspected some error of observation."

M'Lachlan (11) ''suggested that the cocoon of the Chalcis had been mistaken for the egg of the Phasma."

von Brunn (2) records the observation of Wolff von Wülfing, that the young larvae as well as the eggs have many enemies, "hauptsächlich Springspinnen und Hauseidechsen."

Girault (3) in his paper on the "Hosts of the Insect Egg-Parasites in North and South America" does not record an egg-parasite from any Phasmid.

I think that the resemblance of the eggs to seeds has no biological significance as a means of protection against the egg-parasites, if the eggs of the Phasmidae are parasitized. Sharp (16) in all the species which he has examined believes that these resemblances in the eggs have no bionomic importance for the species and I am strongly inclined to accept his view in the case of the egg of *Diapheromera femorata*.

I am indebted to my teacher and friend, Prof. Wm. S. Marshall, for many valuable suggestions in this work and the more than ordinary courtesies extended to me in the use of his excellent entomological library.

Zoological Laboratory, University of Wisconsin, Madison, February 1, 1910.

Bibliography.

1 Bates, H. W., 1867. [Remarks on King's (9) paper.] *Journ. of Proc. of the Ent. Soc. of London.* V, p. 80.

2. v. Brunn, M., 1898. Parthenogenese bei Phasmiden, beobachtet durch einen überseeischen Kauffmann. *Mittheil. aus dem Naturhist. Museum, Hamburg.* XV. pp. 147-161.

3. Girault, A., 1907. Hosts of Insect Egg-Parasites in North and South America. *Psyche* XIV, pp. 27-39.

4. Goldi, E. A., 1886. Die Eier zweier brasilianischen Gespenstheuschrecken. *Zool, Jahrb. Syst.* 1, pp. 724-729.

5. Henneguy, L. F., 1890. Note sur la Structure de l'Enveloppe de l'Oeuf des Phyllies. *Bull. Soc. Philom.* Paris II, pp. 18-25. Summary in: J. R. Micr. Soc. 1890, p. 596.

6. Heymons R, 1897. Ueber die Organisation und Entwickelung vou *Bacillus rossi Fabr. Sitzb. d. Kgl. Akad. d. Wiss.* Berlin. XVI, pp. 363-374.

7. Joly, M., 1871. Contribution à l'historie naturelle et à l'anatomie de la mouche-feuille des iles Seychelles. *Mem. Soc. Toulouse*, III, pp. 1-30.

8. Kaup, J. J., 1871. Ueber der Eier der Phasmiden. *Berl. Ent. Zeitschr.* XV, pp. 17-24.

9. King, C. B., 1867. *Anisomorpha buprestoides. Journ. of Proc. of the Ent. Soc. of London.* V, pp. 78-80.

10. Leuckart, R., 1855. Ueber die Micropyle und dem feinern Bau der Schalenhaut bei den Insekteneiern. *Müller's Archiv. f. Anat. Physiol.* pp. 90-264.

11. M'Lachan, R., 1867. [Remarks on King's (9) paper.] *Journ. of Proc. of the Ent. Soc. of London*, V, p. 80.

12. Morton, W., 1903. Notes sur l'elevage des Phyllies. *Bull. Soc. Vaud. Sc. Nat.* XXXIX, pp. 401-407.

13. Müller, J., 1825. Ueber die Entwickelung der Eier im Eierstock bei den Gespenstheuschrecken und eine neuentdeckte Verbindung des Rückengefässes mit den Eierstöcken bei den Insecten. *Nov. Act. Acad. Caes. Leopold*, XII, pp. 555-672.

14. Murray, A., 1856. Notice of the Leaf-Insect (*Phyllium Scythe*). *Edinburgh new philosophical Journ.* n. s. III, pp. 96-111.

15. Severin, H. H. P., and Severin, H. C. M., 1908. Habits of the American Saw-fly, *Cimbex americana* Leach, with Observations on its Egg-Parasite, *Trichogramma pretiosa* Riley. *Trans. Wis. Acad. Sci. Arts and Letters.* XVI, pt. 1, pp. 61-76.

16. Sharp, D., 1898. Account of the Phasmidae with Notes on the Eggs. *Willey, Zool. Results*, Cambridge. pp. 75-94.

17. Smith, F., 1867. [Remarks on King's (9) paper.] *Journ. of Proc. of the Ent. Soc. of London*, V, p. 80.

18. Stockard, C. R., 1908. Habits, Reactions and Mating Instincts of the Walking Stick, *Aplopus mayeri.* Publ. No. 103. *Carnegie Inst.*, Washington. pp. 43-59.

Explanation of Plate IX.

All figures were drawn with a camera lucida.

Fig. 1. "Hilar area" on the slightly more convex side of the egg: *op*, operculum; *ri*, rim in which the operculum fits perfectly; *m*, margin of the "hilar area"; *s*, semi-circular margin; *r*, buff-colored ridge which passes over into the triangular extension of the black region of the egg; *o*, micropylar orifice.

Fig. 2. Vitelline membrane of egg, after the chorion of the "hilar area" has been removed: *t*, membranous tube, which connects with the opening of the micropylar canal on the inner surface of the chorion.

Fig. 3. Operculum from the outer surface: *vi*, torn so-called "shell membrane" to which the operculum was attached; *br*, brownish rim of chitin from which the irregularly-flattened chitinous rods arise; *c*, large, more or less, central space at the top of the operculum enclosed by the anastomosing rods; *d*, irregular areas which are not constant in number in the different opercula; *p*, rods which project free into these irregular spaces.

Fig. 4. Cross section of a part of the operculum: e, brownish upper surface of the floor of the operculum; *a*, chitinous deposits, between the floor and top of the operculum, resembling somewhat the thin-walled parenchyma of plant tissue except that no middle lamella is discernible.

Fig. 5. Cross section of the micropylar canal *g*, which is surrounded by extremely thick chitin. This canal opens to the exterior by the micropylar orifice.

Fig. 6. Posterior region of the inner surface of the "hilar area" of the chorion: *i*, opening of the micropylar canal in an invagination of the inner surface of the chorion; *o*, micropylar orifice.

Fig. 7. Vitelline membrane in the region of the micropylar apparatus: *v*, opening of the membranous tube, the vitelline membrane micropyle, into the vitelline membrane.

Fig. 8. "Hilar area" on the outer surface of the exochorion; lettering as in Figs. 1 and 6.

Plate IX

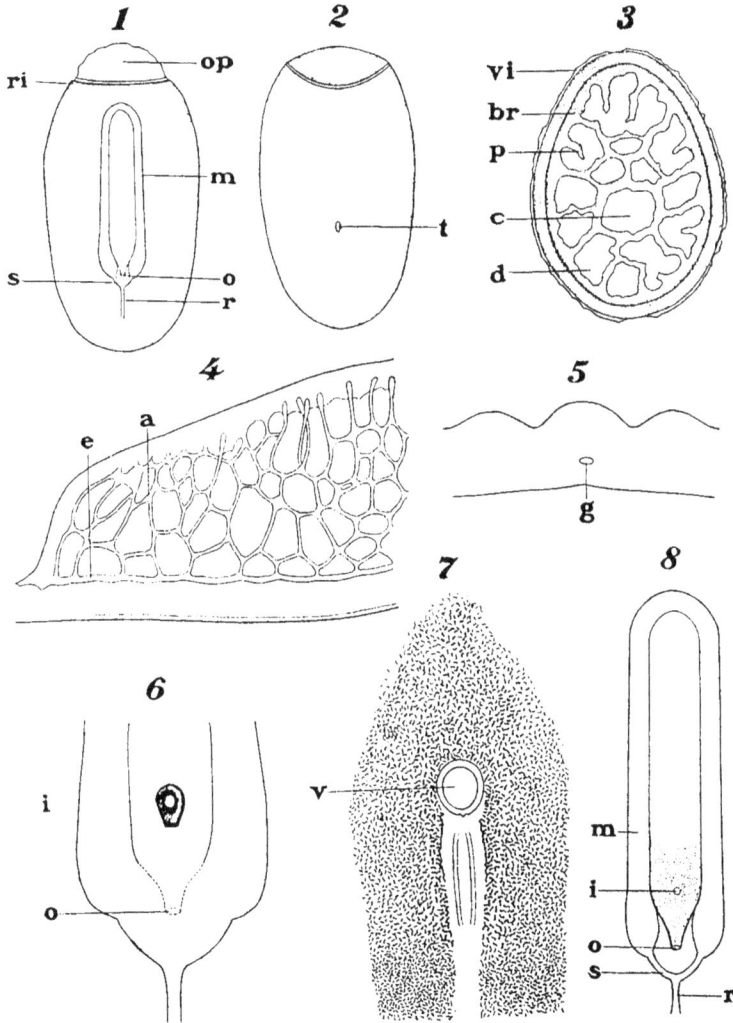

The Effect of Moisture and Dryness on the Emergence from the Egg of the Walking-Stick *Diapheromera femorata* Say

Henry H. P. Severin, Ph. D.,
Professor of Zoology and Entomology, College of Hawaii

and Harry C. Severin, M. A.,
Professor of Entomology, South Dakota
State College of Agriculture and Mechanic Arts

Heymons[1], Godelmann[2] and Stockard[3] have all noticed that in various species of Phasmidæ, some specimens, after issuing from the egg, may have one or more legs caught within the egg-shell and drag it after them for hours. Besides confirming these observations we frequently noticed that one or both antennæ or even the abdomen together with one or more legs may fail to be withdrawn from the egg-capsule. Some specimens, after having withdrawn the prothorax, part of the head and meso-thorax, were unable to extricate themselves further.

A number of experiments were performed in order to determine why the walking-sticks fail to emerge completely from the egg-shell. One thousand eggs were kept on wet sand in a breeding cage, another thousand were put in a tin box and kept perfectly dry from the time they were deposited in the autumn. The following table shows the results of hatchings of two hundred eggs kept in dry and moist surroundings.

Table 1

	Wet conditions	Dry conditions
Number of eggs hatched	200	200
Specimens which emerged completely from the egg-shell	174	12
Specimens unable to emerge completely from the egg-shell	26	188

From: *Journal of Economic Entomology*, Vol. 3, December 1910, pp. 479-481.

The table shows that 13% of the 200 specimens hatched under wet conditions, and 94% of the 200 specimens hatched under dry conditions failed, after springing off the operculum, to extract themselves completely from the egg-shell. It is evident from this that dryness has a marked effect upon the complete emergence of the walking-stick from the egg.

In the next experiment, some of those specimens, which failed to free themselves fully from the egg, were put into a glass jar containing about an inch of wet sand covered with moistened filter paper. Those walking-sticks, which had one or more legs caught within the egg-shell, usually succeeded in withdrawing all the appendages, while those that had all the legs, antennae and abdomen caught, ordinarily failed to free themselves.

In another experiment, some of the walking-sticks, which failed to extricate themselves completely from the egg, were put into a glass jar under dry conditions. These specimens, without exception, failed to withdraw the parts caught within the egg-capsule and all died with the same parts still held securely within the egg.

Godelmann[1] observed in *Bacillus rossi*—? that "die jungen Larven die Eihülsen auf die Dornen der Brombeerranken zu stulpen versuchten und dann mit den Vorderfüszen klimmzuartige Bewegungen ausführten, um sich zu befreien, wobei nicht selten ein Bein oder mehrere verloren gingen, die dann später nach der Häutung regenerirt wurden." In only a few cases, have we observed a walking-stick throw off a leg which was caught within the shell-egg. When a specimen, which had one or more legs caught, was put in a glass jar containing a twig from a hazel-nut shrub, the leaves furnished enough moisture by transpiration to allow nearly all of the young walking-sticks to withdraw the appendages.

The eggs, which still remained unhatched, were now interchanged, the remaining 800 eggs, which had been on the wet sand being transferred to the dry conditions and vice versa. The following table shows the results of the hatching of the next 100 eggs in each ease:

Table 2

	Transferred from wet to dry conditions	Transferred from dry to wet conditions
Number of eggs hatched	100	100
Specimens which had emerged completely from the egg-shell	8	80
Specimens unable to emerge completely from the egg-shell	92	20

The table shows that 92% of the 100 specimens which hatched from the eggs that were kept formerly under wet conditions and then transferred to dry, and 20% of the 100 specimens which hatched from the eggs that were formerly kept under dry conditions, and then transferred to wet, failed, after pushing off the operculum, to extricate themselves completely from the egg capsule. It is evident from these experiments that dryness at the time of hatching has a marked effect upon emergence of the walking-stick from the egg.

Bibliography

[1] Godelmann, R., 1901. Beiträge zur Kenntnis von Bacillus rossii Fabr. mit besonderer Berücksichtigung, der bei ihm vorkommenden Autotomie und Regeneration einzelner Gliedmassen. *Arch. Entwickmelk.* XII, pp. 265-301.

[2] Heymons, R., 1897. Uber die Organisation und Entwickelung von *Bacillus rossii Fabr.* *Sitzb. d. Kgl. Akad. d. Wiss, Berlin* XVI, pp. 363-374.

[3] Stockard, C. R., 1908. Habits, Reactions and Mating Instincts of the Walking-stick, *Aplopus mayeri.* Publ. No. 103, *Carnegie Inst.,* Washington, pp. 43-59.

The Life-History of the Walking-Stick, *Diapheromera femorata* Say

By Henry H. P. Severin, Ph. D.,

Professor of Zoology and Entomology, College of Hawaii

and Harry C. Severin, M. A.,

Professor of Entomology, South Dakota State College
of Agriculture and Mechanic Arts

A number of naturalists have worked on the life-history of *Diapheromera femorata*, without as yet having accurately determined the number of molts that this insect undergoes. Riley (63, 73, 74 and 76) claims in several papers that this species "molts but twice," and this mistake has been carried into a number of text books on entomology as well as into some bulletins and reports of the State Experiment Stations. Thomson (97) had some eggs of *Diapheromera femorata* sent to him from Toronto, Canada, and reared the walking-sticks which hatched from these in the Zoölogical Society's Garden at London. He claims that his specimens molted but four times. During the last four years we reared one hundred *Diapheromera femorata* under conditions which we made as normal as possible and found that twenty-three per cent. molted four times, seventy-six per cent. five times, and only one per cent. six times.

Bordage (8), in working with the walking-sticks, *Monandroptera inuncans* and *Raphiderus scabrosus*, found that there were five or six molts in both of these species. De Sinéty (90) found that the Asiatic species, *Menexenus obtusespinosus*, molted either four or five times and *Dixippus morosus* five or six times. Meissner (55), however, in a recent paper on *Dixippus morosus* claims that "samtliche 42 von mir bis zum Imaginalstadium gezogenen Tiere haben sechs Häutungen durchgemacht; ich halte es auch für unwahrscheinlich, dass weniger vorkommen sollten." Evidently, this author was not acquainted with de Sinéty's (90) work on this same species. La Baume (4), in a recent paper on *Dixippus morosus*, writes as follows concerning the number of molts of this insect: "Die Anzahl der Häutungen gibt de Sinéty auf 4 bis 6 an . . ." Evidently La Baume has erred, for de Sinéty writes, "Dans les espèces asiatiques, nous en avons constaté tantôt un nombre fixe, ... peut-être faute d'un nombre suffisant d'experiences 7 chez *Clitumnus patellifer* tantôt un nombre variable; 5 et 4 (*Menexenus obtusespinosus*), 6 et 5 (*Dixippus morosus*)."

From: *Journal of Economic Entomology*, Vol. 4, June 1911, pp. 307-320.

The question naturally arises, what is the probable explanation of this discrepancy concerning the number of molts of *Diapheromera femorata*? *Diapheromera*, after casting its exoskeleton, eats a large part of or even the entire exuvium, and it may be possible that Riley overlooked some of the molts on this account. If Thomson did not fall into this same error, it is difficult to explain why all of his walking-sticks should have molted four times. He writes, "the first specimen emerged on the 11th of June, and others from time to time during the summer. They changed their 'skins' four times before reaching maturity." In Wisconsin, the walking-sticks hatch in June also, but we noticed, as Riley (63, 73 and 74) also describes, that "some of them, however, continue hatching much later, so that all through the summer and even into fall, young individuals may be found."[1] In their natural habitat in Wisconsin, the walking-sticks feed most abundantly upon the leaves of the hazel-nut shrubs (*Corylus americana* Walt.) and to some extent upon the leaves of the linden (*Tilia americana* L.).

The following table shows the number of male and female walking-sticks which molted four, five or six times. All of these specimens were reared from fertilised eggs under normal conditions.

Table 1

Number of male and female *Diapheromera femorata*
which molted four, five or six times.

	♂	♀
Number of walking-sticks which molted four times	18	5
Number of walking-sticks which molted five times	34	42
Number of walking-sticks which molted six times		1
	52	48

It is evident from this table, that in those specimens which molted four times, the males greatly outnumbered the females.

---

[1] The development of *Diapheromera femorata*, however, is often retarded by parasitism, which fact may account for some of the immature walking-sticks being found late in autumn in Wisconsin. We have reared a leaf-ovipositing Tachinid, which Townsend (98) has recently described as *Phasmophaga antennalis* for us. This year (1910) a large number of walking-sticks parasitized by a host-ovipositing Tachinid were found. We succeeded in obtaining the egg, larval and pupal stages of this parasite but at the present writing the imago has not yet been bred.

The interval or periods between the molts (stages or stadia) and the total duration of these periods (or the post-embryonic development) in *Diapheromera* reared under normal conditions during June, July and August, which time corresponds to the normal period of development of this Phasmid in its natural habitat in Wisconsin, is shown in the following table. In this table the specimens are arranged in groups, the grouping being made according to sex and the number of molts.

Table II

Stages in molting in days of *Diapheromera femorata* reared in June, July and August.

Date of hatching	Sex	Number of molts	Stadium I	Stadium II	Stadium III	Stadium IV	Stadium V	Stadium VI	Post-embryonic development	Date of last molt
1909 6/9	M	4	14	7	10	9			40	7/19
1909 6/9	"	"	15	7	10	10			42	7/21
1909 6/11	"	"	13	7	9	9			38	7/19
1909 6/12	"	"	11	8	10	11			40	7/22
1909 7/22	"	"	10	9	11	13			43	9/3
Averages			12.6	7.6	10	10.4			40.6	
1909 6/9	F	4	15	7	9	7			38	7/17
1909 6/9	"	"	15	9	11	9			44	7/23
1909 6/12	"	"	13	9	10	8			40	7/22
1909 6/12	"	"	16	13	8	10			44	7/26
1909 6/13	"	"	13	9	10	9			41	7/24
Averages			13.8	9.4	9.6	8.6			41.4	
1907 6/13	M	5	8	7	9	9	10		43	7/26
1907 6/22	"	"	10	9	9	9	8		45	8/6
1908 7/6	"	"	9	9	7	9	11		45	8/20
1908 7/9	"	"	12	8	9	11	13		53	8/31
1908 7/13	"	"	10	7	7	11	13		48	8/30
Averages			9.8	8	8.2	9.8	11		46.8	
1908 6/23	F	5	13	8	9	7	9		46	8/8
1908 6/24	"	"	13	10	9	8	13		53	8/16
1908 6/30	"	"	12	9	9	9	12		51	8/20
1908 7/17	"	"	10	6	8	10	13		47	8/31
1908 7/22	"	"	10	9	9	12	10		50	9/10
Averages			11.6	8.4	8.8	9.2	11.4		49.4	
1907 6/13	F	6	8	7	9	8	9	12	53	8.5

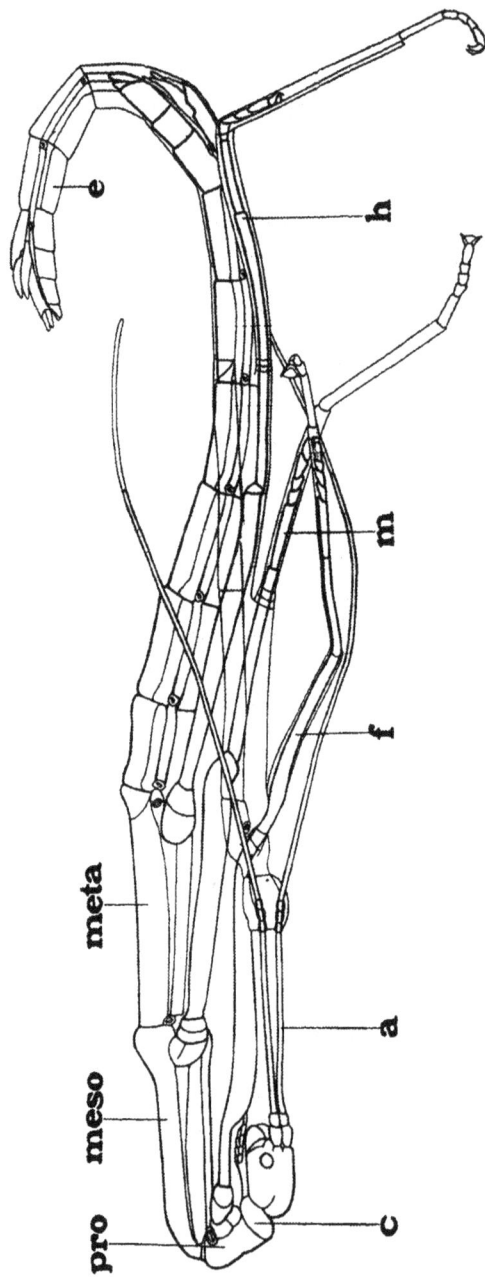

Fig. 7. Female *Diapheromera femorata* in the process of molting: *pro*, prothorax; *meso*, mesothorax; *meta*, metathorax; *c*, cervical ampulla, which is a soft membrane joining the head dorsally to the prothorax; *e*, exuvium; *f*, front leg; *m*, middle leg; *h*, hind leg; *a*, antenna.

From this table, it is evident that there is a wide variability in the interval between the different molts in the same walking-stick and also a considerable amount of variation in the time of corresponding periods in different specimens. The period between molts varies, under normal conditions, from six to fifteen days, the first and last stadia being usually somewhat more prolonged than the intermediary ones. And yet Trouvelot (99) writes, that in the case of *Diapheromera femorata* "he had observed many specimens and the interval of molting was always seventeen days." What wonderfully regulated specimens he must have observed!

The following table shows the average measurements of various parts of the body of ten walking-sticks after the first and second molts and of five or ten male and female specimens after the third, fourth and fifth molts:

Table III

Average measurements in mm. of *Diapheromera femorata* after each molt.

	I Instar	II Instar	III Instar M	III Instar F	IV Instar M	IV Instar F	V Instar M	V Instar F	VI Instar M mature	VI Instar F mature
Length, distal end of front legs to end of abdomen	18.5	31	46.5	46	66.5	68.5	96.5	91.5	126.5	121.5
Length, head and body	10.7	19.8	30.5	30.7	43.5	45	56.5	61.5	75	80
Length, head	1.1	1.3	2	2	2.5	2.5	2.5	3	3	4
Length, pronotum	.6	1	1.5	1.5	2	2	2	2.5	3	3
Length, mesonotum	2.5	4	6.2	6.2	9	9.5	12	12.5	16	16.5
Length, metanotum (with median segments)	2	3.5	5.5	5.5	8	8	11	11	15	14
Length, abdomen	4.5	10	15.3	15.5	22	23	29	32.5	38	42.5
Length, front femora	3	5	7	7	10	10	15.5	13	21.5	17
Length, middle femora	2	3.5	5	4.8	7	7	10	9	14.5	12
Length, hind femora	2.5	4	6	5.8	9	9	14	11	17	15
Length, antenna	8.5	11.5	16.5	16.3	24	24	46.5	37	56	46

A comparison of the average measurements of the male and female walking-sticks, which completed five molts, shows that the males excel the females in the lengths of the antennæ, all of the femora and in the distance from the distal end of the extended front legs to the end of the abdomen; the females, however, excel the males in the length of the abdomen.

There are certain indications which appear when the walking-stick is about to molt. The body becomes greatly distended, the lateral folds of the abdomen as well as the membranous connections between any two adjacent segments becoming greatly stretched; the body, in short, shows a rounding out, a certain fullness and plumpness. Previous to ecdysis, the Phasmid also stops eating and empties out most of the material from the digestive canal; but if, after molting, the chitinous lining of the fore-intestine and hind-intestine of the exuvium is examined, it is evident that not all of the contests have been evacuated. When hatched from the egg, the young creature is of a uniform pale green color which a day or two before the first or second ecdysis deepens into a darker green; after either of these molts, the young walking-stick again assumes the uniform pale green color.

La Baume (4), in discussing the coloration in *Diapheromera* claims that, "Die Jungen sind nämlich vom erwachsenen Tier gänzlich verschieden: sie sind vollkommen grün gefärbt. . . . Erst kurz vor der letzen Häutung geht diese Färbung allmählich in Braun über." Although we are dealing with the same species, our observations not only upon specimens reared in captivity, but also upon hundreds of individuals collected in their natural habitat are very different from those of this investigator. Many walking-stick change their color from green to various shades of brown during the interval between the second and third molts, but more often after the third ecdysis. Many female walking-sticks retain the green color throughout their natural life; in others, however, a marked individual variation in the color patterns exists after the last ecdysis, such as various shades of grey, brown or brick red often combined with various mottlings. Males which pass through four, five or six molts to complete their post-embryonic development, always have the characteristic adult color pattern after the last ecdysis; a day or two before the last molt, the newly developing color pattern becomes very prominent, especially in those specimens which have retained the green color up to this time.

In molting, the Phasmid bends down the prothorax at its union with the meso-thorax so that the head lies beneath the latter (Fig. 7, pro). The top of the head may be in contact with a leaf, stem or other object, while the front legs and antennæ are thrown back along the sides of the body.

In the Phasmidæ, Mantidæ, Blattidæ and Acridiidæ, the cervical ampulla plays an important role in the process of molting. It consists of a soft membrane joining the head dorsally to the prothorax (Fig. 7, c) and can be transformed by the afflux of blood into a greatly swollen pouch, which projects out immediately behind the head. The turgidity necessary to break the old chitinous integument in the Acridiidæ is produced as follows according to Kunckel d' Herculais (50): "ils remplissent leur jabot d'air au point de le distendre complétement; des contractions musculaires, même peu énergiques, peuvent alors aisément chasser le sang dan l'ampoule cervicale. On comprend, d'après cela, que l'effort exercé par l'ampoule est d'autant plus energique que le jabot est plus gorgé d'air."

The old chitinous exoskeleton splits longitudinally at the region of the cervical ampulla and this split increases in length during the process of extrication. After the insect has completely withdrawn itself from the exuvium, the cleft extends along the dorsal median line from the head region to the posterior end of the thorax.

During the process of ecdysis, the dorsal surface of the prothorax pushes out first from the old integument; next comes the head, followed then by the rest of the thorax, and finally by the abdomen (Fig. 7). Of the appendages, the middle legs are liberated first, then the antennæ, followed by the front and finally by the hind legs. One can easily observe the body and legs gradually withdrawing as the old skin becomes empty (Fig. 7, e).

A molting specimen examined under a binocular microscope, shows that a peristaltic-like movement passes from the posterior end of the abdomen forward at intervals. With each series of these movements the body is withdrawn a short distance out of the old skin, the legs assisting in this process of extraction from the old integument. At each attempt to withdraw the legs from the old exoskeleton, such an energetic pull is exerted upon the limbs, that each coxa presses against the body and forms there a temporary indentation.

After the walking-stick has withdrawn its appendages, it appears to be exhausted by the tedious task of ecdysis. It frequently happens that the entire body is not completely withdrawn from the cast skin, and in such instances the insect may remain suspended by the tip of the abdomen within the exuviated integument for half an hour or longer. In this position the head hangs downward, the legs are sprawled out and the antennæ are held forward parallel to the long axis of the body. This attitude does not have any resemblance to the characteristic resting posture which the walking-stick assumes during the day-time; but in all probability it allows the nearly exposed integument to harden and prevents any malformations from developing.

The body of the walking-stick, as well as the legs and antennæ may assume all sorts of abnormal shapes when the insect is unable to extricate itself entirely from the exoskeleton. If, in the process of molting, a specimen falls from the leaf or branch to which it was clinging to the bottom of the breeding cage, many malformations may result, especially if the insect experiences difficulty in withdrawing from the old skin. If any leg should happen to be caught in the exuvium that leg is usually thrown off. We have observed one male individual throw off all of its legs during the last molt and even then it was unable to free itself entirely (Fig. 8) After the newly exposed integument of this specimen hardened, the body assumed an S shape (Fig. 8). It may be possible, that whenever difficulty of this nature occurs during the process of molting that the exuvial or molting fluid which lubricates the two skins at the time of ecdysis, hardens and prevents the parts from being extricated. In all probability autotomy among the Phasmidæ owes its origin to the difficulty experienced in withdrawing the appendages during the process of ecdysis.

An exuvium immediately after being shed, may be stretched out without tearing, but after a short time the old integument hardens and it cannot then be extended to its full length.

After molting, the walking-stick usually eats its cast-off skin. The following observations of a specimen eating its former exoskeleton are copied in detail from our notebook:

The insect was suspended by the posterior end of the abdomen in the molted skin for forty minutes. The tibiæ were then flexed at the knee producing a twitching movement. Suddenly the Phasmid bent its body upward, the legs

Fig. 8. Male *Diapheromera femorata* which threw off
all of its legs during the last molt.

caught hold of the petiole of the leaf, and the terminal end of the abdomen was pulled out of the exuvium. It began to feed on the head of the molted skin at once and bit off both antennæ and one of the front legs, the latter adhering to the leaf by the tarsus. The basal ends of both antennæ were consumed at the same time, the antennæ swaying around in all directions with each bite. Next the front leg which adhered to the leaf was bitten in two through the femur after which this free portion of the leg was devoured, femur first. The walking-stick now bit off the other front leg at the coxa and left it hanging on the leaf by the tarsus. Next it started to eat the mesothorax of the discarded integument. When the walking-stick came to the middle legs it took the bent knee of one of these legs into its mouth and consumed the femur and tibia at the same time. The creature then bit off the other middle leg at the coxa and ate it. It now began to eat at the posterior end of the abdomen and met with one of the hind legs lying along the side of the abdomen. The tarsus of this leg was bent at the joint with the tibia and this bent portion entered the mouth first, the tarsus and part of the tibia being consumed at the same time. It ate the rest of the tibia and left the femur untouched. Next the Phasmid tasted the metathorax, but soon it came back to the femur and ate this portion of the leg. Then the insect bit off the other hind leg at the coxa, but the leg dropped to the ground. Finally the walking-stick devoured the remaining portion of the metathorax and abdomen. The appetite of the creature was still not satisfied, for it went carefully over the leaf, vibrating the palps continually in search of more of its integument. Finally the walking-stick discovered the front leg which was still adhering to the leaf and devoured it. Again it began to search actively for more of its former exoskeleton. We then took another molted skin of a different walking-stick and offered it to the greedy creature, and the Phasmid began to devour this skin also. It ate, however, only the head and front leg, when it was disturbed at its meal by another walking-stick coming in contact with it. Apparently the instinct of the walking-stick does not carry it far enough to recognize its own molted skin.

Godelmann (33) in his work with *Bacillus rossii* writes, "Nach der letzten Häutung, die bei meinen Zuchten etwa in December erfolgte, beginnt das Thier sofort Eier zu legen." Meissner (55), however, found that with *Dixippus morosus*, "Etwa 8-10 Tage nach der VI Häutung beginnen die Imagines Eier abzulegen und setzen dies nun ständig fort." With *Diapheromera femorata*, we also found that the females do not begin egg-laying immediately after the last molt, but that there is an interval of 6 to 10 days between the last molt and the laying of the first egg. These intervals in three specimens, which had been reared under as nearly normal conditions as possible and which had molted four times, were 7, 9, and 10 days, or on an average 8.66 days; the intervals in twelve walking-sticks which had molted five times, were 6, 6, 7, 8, 8, 8, 8, 8, 9, 10, 10 and 10 days, or on an average 8.16 days. From the averages it is apparent that no very great difference exists in the interval between the last molt and the laying of the first egg in the walking-sticks which molt four or five times.

Specimens of *Diapheromera*, which molted four times, reached sexual maturity, on an average, in 50.06 days, while individuals which molted five times required 57.56 days on an average, or an extra 6.6 days before beginning the egg-laying period. It is evident thus, that those walking-sticks which molted four times, omit the fifth molt and yet reach sexual maturity nearly a week earlier than those specimens that pass through five molts. In all probability, temperature plays an important role in the rate of development, but temperature alone does not explain why some walking-sticks molt four times and others five times. We have repeatedly reared a number of *Diapheromera* which were hatched on the same day, fed with the same kind of food and kept in the same breeding cage throughout their entire life history under exactly the same conditions of temperature and yet some specimens molted four times while others molted five times. Further experiments are necessary to determine a solution of this problem.

The eggs, after passing out of the vaginal orifice, may be retained for a number of hours within the peculiar "external uterus" formed by the ovipositor (Fig. 9, *e*).

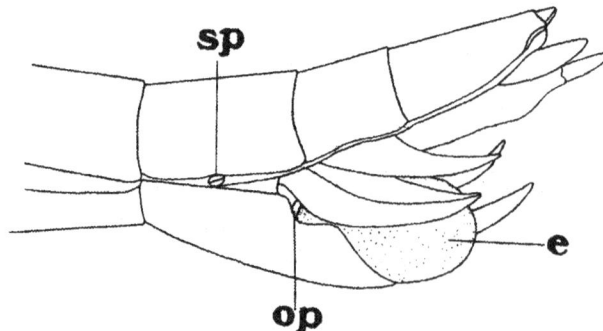

Fig. 9. The posterior end of the abdomen of a female *Diapheromera femorata*, showing an egg held within the "external uterus" formed by the ovipositer; *sp*, spiracle; *e*, egg; *op*, operculum.

After being released by the ovipositor, the eggs are dropped, one at a time, to the ground from wherever the female may be. In this way the eggs are scattered upon the ground below the natural food plant and here they remain over winter. Riley (63, 73 and 74) gives an interesting account of the egg laying in *Diapheromera femorata*, an insect which may, at times, become exceedingly abundant and very injurious. He writes, "The eggs are simply dropped loosely upon the ground from whatever height the female may happen to be, and, during the latter part of the autumn where the insects are common, one hears a constant pattering, not unlike drops of rain, that results from the abundant dropping of these eggs which in places lay so thick among and under dead leaves that they may he scraped up in great quantities."

Concerning the egg-laying of *Bacillus gallicus*, Dominique (21 and 25) emphasizes the fact that "jamais nous n'avons en à enregistrer une seule ponte diurne." *Diapheromera femorata*, however, lays its eggs during both day and night.

Bibliography.

1. Annandale, N., 1902. Notes on the Habits of Malayan Phasmidæ, and of a Flower-like Beetle Larva. *Proc. R. Phys. Soc. Edinb.* XIV, p. 439-444.

2 v. Baehr, W. B., 1907. Über die Zahl der Richtungskörper in parthenogenetisch sich entwickelnden Eiern von *Bacillus rossii. Zoöl. Jahrb. Anat.* XXIV, p. 175-191.

3. Bates, H. W., 1867. [Remarks on King's (47) paper.] *Journ. Proc. Ent. Soc. London* V, p. 80.

4. Baume, La, W., 1908. Beobachtungen an lebenden Phasmiden in der Gefangenschaft. *Zeit. f. wiss. Ins. Biol.* IV, p. 52-7.

5. Becquerel, H. and Brongniart, C. 1894. La matière verte chez les Phyllies Orthoptères de la famille des Phasmides. *C. R. Ac. Sci.* CXVIII, p. 1299-1303.

6. Blatchley, W. S., 1902. *The Orthoptera of Indiana.* 27th Ann. Rept. Dept. Geol. and Nat. Resources of Ind. p. 204-7.

7. Bordage, E., 1898. Sur la régénération chez Phasmides. *Ann. Soc. Ent. Fr.* LXVII, p. 87-91. Summary in: *Zoöl. Centralbl.* 1899. p. 341-2.

8. —— 1905. Recherches anatomiques et biologiques sur l'autotomie et la régénération chez divers arthropodes. *Bull. Sci. Fr-Belg.* XXXIX, p. 307-454.

9. Brigham, W. F., 1866. *Proc. Bost. Soc. Nat Hist.* XI, p. 88-9.

10. Brogniart, C., 1881. Sur la structure des oothèques des Mantes et sur l'eclosion et la première mue des larves. *C. R. Ac. Sci. Paris*, XCIII, p. 94-6.

11. —— 1881. Observations sur la Manière dont les Mantes construisent leur oothèques, sur l'éclosion et la première mue des larves. *Ann. Soc. Ent. Fr.* I, p. 449-452.

12. —— 1884. Sur un gigantesque Neurorthoptère provenant des terrains houillers de Commentery (Allier). *C. R. Ac. Sci. Paris*, XCVI, p. 832-3.

13. v. Brunn, M., 1898. Parthenogenese bei Phasmiden, beobachtet durch einen überseeischen Kaufmann. *Mittheil. Naturhist. Mus. Hamburg*, XV, p. 147-161.

14. Buckout, W. A., 1892. The Walking-Stick—*Diapheromera femorata* Say. *Rept. Penn. State Bd. Agric.* p. 110-2.

15. Burmeister, H., 1835. *Handbuch der Entomologie.* II p. 566.

16. Caudell, A. N., 1903. The Phasmidæ or Walking-Sticks of the United States. *Proc. U. S. Nat. Mus.* XXVI, No. 1335, p. 863-885.

17. —— 1904. Orthoptera from southwestern Texas. Collected by the Museum Expeditions of 1903, 1904. *Bull. Brooklyn Ins.* 1, No. 4, p. 105-116.

18. Charpentier, de T., 1841-'45. *Orthoptera.*

19. Conklin, E. H., 1877. Walking-Sticks or Specters becoming Injurious. *Am. Agriculturist*, Aug. Cumberland County, Penn. Reprint in: *Ann. Rept U. S. Com. Agric.* 1878, Wash. p. 242.

20. Daiber, M., 1905. Beiträge zur Kenntnis der Ovarien von Bacillus rossii Fabr. nebst einigen biologischen Bemerküngen. *Jena. Zeit. f. Naturw.* XXXIX, p. 177-202.

21. Dominique, J., 1894. Observations sur les mœurs du *Bacillus gallicus. Bull. Soc. Sci. Nat. Ouest.* Fr. IV, p. 29-30.

22. —— 1896. La parthénogénèse chez le *Bacillus gallicus* Charp. Ibid. VI, p. 67.

23 —— 1897. Parthénogénèse et parasitisme chez le *Bacillus gallicus.* Ibid. VII, p. 269-271.

24. —— 1899. Parthénogénèse et Thelytokie chez les Phasmides. Ibid. X, p. 127-136.

25. —— 1900. Encore quelques mots sur l'elevage des *Bacillus.* Ibid. X, p. 229-234.

26. Felt, E. P., 1894. On Certain Grass-eating Insects. *Bull.* 64. Cornell Univ. Agric. Exp. Sta. Ent. Div. p. 52.

27 —— 1898. A Walking-Stick. *Country Gentleman.* p. 647.

28. Fernald, H. T., 1898. Report of the Economic Zoölogist. *Bull.* No. 41, Penn. Dept. Agric., p. 109.

29. Ferrisburg, R. E. R., 1874. Walking or Specters becoming Injurious in Vermont. *Rural New Yorker*, Nov. 7. Reprint in *Ann. Rept. U. S. Com.* Agric. 1878, Wash. p. 242.

30. Fisher, L. H., 1854. *Orthoptera Europaea.* p. 135-142.

31. Francois, M., 1899. [Describes in a note the work of H. and Th. Piel de Churcheville on the parthenogenesis of *Bacillus gallicus* Charp.] *Bull. Soc. ent. Fr.* No. 20, p. 398.

32. Froggatt, W. W., 1905. Stick or Leaf Insects, with an account of *Podacanthus wilkinsoni,* as a Forest Pest, and the Spiny Leaf Insect, *Extatosoma tiaratum,* in the Orchard. *Agric. Gaz. N. S. W.* XVI, p. 515-520.

33. Godelmann, R., 1901. Beiträge zur Kenntnis von Bacillus rossii Fabr. mit besonderer Berücksichtigung, der bei ihm vorkommenden Autotomie und Regeneration einzelner Gliedmassen. *Arch. Entwickmeck.* XXII, p. 265-301.

34. Göldi, E. A., 1886. Die Eier zweier brasilianischen Gespenstheuschrecken. *Zoöl. Jahrb.* p. 724-9.

35. Gray, G. R., 1833. *The Entomology of Australia*, p. 1-28.

36. —— 1835. Synopsis of the Species of Insects belonging to the Family of Phasmidæ. *Trans. Ent. Soc. London*, I, p. 1-48.

37. Harris, T. W., 1852. *Harris's Treatise on Insects*. p. 129-130. 1862 ed. p. 146-7.

38. Harvey, F. L., 1898. Insects of the Year. 14th *Ann. Rept Me. Agric. Exp. Sta.* p. 125.

39. Hellmann, A., 1866. Einige Mittheilungen über Leben und Zucht des sogenannten "fliegenden Blattes" (Phyllium pulchrifolium) in Java. *Der Zoöl. Garten.* VII, pp. 308-310.

40. —— 1860. Ueber die "fliegenden Zweige" (*Phasma gigas*) Ambons. Ibid. VII, p. 310-2.

41. Henneguy, L. F., 1890. Note sur la structure de l'Enveloppe de l'Oeuf des Phyllies *Bull. Soc. Philom. Paris*. 8e serie, II, No. 1, p. 18-25. Summary in: *J. R. Micr. Soc.* 1890, p. 596.

42. —— 1904. *Les Insectes*.

43. Heymons, R., 1897. Über die Organisation und Entwickelung von *Bacillus rossii* Fabr. *Sitzb. d. Kgl. Akad. d. Wiss. Ber.* XVI, p. 363-374.

44. —— 1899. Über bläschenförmige Organe bei den Gespenstheuoschrecken. Ein Beitrag zur Kenntniss des Eingeweidenervensystems bei den Insecten. *Sitzb. d. Kgl. Akad. d. Wiss. Ber. Sitz. d. Phys-math.* Classe. 15 Juni. p. 563-575.

45. Johnson, C. W., 1896. The thick-thighed Walking-Stick (*Diapheromera femorata* Say.) 2d *Ann. Rept. Penn. Dept. Agric.* p. 363-4.

46. Kaup, J. J., 1867. Über die Eier der Phasmiden. *Ber. Ent. Zeit.* XV, p. 17-24.

47. King, C. B., 1867. *Anisomorpha buprestoides. Jour. Proc. Ent. Soc. London* V, p. 78-80.

48. Krauss, H., 1897. Jahreshefte des Vereins für vaterländische Naturkunde in Württemberg. 53 *Jgg. Stuttgart* 1897, p. LXX. (Sitz. am 21 Dez. 1896.)

49. Kunckel d'Herculais, J., 1890. Mécanisme physiologiques de l'eclosion, des mues et de la metamorphose chez les Insectes orthopteres de la famille des Acridides. *C. R. Acad. Sci. Paris*, CX, p. 657-9.

50. —— 1890. Du rôle de l'air dans le mécanisme physiologique de l'eclosion, des mues et de la metamorphose chez les Insectes Orthoptères de la famille des Acridides. Ibid. CX, p. 807-9.

51. Le Conte, J. L., 1891. *The Complete Writings of Thomas Say on the Entomology of North America*. I, p. 81-3 and 197-8.

52. Leigh, H. S., 1909. Preliminary Account of the Life History of the Leaf-Insect, *Phyllium crurifolium* Serville. *Proc. Zoöl. Soc. London*, p. 103-113.

53. Leuckart, R., 1855. Ueber die Micropyle und den feinern Bau der Schalenhaut bei den Insekteneiern. *Müller's Archiv. f. Anat. Physiol.* p. 90-264.

54. Lugger, O., 1897. The Orthoptera of Minnesota. *Bull.* 55, Minn. Agric. Exp. Sta. p. 189-191.

55. Meissner, O., 1909. Biologische Beobachtungen an der indischen Stabheuschrecke, *Dixippus morosus* Br. (Phasm., Orth.) *Zeit. f. wiss. Ins. Biol.* V. p. 14-21, 55-61 and 87-95.

56. M'Lachan, R., 1867. [Remarks on King's (47) paper.] *Jour. Proc. Ent. Soc. London*, V. p. 80.

57. Morris, W., 1903. Notes sur l'elevage des Phyllies. *Bull. Soc. Vaud. Sci. Nat.* XXXIX, p. 401-7.

58. Müller, J., 1825. Über die Entwickelung der Eier im Eierstock bei den Gespenstheuschrecken und eine neuentdeckte Verbindung des Rückengefässes mit den Eierstöcken bei den Insecten. *Nov. Act. Ac. Cæs. Leopold.* XII, p. 555-673.

59. Olliff, A. S., 1891. A Walking-Stick Insect Destroying Eucalypts. *Agric. Gaz. N. S. W.* II, p. 350-1.

60. Osborn, H. 1882. Insects of the Forest Attacking Hickory. (The Walking-Stick, *Diapheromera femorata*). *Ia. State Leader*, Oct. 7.

61. Packard, A. S., 1877. 9th *Ann. Rept. U. S. Geol. and Geographical Survey*, p. 630-4.

62 —— 1881. Insects Injurious to Forests and Shade Trees. *Bull. U. S. Ent. Com. Wash.* VII, p. 77-8.

63. —— 1898. Insects Injurious to Forests and Shade Trees. The thick-thighed walking stick (*Diapheromera femorata*, Say). 5th. *Ann. Rept. U. S. Ent. Com. Wash.* p. 317-21. [Taken verbatim from Riley, C. V. (74).]

64. Pagenstecher, H. A., 1864. Die Häutungen der Gespenstheuschrecken (*Mantis religiosa*). *Archiv. f. Naturgesch.* XXX, p. 7-25.

65. Pantel, J., and Sinéty de R., 1903. Sur l'apparition de mâles et d'hermaphrodites dans les pontes parthénogénètiques des Phasmes. *C. R. Ac. Sci. Paris* CXIII, p. 1351-1360.

66. Rehn, J. A. G., 1901. The Forficulidæ, Blattidæ, Mantidæ and Phasmidæ Collected in Northeast Africa by Dr. A. Donaldson. *Smith. Proc. Acad. Nat. Sci. Phila.* LIII, p. 273-295.

67. —— 1902. Notes on some Southern California Orthoptera. *Can. Ent.* XXXIV, p. 141-6.

68. —— 1904. Studies in the Orthopterous Family Phasmidæ. *Proc. Acad. Nat. Sci. Phila.* LVI, p. 38-107.

69. —— 1904. Notes on Orthoptera from Northern and Central Mexico. Ibid. LVI, p. 513-549.

70. Riley, C. V. 1869. Habits of *Spectrum [Diapheromera] femorata* Say. *Amer. Ent.* II, p. 96.

71. —— 1871. Mimicry as Illustrative of these two Butterflies (*Anosia plexippus*, and *Basilarchia archippus*), with some Remarks on the Theory of Natural Selection. 3d. *Ann. Rept. Noxious, Beneficial, and other Insects of this State of Mo.* p. 159-175.

72. —— 1875. 7th *Ann. Rept. Noxious, Beneficial and other Insects of the State of Mo.* p. 180-1.

73. Riley, C. V., Packard, A. S. and Thomas, C., 1878. 1st *Ann. Rept. U. S. Ent. Com.* 1877. Relating to the Rocky Mountain Locust. Wash. p. 277-284.

74. Riley, C. V., 1879. The thick-thighed walking-stick (*Diapheromera femorata* Say). *Ann. Rept. U. S. Com. Agric.* 1878. Wash p. 241-5.

75. Riley, C. V., Packard, A. S., and Thomas, C., 1883. 3d. *Rept U. S. Ent. Com. Wash.* p. 312-3.

76. Riley, C. V. 1884-'86. Orthoptera. *Standard Nat. Hist.* II. p. 176-7.

77. Scudder, S. H., 1868. *Proc. Bost. Soc. Nat. Hist.* XII, p. 99.

78. —— 1876. Odoriferous Glands in Phasmidæ. *Psyche* I, p. 137-140.

79. —— 1880. Annual Address. Before the Entomological Club of the American Association for the Advancement of Science. *Amer. Ent.* 2d ser. I, p. 207-210.

80. —— 1885. Dictyoneura and the Allied Insects of the Carboniferous Epoch. *Proc. Amer. Acad.* p. 167-173.

81. — 1895. Summary of the U. S. Phasmidæ. *Can. Ent.* XXII. p. 29-30.

82. — 1897. *Diapheromera femorata. Psyche* VIII, p 30-1.

83. — 1901. The Species of *Diapheromera* (Phasmidæ) found in the United States and Canada. Ibid. IX, p. 187-9.

84. Scudder, S. H. and Cockerell, T. D. A., 1902. A First List of the Orthoptera of New Mexico. *Proc. Dav. Acad. Sci.* IX, p. 20.

85. Serville, A., 1839. Histoire Naturelle des Insectes. *Orthoptères*, p. 214-292.

86. Sharp, D., 1898. Account of the Phasmidæ with Notes on the Eggs. *Willey Zoöl. Results*, Cambridge, p. 75-94.

87. v. Siebold, T., 1843. Bemerkungen über eine den *Bacillus rossii* bewohnende, Schmarotzer-Larvæ. *Germar's Zeit. f. Ent.* IV, p. 389-394.

88. Sinéty, R. de, 1900. Sur la parthénogénèse des Phasmes [Orthopt.]. *Bull. Soc. ent. Fr.* No. 9, p. 195-7.

89. — 1900. La mue chez les Phasmes du genre Leptynia [Orthopt.]. Ibid. No. 11, p. 228-9.

90. — 1901. Recherches sur la Biologie et l'Anatomie des Phasmes. *La Cellule* XIX, p. 118-278.

91. Smith, F., 1867. [Remarks on King's (47) paper.] *Jour. Proc. Ent. Soc. London*, p. 80.

92. Snow, G. C., 1874. Walking-sticks or Specters becoming Injurious. N. Y. *Weekly Tribune*, 11 Nov. Sb. No. 23, p. 103. Yates Co., N. Y. Reprint in: *Ann. Rept. U. S. Com. Agric.* 1878. Wash. p. 242.

93. Stockard, C. R., 1908. Habits, Reactions, and Mating Instincts of the Walking-Stick, *Aplopus mayeri.* Publ. No. 103. *Carnegie Inst.*, Wash. p. 43-59.

94. — 1909. Inheritance in the Walking-Stick, *Aplopus mayeri. Biol. Bull.* XVI, p. 239-245.

95. Thurau, F., 1899. *Ber. Ent. Zeit.* LXIV, Sitz. Oct. p. (15).

96. Thomson, A., 1882. Notes on a Species of Stick Insect reared in the Insect House in the Society's Garden. *Proc. Zoöl. Soc. London*, p. 718-9.

97. — 1890. Report of the Insect-House for 1889. (Orthoptera; *Diapheromera femorata*) Ibid. p. 96.

98. Townsend, C. H. T., 1909. Descriptions of Some New Tachinidæ. *Ann. Ent. Soc. Amer.* II, p. 243-250.

99. Trouvelot, L., 1866. *Proc. Bost. Soc. Nat. Hist.* XI. p. 89.

100. Wallace, A. R., 1878. *Tropical Nature and other Essays.* p. 91-3.

101. Walsh, B. D., 1864. On Phytophagic Varieties and Phytophagic Species. *Proc. Ent. Soc. Phila.* III, p. 409 and p. 427.

102. Walsh, B. D., and Riley, C. V., 1868. The Stick-bug. *Amer. Ent.* I, p 58.

103. Westwood, J. O., 1839. *An Introduction to the Modern Classification of Insects.* p. 430-6.

The Mechanism in the Hatching of the Walking Stick, *Diapheromera Femorata* Say.

Henry P. Severin, Ph. D.,

Professor of Zoology and Entomology, College of Hawaii,

and Harry C. Severin, M. A.,

Professor of Entomology, South Dakota State College of Agriculture and Mechanic Arts

In the Phasmidae, Mantidae, Blattidae and Acridiidae, the cervical ampulla is said to play an important role in the process of molting, and in some Orthoptera, also in the process of hatching. This ampulla, consisting of a soft membrane joining the head dorsally to the prothorax, can be transformed by the afflux of blood into a greatly swollen pouch, which then projects out immediately behind the head.

The process of hatching of various Orthoptera has been studied by a number of entomologists. Riley (7) does not mention the cervical ampulla while describing the phenomenon of hatching in the Rocky Mountain Locust, for he writes as follows: "The hatching consists of a continued series of undulating contractions and expansions of the several joints of the body, and with this motion there is slight but constant friction of the tips of the jaws and of the sharp tips of the hind tibial spines, as also of the tarsal claws of all the legs against the shell, which eventually weakens and finally gives away. It then easily splits up to the eyes or beyond, by the swelling of the head."

Packard (5) objects to Riley's account of the supposed action of the jaws and spines and believes that "the egg-shell is without doubt burst open by the puffing out or expansion of the membrane connecting the head and prothorax, just as the common house-fly or flesh-fly bursts off the end of its pupa-case by the puffing out of the front of the head."

Kunckel d'Herculais (3 and 4) gives the following account of the physiological mechanism in the hatching of the Acridiidae: "Les Acridiens rompent la coque de l'oeuf, * * * par la pression exercee a l'aide de la membrane unissant dorsalement la tête au prothorax que se transforme par afflux de sang en une ampoule cervicale."

In *Diapheromera femorata* the mechanism, which ruptures the various membranes and springs off the operculum when the walking-stick is about to emerge from the egg, cannot be observed in action on account of the hard, thick, opaque chorion. If the operculum is carefully removed from an egg shortly before hatching, the embryo will be found with its head and prothorax situated directly beneath the portion of

From: *Annals of the Entomological Society of America*, 1911; IV: 187-190, Plate XIV.

the egg removed (Fig. 1, *h* and *p*). The pressure exerted by the cervical ampulla is, therefore, directly against the operculum.

Hatching spines for the purpose of rupturing the embryonic envelopes and also for breaking or cutting open the egg-shell have been described from many insect eggs. Above the prothorax of *Diapheromera*, the thin amnion is covered by numerous long spines which point toward the operculum. These spines, like the egg-burster (or ruptor ovi as Riley (6) calls it) of *Corydalus cornutus*, are portions of the amnion itself. If the prothorax of a walking-stick is examined after its emergence from the egg, no spines are found, but simply short blunt protuberances. In all probability, the long spines of the amnion above the prothorax assist in rupturing the vitelline membrane which is especially thick beneath the operculum.

"When the young walking-stick is in the egg, ready to emerge, the meso- and meta-thorax are not remarkably elongate, but before the little creature is fairly out of its narrow prison, the thoracic segments assume their usual proportions. It is said to be a most curious sight by those who have observed this almost instantaneous development." (Caudell [2]).

An attempt was made by us to secure an explanation for this curious phenomenon observed by Caudell. After the chorion of the egg was removed, the embryo was found to be so curled up in the egg that the posterior end of the abdomen lay near the head region. A longitudinal section through the embryo showed that the thorax was folded transversely in a dorso-ventral direction (Fig. 2). In all probability it is simply the straightening out of these folds as the young walking-stick emerges, that causes the thoracic segments to assume their usual proportions. If the pressure exerted by the cervical ampulla at the time of hatching is not sufficient to rupture the amniotic and vitelline membranes and also to throw off the operculum, it may be possible that the straightening out of some of these thoracic folds assist in the process.

After pushing off the operculum, the young walking-stick, with the prothorax bent down at its union with the mesothorax, begins to emerge from the egg (Fig. 3). The cervical ampulla is now slightly swollen, and the prothorax possesses a deep green color, due to the blood which has accumulated within it.

The method employed during the process of emerging from the egg is almost identical with that which we (10) have described of a walking-stick withdrawing itself from its old skin during the process of ecdysis. A specimen examined under a binocular microscope during the process of emergence from the egg, will be seen to undergo a series of peristaltic-like movements of the segments of the body; these movements pass from the posterior end of the abdomen towards the head. With each series of these movements, the body is drawn out of the eggshell a short distance, the legs also assisting somewhat in this process of extraction. At each pull of the legs in their attempted withdrawal from the egg-capsule, the strength of the pull is such, that the coxa of each leg presses against the body, causing in that region a temporary indentation. When the peristaltic-like movements reach the head, the walking-stick often raises the head vigorously upward in an attempt to withdraw the antennae.

The first part of the walking-stick to leave the egg is the dorsal surface of the prothorax (Fig. 3, *p*); then comes the head (Fig. 3, *h*), followed by the rest of the thorax. The antennae are freed next, and these may come forth either simultaneously or one soon followed by the other. The following order was often observed in the withdrawal of the legs: one middle leg was followed by the other; then the front legs were pulled out of the egg at the same time, and finally the hind legs. The abdomen does not leave the egg at any definite time in relation to the withdrawal of the other parts, but it may emerge after the antennae or, in other specimens, after the middle or front legs. The extrication of the antennae, legs and abdomen, however, does not always take place in the order just given, as is shown in the following table:

Table I.

Order of Withdrawal of the Antennæ, Legs and Abdomen
from the Eggs of Six *Diapheromera femorata*.

A	B	C
{ antenna	antenna	antenna
{ antenna	antenna	antenna
front leg	middle leg	abdomen
middle leg	abdomen	middle leg
middle leg	middle leg	middle leg
front leg	front leg	front leg
abdomen	front leg	front leg
{ hind leg	{ hind leg	hind leg
{ hind leg	{ hind leg	hind leg

D	E	F
middle leg	abdomen	abdomen
antenna	{ antenna	antenna
middle leg	{ antenna	antenna
antenna	middle leg	middle leg
abdomen	front leg	middle leg
front leg	front leg	front leg
front leg	{ middle leg	front leg
{ hind leg	{ hind leg	hind leg
{ hind leg	hind leg	hind leg
	thrown off	

Braces indicate that the two included appendages were extricated simultaneously.

Stockard (11) describes the hatching of *Aplopus mayeri* as follows: "When hatching the embryo's head and body come forth from the egg first, the antennae are then pulled out, the legs being the last parts liberated from the shell." The specimens noted under E and F in the above table agree with Stockard's observations on *Aplopus*, but both of these specimens had their appendages caught in the amniotic membrane (Fig. 4). In a previous paper we (9) have already called attention to the fact that dryness, at the time of hatching, has a marked effect upon the emergence of the walking-stick from the egg. With the addition of water which was added drop by drop to the egg-shell, within which the above-mentioned specimens were caught, these walking-sticks succeeded in freeing themselves.

Bibliography.

1. Bourgeois, J., 1900. Sur un mode particulier de progression souterraine chez quelques larves d'Insectes. *Bull. Soc. ent. Fr.* LXVIV, pp 261-2.

2. Caudell, A. N., 1903. The Phasmidae, or Walking-Sticks of the United States. *Proc. U. S. Nat. Mus.* XXVI, No. 1335, p. 864.

3. Kunckel d'Herculais, J., 1890. Mécanisme physiologiques de l'éclosion des mues et de la metamorphose chez les Insectes Orthoptères de la famille des Acridides. *C. R. Acad. Sci. Paris*, CX pp. 657-9.

4. ——————, 1890. Du rôle de l'air dans le mecanisme physiologiques de l'éclosion, des mues et de la metamorphose chez les Insectes Orthoptères de la famille Acridides. Ibid. CX, pp. 807-9.

5. Packard, A. S., 1877. 9th *Ann. Rept. U. S. Geol. and Geographical Survey*, pp. 630-4.

6. ——————, 1903. *A Textbook of Entomology*, pp. 585-6.

7. Riley, C V., 1877. 9th *Ann. Rept. Noxious, Beneficial and other Insects of the State of Mo.*, pp. 89-90.

8. Riley, C. V., Packard, A. S., and Thomas, C., 1878. 1st *Ann. Rept. U. S. Ent. Com.* 1877. Relating to the Rocky Mountain Locust. Wash. pp. 277-284.

9. Severin, H. H. P., and Severin, H. C., 1910. The Effect of Moisture and Dryness on the Emergence from the Egg of the Walking-Stick, *Diapheromera femorata* Say. *Jour. Econ. Ent.* III, No. 6, pp. 479-481.

10. ——————, 1911. The Life-History of the Walking-Stick, *Diapheromera femorata* Say. *Jour. Econ. Ent.* IV, No. 3.

11. Stockard, C. R., 1908. Habits, Reactions and Mating Instincts of the Walking-Stick, *Aplopus mayeri*. Publ. No. 103, *Carnegie Inst.*, Wash. pp. 43-59.

Explanation of Plate XIV.

All figures were drawn with a camera lucida.

Fig. 1. View of embryo after the operculum has been removed showing the head and prothorax directly beneath. The pressure exerted by the cervical ampulla, which joins the head dorsally to the prothorax, would be directly against the operculum: *h*, head; *p*, prothorax; *vi*, vitelline membrane; *c*, compound eyes.

Fig. 2. Longitudinal section through the head and thorax of the embryo, showing the transverse folding of the thorax in a dorso-ventral direction; *h*, head; *p*, prothorax; *m*, mesothorax; *met*, metathorax.

Fig. 3. Walking-stick emerging from the egg showing that the prothorax is bent down at its union with the mesothorax: *h*, head; *p*, prothorax; *m*, mesothorax; *op*, operculum still adhering to the egg by means of the so-called "shell membrane."

Fig. 4. Walking-stick with its appendages caught within the egg-shell: *ha*, "hilar area."

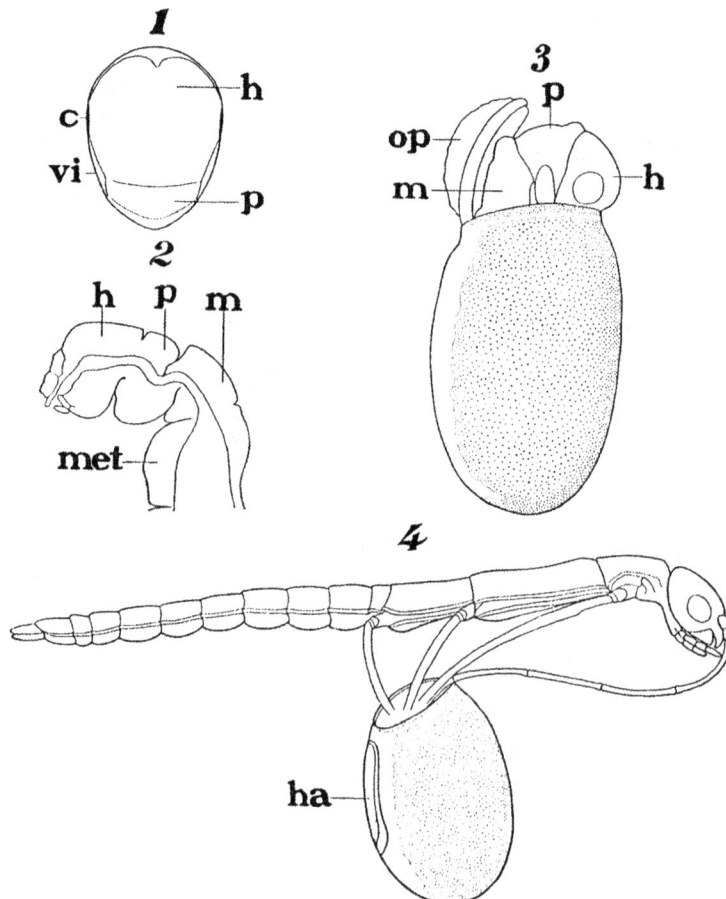

Inheritance in the "Walking-Stick," *Aplopus mayeri*

Charles R. Stockard

Cornell Medical School, New York City, February 6, 1909.

The family Phasmidæ, as is well known, shows some of the most striking cases of "protective resemblance" found among the insects. Several of the genera are typically stick-like to a surprising degree while members of the genus *Phyllium* resemble in detail a leaf-like structure. These animals are no doubt protected by their imitative forms provided they behave in a certain manner. In fact the protection or concealment of such an animal depends as largely on its behavior as upon its resemblance to surrounding objects. In order to ascertain whether these so-called protectively adapted insects really exhibited a "protective behavior" I[1] studied the habits of the "walking-stick," *Aplopus mayeri*, which is abundant on the Tortugas Islands, Florida. These large insects were found to behave in a manner almost ideal for their concealment among the twigs and stems of the plant on which they feed, *Suriana maritima*.

My study was made during a season, June and July, when the enemies of *Aplopus* were extremely rare on these islands. In the spring and fall, however, the great numbers of migrating birds which stop here no doubt devour many of these large Orthoptera in spite of their almost perfect concealment. But for their protective resemblance and habits birds might easily exterminate such slow-moving flightless insects within a few seasons, in fact the existence of creatures like Aplopi on these small islands is really dependent upon their ability to be passed unobserved by birds migrating between the eastern United States, West Indies and South America.

The question arises whether the protective behavior in *Aplopus* is fully developed on hatching from the egg or whether it is attained with their large size and mature condition. In order to investigate this and the further question of first-leg form considered below eggs were collected during the summer and brought to New York where the newly hatched individuals might be observed.

These eggs were kept in small loosely stoppered bottles in the laboratory at ordinary room temperature. They began hatching about the first of December and during January a large number of the insects came out.

---

[1] "Habits, Reactions and Mating Instincts of the 'Walking-Stick,' *Aplopus mayeri*," Science, N. S., XXVII., 1908—*Publication* No. 103, *Carnegie Institution*, Washington, 1908.

From: *Biological Bulletin*, Vol. XVI, No. 5, 1908, pp. 239-245.

Behavior of Newly Hatched Aplopi.

The reactions of the small insect on the day it emerges from the egg are almost identical with those of the fully mature eight-inch females which I studied at the Tortugas. The young Aplopi are a light chocolate-brown in color with yellowish bands about the legs and the sexes are similar. The adult males, however, become greenish in color while the female retains her original brown. The adults also have rudimentary wings which are capable of being raised when the insect is excited, but the young are wingless. Their reactions will be referred to briefly at this time as they are given in some detail in my former paper.

The insects when at rest among the twigs assume an attitude which in consequence of their stick-like shape makes them most difficult to detect. The first pair of legs are stretched directly forward enclosing the head between thin curved portions of the femora which fit perfectly against it. The antennæ are brought together between the first legs, Fig 1, B. (See also Fig 1, Plate I., and the photographs in my former paper.) The anterior end of the insect thus closely resembles a more or less pointed stick. The newly hatched individual habitually assumes this position and the point of especial interest, which I shall return to later, is that the thinned out curved part of the femora fit about the head as perfectly the first time the legs are stretched forward as they do in the adult.

In walking from place to place the adult moves slowly and often exhibits a slow laterally swinging motion suggesting a twig swinging in a light breeze. The young also swings its body from side to side in a similar manner. When a number of young

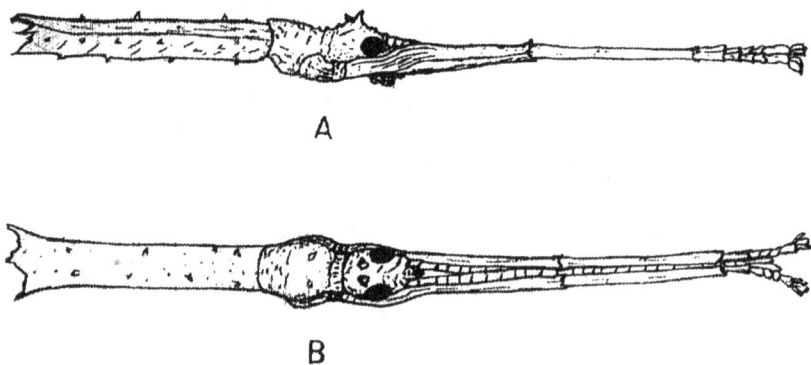

A

B

Fig. 1. A. Lateral aspect of *Aplopus*, head and first two thoracic segments. The first pair of legs are stretched forward in the typical resting attitude. The femur fits perfectly about the ventro-lateral region of the head and leaves the eyes uncovered.

B. Dorsal view of the same specimen showing the approximated antennæ directed forward and enclosed between the first pair of legs.

Aplopi are sitting motionless if the observer blows a current of air over them they all begin to swing very actively from side to side as if being swung by the breeze. This swinging motion no doubt serves to render them less conspicuous among the shrubs.

The newly hatched individuals use the same methods to escape an enemy as those employed by the adult. When they are touched or pinched slightly they move away a short distance and immediately come to rest again, if the stimulus be repeated they begin to walk at a more rapid gait than before and move a greater distance away. If again touched they drop bodily to the floor and feign death just as the adult does. The death-feigning reaction is more readily induced in the young than in the adult, and no doubt serves to great advantage in enabling them to escape an enemy which fails to seize them securely in the first attempt. The chances of escape for this stick-like creature when it drops through the dense foliage and branches of the *Suriana* bush is most favorable. When in the death-feint the legs may be bent in any position and the body twisted without the least move on the part of the animal. They may actually be piled one on another and will remain as motionless as dead insects.

The young walking-stick crawls upwards on any object that it may reach after emerging from the egg. As I previously recorded the female *Aplopus* sits in the *Suriana* bushes and lays its eggs which fall to the ground where they later hatch. Thus the tendency of the young to crawl upwards on the first object with which it comes in contact serves to bring it up the *Suriana* bush to its leafy food. In crawling up the young insect waves its antennæ to feel the way just as does the adult and reaches out with the first legs to grasp the object located by the antennæ.

Finally the young like the adult is more or less nocturnal in its movements. During the day they sit motionless with the first legs extended forward but at night they become active and move about to feed. The food of the adult is limited to the leaves of *Suriana*. I have made no attempt to feed the young since they may be kept alive for about one week after hatching without taking food.

The Thin Curve of the Femora which Fits Against the Ventro-Lateral Surfaces of the Head.

When the first pair of legs are extended forward the femur of each is so curved near its proximal joint as to fit perfectly against the ventro-lateral parts of the head and at the same time leaves the eyes uncovered; Fig. 1, A and B. The curved portion of the femur is also very thin in a lateral direction and thus when pressed closely to the head the legs go out as almost straight lines instead of bulging around the head to any great extent. It seems difficult to believe that the first pair of legs could through chance variations or mutations have come to fit so perfectly around the sides of the head and at the same time to have their dorsal line so curved as to leave the eyes uncovered. It must be remembered that when the first legs are in the extended position the head presses against the dorso-lateral surfaces of the femur and not straight against the inner lateral surface only. This arrangement may be better understood by a close examination of the dorsal and lateral views given in Fig. 1, A and B.

The possibility suggests itself that the perfection of the fit is attained during the life of the individual since the legs are so habitually pressed against the head for about twelve hours daily. To test this it became desirable to study newly hatched individuals in order to find whether the femur curve was as perfectly adjusted in them as in the adult. A careful examination of about one hundred Aplopi shortly after emerging from the egg has convinced me that the curve of the femur is as true to the head pattern in the newly hatched young as in the mature insect when several months old.

Finally, is this adjustment between the structure of the femora and head due to the position of the insect when enclosed within the inelastic egg shell? If the first

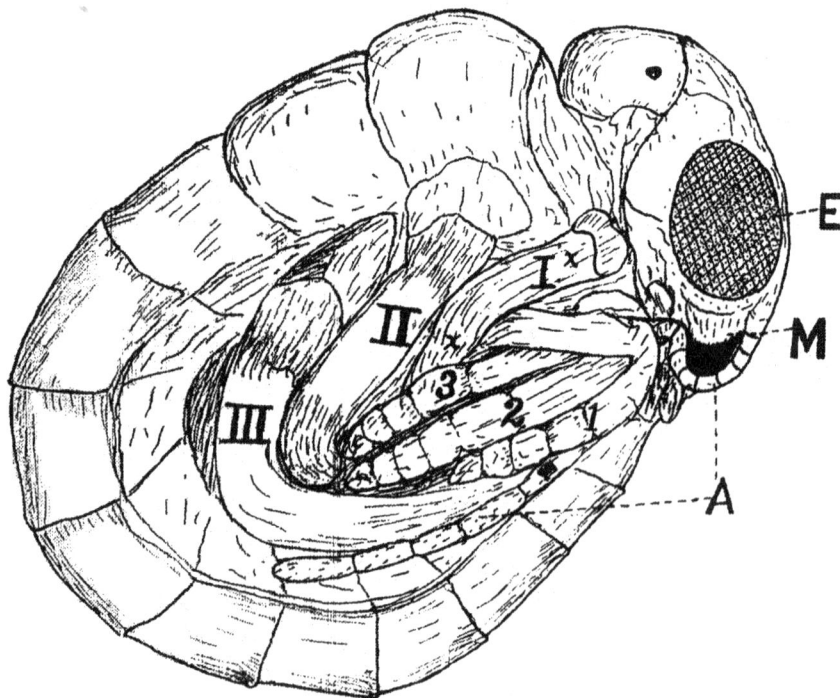

Fig. 2. An unhatched *Aplopus* with its egg membranes dissected away showing its folded position. The femora of the three right legs are marked with roman numerals and the tarsal ends of the same legs are indicated by figures. The part of the first femur which in later life fits against the head is shown between the points x-x, it is not molded against the side of the head in the egg. A, antennæ; E, compound eye; M, mandible.

legs were folded forward against the head the pressure during embryonic life might easily be sufficient to mold the femur curve into pattern for the head. Twenty eggs containing embryos at various stages shortly preceding hatching were dissected with this question in view. The elliptical egg-shell is of a rigid chitonous material with a circular operculum at one end and a hilum-like scar on one side to which the inner egg membrane is attached. The size of the egg ranges from 2 mm. in narrow diameter by 4 mm. in long diameter to 3 mm. by 4.5 mm. The length of the walking-stick on hatching is from 17 mm. to 23 mm. measured from the tip of abdomen to tip of the first pair of legs when extended forward, or from tip of head to tip of tail 9.5 mm. to 13 mm. The embryo within the egg is, therefore, necessarily much folded and bent.

On dissecting the egg the embryo is found to be curled around in a rather constant manner, the head being usually, though not always, near the opercular end. The long legs are folded back and forth upon themselves in a very definite fashion as shown by the camera drawing, Fig. 2. The antennæ (A) pass down the front of the head and then back along the ventro-lateral surface of the abdomen being sometimes bent around the first pair of legs. The point of most importance is that the femoral segments of the legs are all directed obliquely away from the head. The first pair of legs each of which is folded on itself four times does not touch the sides of the head at all. The head and large eyes are entirely uncovered and exposed. The femora of the first pair of legs not only fail to mold their curves against the head but the femora are so pressed against the thorax that the surfaces which will subsequently be concave (in Fig. 2 between x and x) are actually arched convexly. Thus it is seen that the mechanical arrangement of the embryo's parts within the egg is not responsible for the fit of the femur curve against the head. On the contrary the curve seems to develop in spite of these arrangements.

When hatching the embryo's head and body come forth from the egg first, the antennæ are then pulled out, the legs being the last parts liberated from the shell, Fig. 3. It often happens that the shell is carried around for some time dangling to the third pair of legs. In Fig. 3 the well developed curves of the femora are distinctly shown, x to x, and are being pulled in a direction away from the head, yet as soon as the legs are free from the shell the first pair may be straightened forward and their curved femora fit neatly against the sides of the head. We see, therefore, that the curve of the femora to fit the sides of the head is a character transmitted to all of the young and perfectly formed at the time of hatching. It might seem that the origin of this character is most probably due to the habit of the insects to press the first pair of legs against the head. Gradually, this pressure developed a thin concave region of the femur of the first leg which molded itself more and more perfectly to the contour of the head. If this curve arose in any other way the second and third pair of legs might have developed at least a trace of such a character though this is not absolutely necessary. It must be remembered that the curves fit the ventro-lateral contour of the head to a remarkable degree.

When the first pair of legs are so stretched forward the insects antennæ are brought together. The legs have an irregular groove extending along the approximated surfaces and when complete approximation takes place a rather imperfect tube is formed enclosing the antennæ. This is a case analogous to the above and it is difficult to imagine how chance variations bring about such mechanical harmonies between organs only associated through an habitual attitude assumed by the animal when at rest. Yet it must not be forgotten that many other equally as nice morphological arrangements exist which have no habit or action connected with them. Indeed a crucial case of use inheritance is almost impossible to imagine from purely descriptive work. I would not be understood as advocating any principle of inheritance but merely bring forward the present case as being of interest in itself.

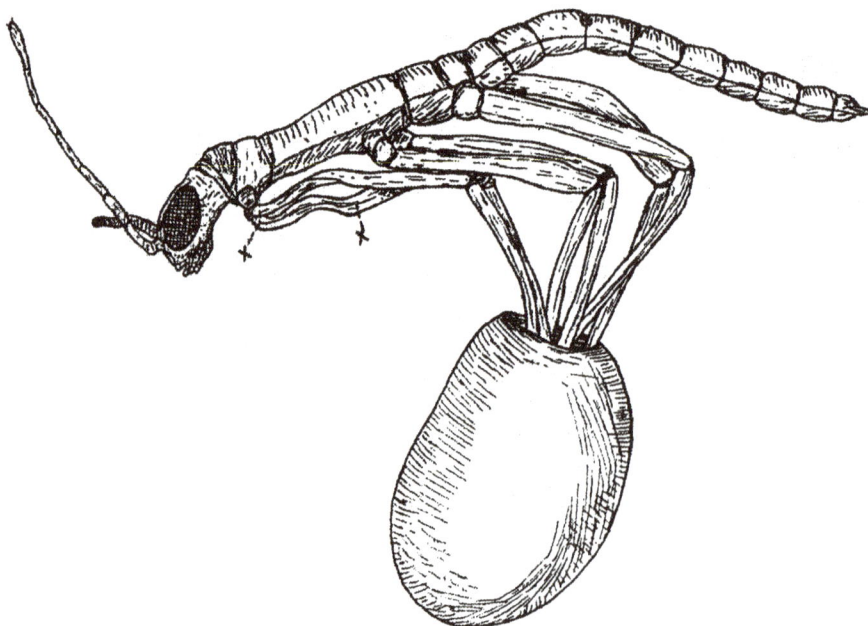

Fig. 3. *Aplopus* in the act of hatching from the egg. The body and head come out first, then the antennæ and finally the legs free themselves from the shell. The parts of the first legs between x-x are curved to fit the head when they are straightened forward although they have never touched the head up to this time.

Habits, Reactions, and Mating Instincts of the "Walking Stick," *Aplopus mayeri*

Charles R. Stockard

An investigation of the behavior of a protectively adapted insect is important to show definitely whether the actions of such an animal are coordinated with its protective structure. If an insect such as the "walkingstick," which forms the subject of the present discussion, was found to move about briskly on exposed portions of the plant on which it lives, and to show other habits which might attract the attention of enemies in spite of its apparent resemblance to the stems and leafy parts of the plant, then, notwithstanding this resemblance, it would scarcely be as well protected as other insects showing no such resemblance but remaining still and concealed among the leaves and branches of the shrub. It is clear to all observers that the behavior of an animal is almost if not quite as important as its structure in determining whether or not the animal is truly protectively adapted to its surroundings.

With the above as a premise, we may ask what would be the theoretical expectation for protective behavior of such an insect as *Aplopus*. Since movement attracts the attention of birds and other enemies almost or quite as readily as conspicuous appearance, we should first expect this insect to remain perfectly motionless during the day, while it may be seen, and to move at night; in other words, nocturnal habits would be ideal for its protection. *Aplopus* is unable to fly or leap; thus its most effective means of escape would be to drop bodily from a position when touched, and become lost by falling and alighting among the lower branches of the bush, where it might remain motionless and concealed. When moving from place to place it would attract less attention should it move slowly, and the extreme perfection of movement would be to vibrate from side to side as it progressed, as a twig swings in a light breeze. The male is colored with more green than the female; therefore, he may move among the leaves to better advantage and she will be less conspicuous on the larger brown stems. Lastly, since these insects vary greatly in color, as do most protectively colored animals, we might expect, for instance, that light-gray females would rest on the lighter-colored stems, while the dark-brown type would be found on darker stems.

From: Stockard, Charles R. 1908. Habits, reactions, and mating instincts of the "walking stick," *Aplopus mayeri*. *Papers from the Tortugas Laboratory of the Carnegie Institution of Washington*. Publication No. 103. 2(2): 43-59.

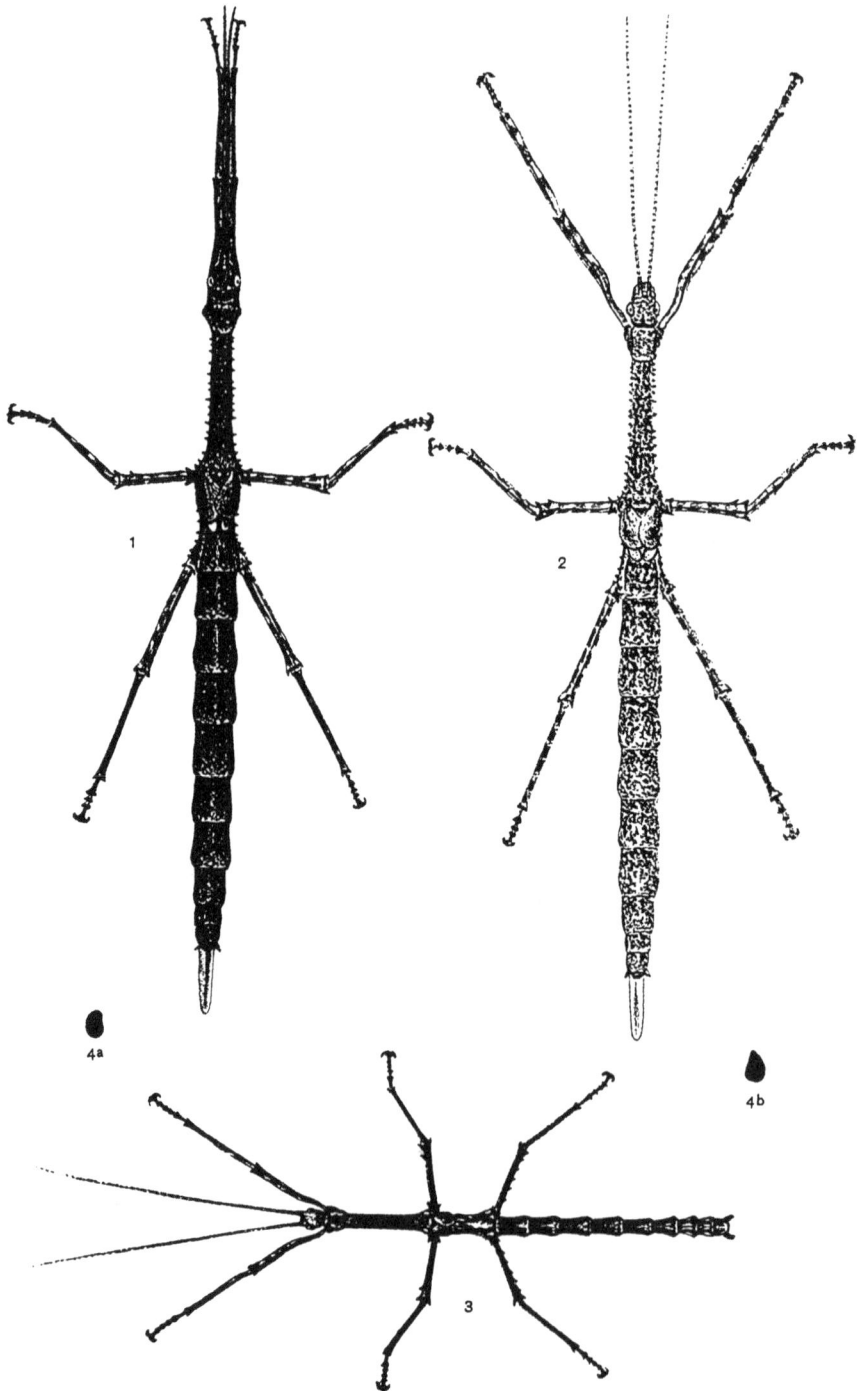

After studying the habits of the "walking-stick" one finds that the foregoing expectations for its behavior are minutely carried out, with the single exception of the last mentioned.

In the following pages I shall discuss the habits of *Aplopus* and enumerate the results of a number of experiments conducted to test its responses to various stimuli and changed conditions. Record will also be made of some experiments concerning their mating instincts, in which males were induced to copulate with the amputated abdomen of a female attached to a small stick supported by wire legs.

The experiments were performed at the Laboratory of Marine Biology of the Carnegie Institution of Washington, Tortugas, Florida, and it is a pleasure to express my thanks to Dr. Alfred G. Mayer, the Director of the Laboratory, for many courtesies extended to me while there, and for the kindly interest he has shown in my work.

Behavior of *Aplopus* in Nature.

Aplopus mayeri is a large insect, the females often measuring more than 8 inches from the tip of antennæ to the tip of abdomen, while for the smaller male 6 inches is an adult length. The male's antennæ are longer than those of the female. The male is much more sensitive to stimuli and in nature is the more active of the two. Figures 1 and 2 of plate 1 illustrate females and figure 3 shows a male, all reduced to two-thirds natural size. A decided difference in color will be noted between the two females, one being very dark, while the other is a pale gray. A large variety of gradations exist between these two extremes. The males are more or less greenish, but they also vary considerably in color. In some males the abdomen is a rich dark brown, in others a pale drab. The legs in all are darker or lighter shades of green. Such variations are common within the family Phasmidæ, all members of which are more or less protectively colored and constructed.

Facing Page

Fig. 1. A dark type *Aplopus* female with first pair of legs extending forward, inclosing the antennæ. This position is often assumed and serves to give the anterior end of the insect the appearance of a straight stick.

Fig. 2. The pale-gray type female with first pair of legs apart showing curve in the femors, which fits closely to the head in Fig. 1.

Fig. 3. Male *Aplopus*, indicating his smaller size and green legs. Figs. 1, 2, and 3 are two-thirds natural size.

Fig. 4a. Egg of *Aplopus*, natural size. 4b. Seed of *Suriana maritima*, natural size. The two resemble each other closely in size and color.

The young males are brown or grayish, resembling the females in color, and can only be distinguished from them by the absence of the oviscapt and the presence of a prominent organ of intromission on their ventral surfaces near the tip of the abdomen. At maturity, however, the males acquire the adult greenish color and may then be recognized at a glance. The wings of both sexes are rudimentary, but are capable of being raised when the animal is greatly excited, giving to it a lively and agitated appearance. *Aplopus* has spines and prominences on its body and legs suggesting the slight irregularities on the bark of twigs.

These insects are found only on their food-plant, *Suriana maritima*, and on this shrub they are extremely difficult to detect. In color and shape the female resembles closely the stems of small branches. The greenish color of the male conceals it among the leaves, while one may find a close resemblance in size and color between the eggs of *Aplopus* and the seed of *Suriana*, both of which fall from the branches to the ground, where they are obscured among the debris (figs. 4a and 4b of plate 1).

The "walking-sticks" are not easily collected during the day, though at night, when they become active, one may obtain them in large numbers by means of a lantern. The following instance may be cited as illustrating the extent to which these insects are concealed as they sit among the branches. A small group of bushes about 10 feet in diameter contained six large females and two adult males. Three of the females were sitting near the edge of the bushes and within about 2 feet of one another. A person unaccustomed to searching for the insects, although familiar with their appearance, attempted to find the three, but failed to locate any of them. I then followed after him and succeeded in locating two, but failed to find the third until a second careful search was made.

As a test of how readily birds might find aplopi while in their motionless attitude, five individuals were placed on the ground near a hen with several small chickens. The mother showed no evidence of recognizing the insects until within a short time the Aplopi became excited at finding themselves on the ground and began to crawl toward a bush. When they began moving the hen immediately started after them.

The observations and experiments that follow were based on the actions of 26 males and 81 females, some of which were kept in cages, while others were allowed to remain in their natural environment on isolated Suriana bushes.

Facing Page

Fig. 1. Female *Aplopus* in normal attitude on *Suriana* branch.
Fig. 2. Female in somewhat different position.
Fig. 3. Light-gray female on a dark stem of *Suriana*.

Attitudes When at Rest.

Aplopus assumes a decidedly protective attitude when at rest. The forelegs, which are slightly grooved on their anterior surfaces, are directed forward, the grooves being approximated to form a tube inclosing the antennae, thus producing a resemblance between the anterior end of the animal and the straight end of a small dead stick (see fig. 1 of plate 1 and also figs. 1, 2, and 3 of plate 2, photographs from life of the insects in such a position). With their forelegs straightened in this manner, the females usually rest in an obliquely vertical position on the leafless stems. The abdomen sometimes points upward, the tips of the forelimbs being directed down, grasping the branch on which they rest. Again, the abdomen may be turned downward and serve as a partial support, while the body, with the extended forelegs free, points obliquely upward. In either attitude the insect closely simulates a dead stick projecting from the supporting branch. The femora of the first pair of legs are curved near their proximal joints so as to fit closely around the insect's head when they are extended forward (fig. 2 of plate 1). The females, as mentioned before, vary considerably in color from dark brown to light gray, as do also the stems of *Suriana*, though the insects do not at all times take advantage of this variation, the dark females being not uncommonly seen on light stems, and vice versa.

The males do not so constantly assume the position with the first legs extended. This attitude is less essential for them than for the females, since they are found as a rule among the leafed branches, where their greenish legs are inconspicuous. Their slenderer proportions and smaller size also make them more difficult to see. At times, however, the males do straighten their first pair of legs forward and assume the position so common to the female.

The more common occurrence of the greenish males among the foliage and of the brown females upon the brown stems of the plant suggest the case of *Mantis religiosa*. Di Cesnola[1] records this mantis as occurring in a green and a brown form in Italy, the green form being always found upon green grass and the brown form upon grass burnt by the sun. He found that when 25 individuals of the green form were tied on brown grass all were killed in 11 days, while 20 tied on green grass were all alive after 17 days. The results were similar when the brown form was tied on green and burnt grass.

---

[1] Di Cesnola, A. P. Preliminary note on the protective value of color in *Mantis religiosa*. *Biometrika*, III, p. 58, 1904.

Movements of *Aplopus*.

Aplopus is nocturnal in its habits. During the day it sits motionless among the branches, but as the sun's rays weaken the males begin to move about first, and later the females. Their manner of walking is peculiarly interesting. They resemble sticks crawling about on legs. The legs are moved in a stiff manner and the insect progresses slowly as a rule, although they sometimes move at a rapid gait. While walking among the branches or on a flat surface they often show a lateral swinging movement, the foothold forming a fixed point, while by bending the tarsal and knee joints the body is swung sidewise, sometimes with an amplitude of more than half an inch. This movement suggests to the observer the swinging or waving motion of branches and stems when shaken, or blown by the wind. The male has also a peculiar quivering movement that is sometimes performed at intervals while moving about the branches. This motion is more to be associated with the mating instincts, as is shown below. In the evening *Aplopus* shows a tendency to climb upward, being negatively geotropic. It will then often turn and go upward if the twig is inverted after it has reached the top.

The males travel greater distances during the night than do the females. Three females under observation did not move more than 2 feet from their original positions within a period of two days, yet others were found to migrate to parts of the bushes 10 or 12 feet distant during a single night. The males usually travel many yards in a night and it is almost impossible to keep track of them for more than one day.

Aplopus avoids or escapes its enemies in the following ways: On several occasions females were touched lightly as they sat in their protective attitude. They remained motionless after being touched, as though they were inanimate bodies. A male under observation about dusk was struck by a large insect which flew against it; the *Aplopus* jerked quickly back and remained motionless for more than a minute, after which it walked swiftly down the branch.

The most effective means of escape for these animals is the "dropping reaction." When one attempting to capture an *Aplopus* fails to seize it the first time, it often drops bodily from the limb on which it rested and catches on some lower branch that it may chance to strike. If seen and unsuccessfully grabbed at for the second time, it will again drop and may sometimes fall entirely to the ground. One male in attempting to escape capture fell entirely to the ground, striking on its back with its legs extended in the air. It feigned death perfectly and remained in this awkward position for more than 8 minutes; then turned itself over and moved away so quickly that it was lost sight of in the dim evening light.

Since "walking-sticks" are unable either to fly or jump, this dropping reaction is a most important means of escape, and the dense growth of the *Suriana* bushes would apparently prevent birds from finding the insect a second time after it had so suddenly fallen out of reach. Their motionless attitudes during the day and close resemblance to the stems of the bushes no doubt serve to protect *Aplopus* to a marked degree from predaceous birds and other enemies.

The food of *Aplopus* consists entirely of the leaves of *Suriana maritima*, the plant on which it lives. The only previously published statement regarding its habits is a brief paragraph in the catalogue from the supply department of the Marine Biological Laboratory at Woods Hole. This states that "the prey is seized by a quick movement of the forelegs." Such an idea is, of course, erroneous, since all members of this family are known to be vegetable feeders. The statement is doubtless based on the opinion of some amateur collector. *Aplopus* usually feeds at night, although those resting on leafy branches are sometimes observed to feed during the day. In feeding they bite the leaf straight across the top and often eat it entirely away, or they may bite the leaf in an up-and-down fashion until it is consumed. They rarely make semicircular cuts in the leaves, as the locust often does. These characteristically bitten leaves serve to furnish a trustworthy index of the whereabouts of Aplopi, as they seem to be somewhat locally distributed on the island.

Mating Instincts.

Mating occurs as a rule during the night, although several pairs were observed *in copulo* during the day. The active process is much the same as in kindred insects. The male takes a position on the back of the female, with his front feet resting on her metathorax, the second pair of feet grasping her abdomen about its middle, his third pair of legs usually hanging freely extended, the tip of his abdomen being firmly attached to a slight pit on the ventral surface of the seventh abdominal segment of the female. The intromissive organ of the male is then protruded and placed between the oviscapt and the last three abdominal segments of the female. In this position the male remains for from 30 minutes to several hours. His copulating organ is then withdrawn, although he may still remain for a long time sitting upon the back of the female (fig. 4, plate 3). One male may copulate with several females during the same day. The male often gives periodical quivering movements while over the female, probably for the purpose of exciting her to the sexual act. He sometimes shows a slow, swinging motion during copulation.

The female is supplied with a long ovipositor, although it seems to be useless, as her eggs are allowed to fall carelessly to the ground as she sits motionless among the branches. The eggs resemble closely in size and color the seed of *Suriana*, as mentioned before, but differ from them considerably in shape. (Compare figs. 4a and 4b in plate 1.)

All of the observations on the habits of *Aplopus* in nature would seem to indicate that the behavior of this insect is as truly protective as is its close simulation of the branches on which it lives.

Experimental.
Experiments With Light.

Aplopus responds to light and darkness in a most interesting manner. The insects were observed to begin moving on the bushes by a much brighter light in the evening than that which served to stop their movement during the morning. They were seen feeding and crawling slowly about, at times, two hours before sunset; while they often came to rest more than half an hour before sunrise. The difference in intensities of the lights causing the two reactions is very great. It occurred to me that perhaps their response was periodic and not entirely due to the effect of light; that is, after being active for several hours during the night they become tired and cease to move for this reason, and not on account of any response to light, since the intensity of the morning light by which they come to rest is even less than that of the moonlight in which they are active. (The quality of the two lights is no doubt different.) The case is, however, made clear by the following experiment:

Sixty-five individuals in a wire cage had come to rest at 4 h 50 m a. m. At this time daylight was scarcely perceptible. It was much darker than when they had begun movement during the evening, or even the moonlight of the earlier part of the night. It would seem, then, that a physiological periodicity had had some influence on their behavior. To test this the cage was placed in a dark-room at 5 a. m. In less than half an hour all were actively crawling, thus showing that they had responded to the faint light of approaching day and not to a tired condition. They continued to move actively for more than an hour in the dark-room, and were then put into the light, where they readily came to rest again.

The fact that they begin movement by brighter light in the evening and stop by paler or weaker light in the morning may possibly be associated with a similar habit of some birds, which go to their roosts by brighter light than that by which they leave.

A number of dark-room experiments were performed during the day to test the manner and time of response to light and darkness. The dark-room was one arranged for photographic work, having a red glass window that might be covered with a black oilcloth, so that no light was admitted. The door of the room opened into the closed side of the laboratory, thus permitting only weak diffused light to enter the room at any time. I was enabled to detect the first movement of the insects in the dark, as the gauze wire of the cage gave a perceptible clicking sound when their feet were moved upon it.

We may first consider the reactions of normal individuals. Since the experiments gave closely similar results, one may be recorded for illustration. Three females and two males were placed in the dark-room at 10 h 25 m a. m. After 15 minutes three were actively moving, while after 20 minutes all were in motion. The door was opened and light admitted at 11 a. m.; they came to rest in a little more than a minute, and remained so in spite of various loud noises until 11 h 11 m a. m., when the room was again darkened. The animals began again to move and all five were in active motion within 8 minutes. Bright daylight was thrown on them after all had been moving for 3 minutes; two were at rest in less than a minute, and all were quiet in about 5 minutes. When they had been at rest for 11 minutes the room was for the third time darkened, and after 11 minutes all were active. Light was then admitted and two ceased to move within 2 minutes, the others stopping after 5 minutes.

The dark-room was again closed at 11 h 45 m a. m. and left until 12 h 30 m p. m., at which time all of the insects were active. On admitting light they became motionless within 2 minutes. The dark-room was closed for the fifth time at 12 h 55 m p. m., after the five "walking-sticks" had been quiet for more than 20 minutes; 10 minutes after they had been in the dark two were moving, and all were in motion after 15 minutes or at 1 h 10 m p. m. Light was admitted at 1 h 11 m p.m, and all came to rest within 30 seconds, a very quick response. They were then exposed to light for 10 minutes, then again put into the dark-room. The first one did not begin to move until 17 minutes had elapsed; the others were moving after being in the dark 20 minutes. The first ones to move had disturbed others by striking against them, so that these probably moved earlier than they would have otherwise. They were allowed to remain active for 10 minutes and were then placed in bright light, where they again stopped all movement in less than 30 seconds. They were observed closely for 10 minutes while in the light, and not a leg or antenna was moved, though some had stopped in apparently awkward positions.

The foregoing experiment was repeated several times on different individuals and at various periods during the day, always giving similar results. *Aplopus* is thus seen to become active in the dark within from 10 to 20 minutes, and at times even more promptly. This activity is continued as long as it remains in the dark. When the insect is placed in bright light it promptly comes to rest within from less than 30 seconds in some cases to several minutes in others. *Aplopus* responds, therefore, more promptly to light than to darkness. The males appear to come to rest more readily than the females; they are also more active in the dark. These insects may readily be made to mate by placing a number of individuals of both sexes in a cage in the dark.

The question next arises whether responses to light and darkness are due to the action of the stimulus on the optic organs or to the effects of light on the body-surface of the insect as a whole. In attempting an answer to this question several experiments were performed. First, a number of Aplopi were chosen and their eyes were well covered with a lampblack paste until they were apparently blind. These individuals were then subjected to darkroom experiments. When only the compound eyes were blackened, the simple eyes being uncovered, they still responded in the dark-room, though slower than the control. On one occasion a male and three females were used; the male moved slightly after 15 minutes, though almost an hour had elapsed before all four individuals had become active.

When both the simple and compound eyes were blackened they responded still more slowly in the dark. Of four treated in this manner only one had moved after 30 minutes in the dark-room, and this one almost immediately came to rest again; so that after 50 minutes all were quiet, three of the four not having moved during this time. After 2 hours three were at rest and one was moving; one of the four had not moved at all during the two hours and the three that had moved did so only for a moment, not becoming really active, as they normally do in the dark-room.

To test further the importance of vision in responding to changes from light to dark, I determined to blacken the compound and simple eyes of a number of Aplopi during the night to ascertain in what manner they would respond when the daylight appeared. Six females and two males were placed in a cage to themselves and their eyes were painted at 9 h 40 m p. m., while they were all very active. At 5 h 30 m a. m. on the following morning three of the females and one of the males were actively moving. These animals were much more active than the control of about 50 individuals, all of which were now at rest, although they were caged nearby so as to experience the same light conditions. At 6 o'clock four of the blind ones were still active, although the sun had been shining for half an hour. At 8 o'clock all were at rest, yet they were more than an hour later than the control in responding to the morning light When these blind insects had been at rest for 2 hours they were placed in the dark-room, where all became active after about an hour. They were then brought into the light and assumed the attitude of rest within 12 minutes.

In the evening the ones with painted eyes became active 30 to 45 minutes earlier than the normal ones did. At 6 h 12 m p. m. not one of 50 normal insects had moved, while 5 of the 8 blind ones had been moving actively for 40 minutes. Aplopi probably appreciate light to some extent through their bodies, but more acutely by means of their eyes; thus night appears to come earlier and day later to the blind ones. The 2 blind males failed to pair with either of the 6 blind females, though normal males and females usually mated when they were caged together.

Blind and normal females were observed in their natural environment on *Suriana* bushes. Here the blind individuals also became active earlier in the evening than the normal ones.

When the strong light of a bull's-eye lantern is thrown on a normal one of these insects at night, it turns its head from side to side and gives evidence of seeing the light.

These experiments seem to show that *Aplopus* may respond to light and darkness through its general body surfaces, but that it does so much less readily, or slower, than by means of its optic organs.

Experiments With Light Rays of Different Lengths.

It became desirable at this stage to know whether the insects responded to white light as a complex whole or to some of its constituent rays. Several experiments were conducted in the attempt to solve this problem.

Light was passed through a vessel containing carbon bisulphide, which serves to eliminate the ultra-violet rays. This is the well-known experiment first performed by Sir John Lubbock on ants. A dark-jar was arranged and two of the "walking-sticks" were placed in it. After they had been quiet for 10 minutes the jar was covered by a vessel containing seawater in order to test the effect of the subdued light which was transmitted by the liquid. The animals under this condition remained motionless for 25 minutes. The vessel containing the sea-water was then removed, and the jar allowed to stand uncovered for 25 minutes. The insects still retained their daylight state of rest. A vessel containing carbon bisulphide was now placed over the jar, thus admitting daylight minus its ultra-violet rays. The Aplopi remained perfectly motionless in this light for 85 minutes and were then removed from the jar. It thus seems apparent that this insect is not brought to rest by the ultra-violet rays of sunlight, since they do not move in the absence of such rays. They probably respond, therefore, to the visible rays of the spectrum.

Ten Aplopi were subjected to light transmitted through blue glass. (Spectroscopic analysis showed this glass to be impure, transmitting blue, green, and a little red and yellow.) The insects gave no definite response in this light, although during one experiment they became more active than usual, moving as if they were in the dark. Such a response was, however, not at all constant and I am inclined to think that the individuals of this experiment had become unduly excited from some other cause.

The influence of red light, containing possibly a little orange, was tried on ten Aplopi. This also failed to give any definite reaction. It seems likely, then, that these insects respond to sunlight as a complex light and not to a limited number of its rays—at any rate not to the few tested above.

Experiments With Sound.

Aplopus seems indifferent to loud noises; a loud voice or a strong rap upon a board is apparently unheard. A 32-caliber pistol was fired three times within 18 inches of three active individuals, one male and two females, yet they gave no indication of having heard the pistol. Before the pistol was fired the second time the "walking-sticks" were made to assume awkward positions; still they remained motionless after the noise.

Movement Experiments.

Aplopus may be made to assume almost any position, it matters not how apparently awkward, and it will often retain such a position for a long period of time. Such a response may be very useful in causing this animal to be passed unnoticed. If it be shaken or struck while resting on a limb it will not at first scamper off as most insects would, but remains perfectly still in almost any position it may chance to occupy after the shock. When such a disturbance is repeated for several times, *Aplopus* may become excited and either drop or attempt to run away. One of either pair of legs may be lifted from its foothold and be straightened or twisted backward or forward and left with the foot free and unsupported. The leg may remain motionless in such a position for long periods of time. Two or even three legs can be raised in such a fashion, and *Aplopus* will stand motionless on its remaining foothold. Not more than three of its feet can be raised at any one time, since it is unable to support its long body upon only two legs. The antennae may be directed in any direction the observer may wish and the insect will permit them to remain in such a position. One may actually lift an unexcited *Aplopus* by its long mesothorax and slowly place it back down upon a flat surface, where it will remain for 10 minutes or more with its legs pointing upward. A second individual may be placed in a similar manner over the first, and both will remain motionless for many minutes. As mentioned above, they show a death-feigning reaction.

This insect suggests to one a papier-mache imitation with wire legs which may be bent or twisted in almost any manner and put in any position. It could scarcely be more stick-like.

When walking, *Aplopus* often stops and waves its antennæ about in a circle, apparently feeling for some object in front of it. If the antennæ strike an object, a stick or a leaf, the first pair of legs reach forward and attempt to grasp it and pull the body of the insect up to it. When the insects have climbed to the top of a branch they usually wave their antennæ, trying to find some object on which to continue their upward journey. The antennæ of several individuals were cut away close to their proximal joints. The insects were slightly excited by the operation, but soon moved off, using their first pair of legs as feelers, stopping at intervals and waving either the right or left leg and at times circling both legs in front of the head, just as if the legs were efficient antennae. One of the first pair of legs was removed, and the remaining one then served the purpose of a feeler. The other first leg was then removed, leaving the animal without antennæ or either first leg. The insect now progressed in a slower but surprisingly normal fashion upon only four legs. The point of especial interest is that first the one and then the other of the second pair of legs was raised and circled about as an antenna or feeler. Both of these legs could not be so used at any one time, since the insect is unable to stand on less than three legs. Normal insects were never observed to use either of the second pair of legs as feelers.

The eyes of such a four-legged, antennaless animal were blackened so that it was unable to see. This confused the subject considerably and it turned several times in a circle before being able to progress straight forward. The progress was then slow and cautious. Such an *Aplopus* often turned its head from side to side, as if attempting to see; it also moved the stumps of its antennæ and legs. It was able to climb among the branches and feed in a typical manner. On the following day it showed marked improvement in its ability to progress. When at rest these crippled individuals directed the remaining proximal portions of their antennæ and first legs forward, just as though they were assuming the attitude with legs and antennæ pointing straight out in front of the head, which is so typical for normal individuals.

A strong electric current causes *Aplopus* to move actively and may often cause its legs to kick violently for some seconds.

Mating of Males With a Portion of a Female Abdomen Attached to a Stick.

Many experimenters have attempted in various ways to determine through what senses the male insect locates and mates with the female. Among the moths and butterflies the sexes are sometimes differently colored and observers have claimed that the adornment of the male or of the female was a factor in the selection of the other sex. This manner of viewing the case was seriously questioned by some interesting experiments performed by Mayer in 1900.[1] A number of female moths were placed in an open-mouth glass jar covered by netting and five males when liberated 100 feet away flew to the jar. The experiment was then repeated with the jar inverted, so as

[1] Mayer, A. G. On the mating instinct in moths. *Annal. and Mag. Nat. History*, v, 1900.

to close the opening. This time the males did not approach, although the females were visible through the glass. It thus appears that the male moth finds the female by the sense of smell rather than the sense of sight. Other females were inclosed in a box with an open chimney, and the males flew to the chimney, although the females were not visible. When abdomens of females were cut off, the males would fly to these rather than to the winged bodies. If the antennæ of the male be removed he does not go to the female.

Mayer also glued the wings of a male over the wings of a female, so that she appeared like a male; nevertheless she was found by a male and mated with normally. Males would pay no attention to other males with female wings, but would pair readily with a female both of whose wings had been cut away.

In all of these experiments, however, the male and female were in healthy conditions during mating, so that they were capable of movement or actions by which the sexes might excite one another. Dr. Mayer informs me that during his experience a male would not mate with a fatally mutilated or dying female.

I wished to conduct an experiment that would eliminate the possibility of anything like a courtship or psychical action between the sexes. Since it seems to be the odor of the abdomen of the female that first attracts the male, I concluded to make papier-mache imitation females and smear the abdomen of these with juices from the abdomen of mature females; then, on caging a number of males with these imitation females, pairing might take place. The papier-mache imitations could not be obtained, however, so this experiment was abandoned, though it is probably well worth trying with a number of insects.

It was then decided to construct an artificial female by fastening a portion of the abdomen of a mature female *Aplopus* on to a small stick. A *Suriana* stick was cut that approximated in thickness the female's body and supported on six wire legs. One end of the stick was trimmed to a conical point and the abdomen of a female minus the first segment was pushed on over this conical end and made fast by winding thread about it. An abdomen thus attached to a stick will remain alive and is capable of moving slightly, and indeed defecating after more than 24 hours. The head and thorax also continue to live and crawl about in the usual manner for several days after the abdomen has been removed.

I induced two male aplopi to pair with such a "stick-female" in a perfectly normal manner (text-fig. 1 and plate 3, fig. 5). The experiment was performed as follows: It had been found, if a male was separated from a normal female while mating with her, that they would remate after a short time if placed in the dark. It had also been found by a previous unsuccessful experiment that the abdomen should be from a female that was mature, but that had not been mated with. This in mind, five males and ten females were put into a dark-room, where after 12 minutes one of the males had paired with a female. The pair was separated and the abdomen of the female cut off at the joint between the first and second segments and fixed to the stick with wire legs as described above. All of the females were now removed from the cage and the abdomen on the wire-legged stick was attached to the side of the cage in a vertical position and placed in the darkroom with four males.

After 1.5 hours the "stick-female" had not been disturbed by any of the males. It was now moved and placed in a horizontal position, as if holding to the gauze-wire top of the cage by its legs, with its body suspended, the attitude of any insect while clinging to the under side of a horizontal surface (fig. 1). In such a position the abdomen was mated with in less than an hour. The male in this instance was not the same individual that had previously mated with the entire female. He was in a perfectly normal copulating attitude, his organ of intromission being inserted between the oviscapt and the raised end of the female abdomen, as is shown in figure 1. Figure 5, plate 3, is a photograph of the pair, although here the male has withdrawn his intromissive organ on account of the disturbance caused by shifting the case into a favorable light for photographing. This male was finally, by the movements of the cage, made to leave the "stick-female."

A point of some interest is that *Aplopus* seems to prefer the female to occupy a horizontal position in mating. During the first experiment with the "stick-female" it was placed in a vertical position and caged with males in the dark for two days without a result. In the experiment above the "stick-female" was first placed vertically and remained so for 1.5 hours without attracting a male. When it was changed to a horizontal position a male paired with it in less than an hour. All of the normal pairs observed were in a more or less horizontal position. It may be that the attitudes of the male are difficult to assume unless the female stands horizontally.

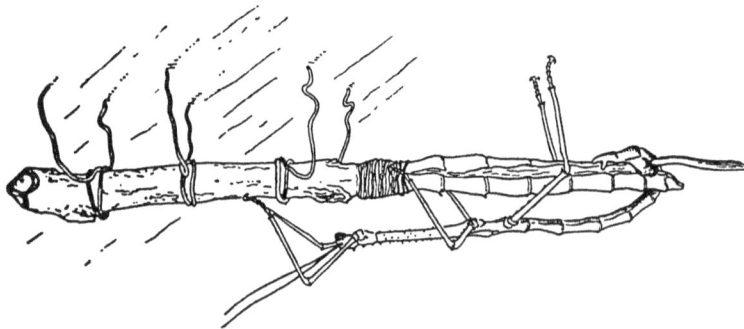

Fig. 1.—Drawing of male *Aplopus* in full copulating attitude with
the end of a female abdomen fixed to a wire-legged stick.

The cage with the "stick-female" and four males was again returned to the dark-room and after 2.5 hours a second male was found standing on the decoy. He remained in this position for over 3 hours, which was a much longer time than I had known a male to stand over a normal female without copulating with her. After this time, however, he began the usual mating movements and copulated perfectly with the abdomen. This was, then, the second time that the amputated abdomen of the female had been paired with, and each time by a different male. No doubt, therefore, remains that the male *Aplopus* may pair normally with the female without any "communication," "courtship," or psychical processes having taken place between them.

Summary and Conclusions.

1. The habits of *Aplopus mayeri* on its food-plant *Suriana maritima* are as truly protectively adapted as is its singular stick-like appearance. The large females in their color and shape resemble the stem of this plant; the males are greenish and well concealed among the leafed twigs, while the eggs are peculiarly similar to the seeds of *Suriana* in size and color, although differing in shape. The insect is nocturnal and only occasionally moves in the daylight; then as a rule with a slow, waving motion suggesting the movement of a branch swinging in a light breeze. To escape enemies it may fall bodily from its position and become lost among the lower branches of the shrub, or at times it may fall entirely to the ground, where it will lie motionless for several minutes as if feigning death.

2. *Aplopus* becomes active by a much brighter light in the evening than that by which it comes to rest in the morning. Both reactions are, however, responses to light and not to a physiological periodicity, as may be shown with dark-room experiments. If these insects are blinded by painting their eyes with lampblack paste, they still respond to light and darkness, although much slower than normally.

3. They gave no response to sunlight lacking the ultra-violet rays, and were equally indifferent to red and blue lights, acting in all as though they were in ordinary daylight.

4. *Aplopus* gives no indication of hearing sounds of various intensities.

5. These insects during the day, while inactive, may be made to assume an almost endless variety of positions, any of which they will maintain for considerable period of time. They may actually be piled over one another, with their backs down and legs extended in the air, as if they were inanimate sticks. Such stick-like indifference may often assist them to pass unnoticed by enemies that might otherwise be attracted by their movements.

6. While moving about, the antennæ are often waved or circled in front of their heads, as if feeling the way. Should the antenna be removed, the forelegs are readily

pressed into service as feelers, these being waved much as if they were true antennæ. If now the first pair of legs are removed it is interesting to find that the legs of the second pair are alternately waved about and used as feelers, although normal insects were never seen to use either leg of the second pair in such a manner. *Aplopus*, considering the length of its body, progresses remarkably well with only four legs. If such a four-legged, antennaless individual has its eyes blinded, it becomes much confused and often turns in a circle, and twists its head from side to side as it walks. It improves in its movements with practice.

7. The abdomen of a mature female was cut off between the first and second segments and tied to a stick which was supported on wire legs. Males in a dark-room were found to copulate in a normal manner with this amputated female abdomen fastened on the stick. This is a unique case of a male insect's pairing with a removed portion of the female. Such an experiment makes it evident that a courtship or psychical response is not essential between the two sexes in mating.

Fig. 4. A mating pair of Aplopi. The male has withdrawn his intromission organ but still grasps abdomen of female.

Fig. 5. Male *Aplopus* immediately after he has withdrawn his intromission organ while copulating with the amputated abdomen of a female fixed to a wire-legged stick.

An Unusual Occurrence of Walking-sticks

Hortense Butler
State College, N. M.

During the past summer (1913) the woods in the vicinity of Peterson, Iowa, showed walking sticks, *Diapheromera femorata*, in numbers which constituted a veritable pest. The woods are principally oak, with smaller numbers of elm, ash, aspen, linden, hickory and black walnut trees and a heavy undergrowth of hazel. On the 30th of May it was observed that the hazel bushes were quite covered with recently hatched walking-sticks, varying from three or four millimetres to a centimetre in length, in color they were a very pale yellowish green.

By the first of August they had begun to leave the timber and appear in the orchard and around the house. In the orchard they infested particularly one tree of early apples, devouring nearly all the leaves; on a single twig six inches in length I counted sixteen clustered together and they were equally numerous over the entire tree.

The woods had become forbidden ground to us; if one were sufficiently brave to start through them, the walking-sticks fell to the ground from every tree in such numbers as to sound like hail. Through August and September there were seldom fewer than fifty on our screen door each morning. The little chickens were particularly enthusiastic over them and soon learned to appear when we swept them off the doors in the morning. In spite of the long awkward bodies and clinging legs of the insects, they were soon able to devour them quickly and deftly.

By mid-September the timber showed stretches a couple of hundred feet broad and half a mile long where the trees had been completely defoliated. The walking sticks began to cross the road to another piece of timber in which there had been almost none of the insects and every passing carriage or motor crushed them by hundreds. This extremely local character of the infestation was a curious feature. One piece of timber containing about two hundred acres was almost wholly stripped, while a similar piece across the road was scarcely touched. It would appear that no walking-sticks matured there, and the light damage done was by migrants from the other timber. There was an apparent disparity in numbers between the males and the females, though the apparent scarcity of females may be due to their greater sluggishness. During the latter part of the season the females appeared in slightly greater numbers.

From: *Journal of Economic Entomology*, June 1914. 7: 299.

Vaporous discharge by *Anisomorpha buprestoides*.
(Orthoptera: Phasmidae).

W. L. McAtee

Biological Survey, U. S. Dept. Agriculture, Washington, D. C.

A review of information on the secretions of this phasmid and their ejection was published by Samuel H. Scudder in 1876 (*Psyche*, Vol. 1, pp. 137-9). C. J. Maynard gives (*Contr. to Science*, Vol. I, 1889, pp. 31-35) a full account of the thoracic glands and their discharge. An interesting note on the subject will be found also under the name of H. M. Russell (*Proc. Ent. Soc. Wash.* Vol. XIV, No 3, July-Sept., 1912, p. 117). Observations on the nature and source of the discharge by the insects vary; it is a milky fluid or a very fine mist; it is discharged from definite pores on the sides of the thorax or from some part of the abdomen. An observation differing somewhat from the previous accounts should be put on record, and the diversity of opinions should induce someone to make a thorough study of the matter and publish a full account. The observation to which I refer was made by Mr. C. H. M. Barrett, taxidermist of the United States Biological Survey, while on a collecting trip in Florida. At Miakka Lake, Manatee County, during a thunderstorm, June 19, 1918, Mr. Barrett found a number of pairs of *Anisomorpha buprestoides*, *in copula*, in the interstices of a pile of boards in a deserted cabin. When suddenly uncovered or otherwise disturbed, the insects discharged from the end of the abdomen vapor in the form of small puffs appearing two inches from the abdominal apex. The discharge in each case was immediately preceded by a crackling sound similar to that made by a small electric spark. Mr. Barrett's observation that *Anisomorpha buprestoides* discharges a vapor from end of abdomen and that the discharge is preceded by a peculiar crepitation, differs, so far as I am aware, from any previously recorded.

From: *Entomological News*, Vol. XXIX, No. 10, 1918, p. 388.

www.ingramcontent.com/pod-product-compliance
Lightning Source LLC
Chambersburg PA
CBHW081150270326
41930CB00014B/3097